Destination Heartland

Destination Heartland

A Guide to Discovering the Midwest's Remarkable Past

CYNTHIA CLAMPITT

3 FIELDS
B O O K S

3 Fields Books is an imprint of
the University of Illinois Press.

Library of Congress Cataloging-in-Publication Data
Names: Clampitt, Cynthia, author.
Title: Destination Heartland: a guide to discovering the
    Midwest's remarkable past / Cynthia Clampitt.
Description: [Urbana, IL]: 3 Fields Books, an imprint of
    University of Illinois Press, [2022] | Includes bibliographical
    references and index.
Identifiers: LCCN 2021052449 (print) | LCCN 2021052450
    (ebook) | ISBN 9780252044298 (hardback) | ISBN
    9780252086373 (paperback) | ISBN 9780252053283 (ebook)
Subjects: LCSH: Historic sites—Middle West—Guidebooks. |
    Historical museums—Middle West—Guidebooks. | Middle
    West—Guidebooks.
Classification: LCC F355 .C54 2022 (print) | LCC F355 (ebook) |
    DDC 917.704—dc23/eng/20211026
LC record available at https://lccn.loc.gov/2021052449
LC ebook record available at https://lccn.loc.gov/2021052450

To my dad, who taught me to explore,
and my mom, who taught me to always take notes.

Contents

Acknowledgments

This book would not have turned out nearly so well without the assistance of a wide range of friends and acquaintances who introduced me to experts, directed me toward resources or destinations, sent articles, joined me for an occasional adventure, or in some other way aided the process. For these helpful kindnesses and others, thanks to Maggie Kohls, Mira Temkin, Terese Allen, Jane Hanson, Ro Sila, Judy Dollard, Barb Pohl, Ralph Haynes, Catherine Lambrecht, Katherine Garrett, Donna Douglas, Blane Nansel, Francene Sharp, Ellie Carlson, and Mike & Peggy Leslie.

Warmest thanks to all the interpreters, historians, educators, reenactors, and other experts who populate the world of museums and living-history venues, as well as the families that keep long traditions alive across the Midwest.

Special thanks to Teresa Tucker, for encouragement and feedback at early stages, to Steve Levinthal, for keeping my technology fit for work, and to Bob Ahern for advice and assistance when it was needed.

Destination Heartland

Introduction

Why Midwestern history? Because I love American history, and the history of the Midwest is, to a greater extent than most people realize, a key element of that history. Ralph Waldo Emerson believed that "Europe stretches to the Alleghenies; America lies beyond." Abraham Lincoln said of the Midwest, "this great interior region is naturally one of the most important in the world." And historian of the frontier Frederick Jackson Turner related that individualism, independence, egalitarian spirit, and a sense of nationhood grew on the frontier, which in the 1800s meant what we now call the Midwest.[1] It's big, exciting history—and I think people need to know not only how foundational it is, but also how many sensational, fun places there are to explore the events that shaped both the region and the nation.

Being Inspired

I grew up in the Midwest. I went to summer camp in Wisconsin, visited the Lincoln sites in Springfield, Illinois, and played tourist among some of the area's offered delights, both urban and rural. However, it was my work as a food historian that created the need to seriously explore the region. While much time was spent in libraries and archives, early in the research for my book *Midwest Maize*, I also visited historic farms and living-history venues in the states I was exploring. As I continued, in each new location, I found something additional of interest—not related to what I was working on, but still attractive to a historian: Fort Snelling in Minnesota, Pioneer Village in Nebraska, Tippecanoe Battlefield in Indiana, the Herbert Hoover birthplace in Iowa, Mark Twain's boyhood home in Missouri, and more. My next book, *Pigs, Pork, and Heartland Hogs*, carried me across the Midwest again. More discoveries. I joined the newly formed (2014) Midwestern History Association and began to travel the Midwest with a new focus—I wanted to see just how much the region had to offer.

It offers a lot. Waterways, which helped define our early history, when water was the easiest way to travel, are abundant—and often stunningly impressive. The Great Lakes, which stretch to distant horizons and look quite ocean-like when one stands on their shores, hold one-fifth of the planet's fresh water. The mighty Mississippi River, one of the longest and most important rivers in the world, definitely lives up to the Ojibwe word from which we get its name: *Messipi*, which means "Big River" or "Father of Waters." And the Missouri River, nicknamed the "Big Muddy," vital to the Great Plains, is the Mississippi River's equal in all but destination.[2] Many state borders are defined by rivers, and river features often gave names to towns that grew up nearby (such as Sioux Falls and Cedar Rapids).

In addition, the Midwest is remarkably beautiful. As John Steinbeck wrote during a driving trip that carried him across the region, "I had forgotten how rich and beautiful is the countryside—the deep topsoil, the wealth of great trees, the lake country of Michigan handsome as a well-made woman, and dressed and jeweled. It seemed to me that the earth was generous and outgoing here in the heartland, and perhaps the people took a cue from it."[3] And the beauty is so varied. The North Woods are spectacular, dark with pines and brightened by the white trunks of birch trees, floored with pine needles or mosses, and crowded with ferns. The tallgrass prairies are magnificent, undulating in the almost constant breeze like a green and gold ocean. Rolling hills and handsome farms abound. However, I think that perhaps it is the immense size and openness of the Midwest that is its most striking feature. The sky dominates, and one is almost overwhelmed by the sense of space.

The region's grandeur did not merely impress; it shaped our history. And the history it shaped is quintessential Americana, with so many of the iconic images we associate with our past. It was *Little House on the Prairie* and the Pony Express. It was the birthplace of Buffalo Bill's Wild West Show and Antonin Dvorak's *New World Symphony* (both in 1890s Iowa). It gave us revolutionary farming equipment, but also gave us the first airplanes (the Wright Brothers lived in Ohio) and cheap cars (thank you Mr. Ford). It was and is a place where wide-open spaces led to big ideas.

The region's history was not without pain and conflict. Native Americans were relocated. The War of 1812 challenged American independence. The Dred Scott Case reinforced the rights of slave owners, while the Underground Railroad and "Bleeding Kansas" fought to liberate the enslaved. Of course, even when there was no conflict, there was always tremendous challenge. But challenge drove change, and things progressed with astonishing speed.

Of course, all the regions of the United States have rich and remarkable histories. However, of all these regions, the Midwest is the most often overlooked, even by those in the Midwest. I'd like to help change that. Because the region sometimes dismissively called "flyover country" offers a multitude of great places to land. *Destination Heartland* is a celebration of what is here and what has happened, as well as why it matters to Midwesterners, to the nation, and to the world.

What This Book Is and What It Is Not

The purpose of this book is to encourage readers to seek out the many delightful places where one can, in fact, "visit" Midwestern history, from seeing history come alive in wonderful living-history venues and reenactments to perusing astonishing collections and ancient sites. The information is organized by the various ways of interacting with history, from simply viewing to exploring and engaging, though featured destinations are listed by state in Appendix A. To help give everything context, I include enough background and history to help make it clear why a place is significant—though significance can range from a general idea or trend of a period to specific important events and people.

Now, for the things the book is not.

One important thing it is not is the tale of an inexperienced provincial emerging from a cocoon and making a first, tentative foray outside the neighborhood. At this writing, I have visited thirty-seven countries on six continents, have traveled through most of the U.S., including Alaska and Hawaii, and have lived in both other regions and other countries. So, my enthusiasm for the Midwest and its many delights is not a case of not knowing any better. It is a case of wondering why it took me so long to realize that exploring the Heartland is so worthwhile.

The book is also not a comparison with other regions, except in cases where it shows interconnectedness. All the nation's regions are worthwhile. All are pieces of the larger picture. But the Midwest is a very important piece of that picture, and the image is not complete if it is left out.

It is far from being a comprehensive look at all the region offers. There is a lot more than history to explore and enjoy. The Midwest is home to fabulous geological features—from the bluffs and towers of the Driftless Area, where Minnesota, Wisconsin, and Iowa come together (an area missed by the glaciers) to the colorfully layered canyons of South Dakota's Badlands to the dramatic Garden of the Gods in the Shawnee National Forest in Illinois, and more. Some of the nation's best zoos are in the Midwest, along with wildlife research organizations, such as the International Crane Foundation in Wisconsin or the Wolf Park in Indiana, and nature reserves where you can see creatures that live here (bison anyone?). Museums that range from cozy to immense offer collections that focus on areas of interest besides history or examine histories of places beyond the Midwest. These are all worth seeing. But first, I want to establish that the Midwest has both a remarkable history and wonderful opportunities to explore that history. I want to get you on the road—and then you can enjoy whichever other sites and wonders capture your interest as you travel. And to be honest, there are a lot of places in the country with nice rocks and good zoos, but the history of the Midwest is unique and often surprising, and it should be explored.

Even focusing on history alone, it would be impossible to fit in every place in the Midwest that gives us access to history. There are hundreds of town and county historic societies with collections that offer insights into local history, as well as topical museums (transportation, inventions, agriculture, various people groups) and state museums. So, the book is far from comprehensive even for history. However, I think the many locations that are included will help underscore just how abundant opportunities are. This book spotlights places across the region that are not merely old but that actually help connect us with Midwestern history, often in delightfully engaging and entertaining ways. (Yes, history can be fun.)

The book has not been subsidized in any way. It is my love letter to the Midwest and its history. This had an impact on the number of places I have been able to visit thus far (though I'll never stop searching—keep an eye on my MidwestMaize.com blog), but it means there was no pressure on me to promote any destination. I have included places I've seen and that I think are worth mentioning.

For this volume, I am including the twelve states of the "Greater Midwest." Kansas and Nebraska, both on the Great Plains, were actually the first states to be labeled "the Middle West"—so it seems imperative that they be part of this tale. So, we will be traveling through (in order of statehood) Ohio, Indiana, Illinois, Missouri, Michigan, Iowa, Wisconsin, Minnesota, Kansas, Nebraska, North Dakota, and South Dakota. (And this is the order in which destinations will be listed within each chapter. Appendix B reiterates this order and gives specific dates for statehood.)

Finally, there will be some difference in the number of places identified for each state. This is not a reflection on a state's importance but rather on its population. The number of people who live in the states of the Midwest range from 13 million in Illinois to less than one million each in South Dakota and North Dakota. And some states are older. Ohio became a state on March 1, 1803, and North and South Dakota were admitted into the Union on November 2, 1889, with the other Midwestern states ranging between those two dates. States that are older and that have larger populations will have more places to visit. So, if it appears that the distribution is not perfectly balanced, it can't be. That said, there is no state that is without its delights. All twelve states have remarkable pasts and wonderful places to explore.

What Lies Ahead

The first chapter traces the Midwest's history from the arrival of early groups of Native Americans through the French explorers, to the tsunami of settlers that flooded in after the American Revolution and Louisiana Purchase, and then on to the development of the region and continued growth into the beginning of the 20th century. The cutoff for the historical narrative is the beginning of World War I, often recognized as the beginning of the modern world. This chapter relates how the region came by the titles of Middle West and Corn Belt, and how the region became identified with hard work and innovation, from the John Deere plow to refrigerated train cars, stockyards to the auto industry and aviation. It also shows why even these are not the totality of Midwestern identity, with such familiar names as Wyatt Earp, Johnny Appleseed, Annie Oakley, Frank Lloyd Wright, and many more being part of the tale.

The book then launches into where and how one can visit history, the "how" being the different ways of connecting, from simply looking and listening to actually participating. Also, in order to discuss as many places as possible, some decisions had to be made as to where a venue fit in. As a result, a place might qualify for more than one chapter, but I had to pick one. For example, historic towns are in a different category from museums or historic restaurants, even though many vintage communities will be home to at least one museum and possibly an early restaurant. When lines cannot be easily drawn, I focus on an obvious or dominant characteristic, though I also note what is nearby, when appropriate. I hope that the index will help folks find anything that might not have ended up in the category they expected.

Finally, the "Locating" chapter includes resources, websites, and other ways to find museums, Carnegie libraries, historic markers, and more. It also offers recommendations for how to pursue your own research—because all of us are surrounded by history. There are half a dozen historical societies within 10 minutes of my home. Expand to half an hour from home, and we add three historic farms (two of them living history farms), a dozen more historical societies, a historic village, and the state's oldest tavern. If you begin to look, you may be surprised by what you find, both near and far.

In addition, to add a bit more breadth, I invited a few historians, authors, and others to contribute their voices to the discussion. So, the book is dotted with inserts where these other Midwesterners share experiences, insights, and historic tidbits—because I am not alone in loving this region.

I hope you will gain inspiration from the places identified here, as well as some potential ideas for travel destinations, but keep in mind that there is even more out there than I could include.

Why Does This Matter?

There are so many reasons this—the pursuit of history—is important. We can't know where we're going if we have no idea where we've come from. Understanding how things have changed can help us face the changes that lie ahead. Knowing what life was like can and should make us grateful for how far we've come. And the past here might be the future somewhere else.

Another reason it is important is purely practical: we lose all this rich heritage if we don't visit it and support it. It takes money to keep these places going, to provide programs and pay employees and repair log cabins or ancient stagecoach stops. And even volunteers need encouragement to keep working on these places.

People are rushing off these days to find out what their DNA tells them about their past. These places represent the DNA of the Midwest—the stories and people and events and developments that created who we are today.

Get Out of Town

The Midwest's history is remarkable, and I believe there is enough of that history included here to make the book worth reading even if you can't visit the destinations described. However, there is so much that is delightful in the region and in these places, I hope you will at least consider doing a bit of exploring.

Some of the places mentioned in this book are destinations around which a trip can be planned. Some are simply possible brief stops en route to other places. But start planning to wander—and expect to find more than you imagined.

I can remember driving from Chicago to a historic spot in northern Iowa, and as I drove, I passed through numerous beautiful little towns with charming nineteenth-century downtowns, streets lined with Victorian houses, impressive buildings from a bygone age, whether a mansion, farm, or early and ambitious government building. If I had not had a schedule to keep, I could have probably spent weeks making my way across the state. During another driving trip, I saw dozens and dozens of signs along the road for birthplaces of notable individuals, sites of historic events, and museums for the wide array of ethnic groups that settled the Midwest. I couldn't always stop—but with increasing frequency, I did.

The goal is to get you started—and excited—but also to show you how to find more of what is available. Because there is always more. So, read about the region's past events and present destinations, and then try to get out of town and discover the Heartland. You may be surprised by how much of the region's history resonates, how much is familiar, and how much of the world today was created by what happened here not so very long ago.

CHAPTER 1

Creating and Defining the Midwest

Most of the remarkable stories and historic details in this book will be connected to the places described. However, the purpose of this chapter is to give context to the many tales and destinations that follow. There will be some intriguing details here, but the main purpose of the chapter is to set the stage for what is to come.

After the Ice

The one thing most responsible for the features that define the Midwest was ice. The massive glaciers of the last great Ice Age, more than two miles thick, scraped and carved and compressed the land as they advanced, creating broad plains, jumbled moraines, and numerous lakes. Then, as the glaciers retreated 12,000 years ago, they left behind deep layers of loess, a rich soil material created by the glaciers grinding across the continent. The melting ice created rivers and filled lakes. Then, as temperatures rose, vegetation began to return to the scoured landscape.[1]

This would not be the end of changes. The region's flora and fauna were affected by the alternating warm and cold periods that occurred planet wide,[2] including a Little Ice Age that ran from the mid-1300s to the mid-1800s. There were floods and droughts. The New Madrid Seismic Zone, a fault the runs north and south through the region, ruffled the landscape and changed the course of the Mississippi River roughly every 500 years (most recently, 1811–1812).[3]

The arrival of humans would also have an impact. Once the ice was gone and plants were growing, people began to move into the region. Archaeological evidence so regularly upends theories of the earliest part of the story (who came, from where, and when) that the best description of the millennia immediately after the ice sheets left is "we don't really know." Paleoindians hunted mammoths, leaving spear points behind as evidence of their having existed. Then Archaic hunter-gatherers hunted smaller animals and gathered wild foods. However, we have more evidence of later people. The Early Woodland Period saw the introduction of pottery and gave rise to the Adena (800 B.C.–A.D. 1) and Hopewell (200 B.C.–A.D. 400) cultures, and the mound builders of the Mississippian people (A.D. 700–1400). The impact these groups had was considerable. They burned large areas to make hunting easier, introduced agriculture (especially crops brought in from Mesoamerica: corn, squash, beans), cut down trees, rerouted streams, and, in the case of the mound builders, moved tons of earth. We tend to think of the Midwest that the first European settlers saw as being pristine and untouched (they certainly thought it was), but most of it had not been purely natural for millennia.[4]

Each of these cultures disappeared. Reasons varied: overhunting, conflicts with other groups, exhausted resources, climate change. The Native Americans who would in time come into contact with Europeans arrived in the Midwest long after these earlier groups had vanished. Of course, because most Native American groups were migratory, different groups kept arriving and leaving. Some followed herds. Some moved when land was exhausted. Most groups also traded across large areas, and some were "snow birds," heading south when winter came and returning to the Midwest when spring arrived. So, it was a pretty dynamic population. Some groups of Native Americans trace their arrival to the late Mississippian era, but others arrived later. And, of course, some moved to the Midwest after Europeans started settling the East Coast. Many of these groups are still in the Midwest, preserving their cultures—and often sharing them with visitors.

Though "the three sisters"—corn, beans, and squash—had arrived with earlier groups, each successive group of Native Americans brought new varieties of these three, along with new traditions. They also incorporated new foods provided by the new region they'd entered, from maple syrup to wild rice. Different regions had different foods, dependent as much on the terrain as on tradition. Many Native Americans planted crops in the soft, rich soils of Iowa and the states around the Great Lakes. On the Great Plains, the tough, heavy layer of sod resisted agriculture, but it was perfect for hunting. High winds and grass fires kept the plains free of trees, making them ideal for game animals, including the iconic American bison. Fish were abundant in the lakes and rivers, and there were numerous wild foods to be foraged or domesticated. Trade, migration, and warfare kept the region's population evolving, but change sped up as entirely new people began to arrive.

Trappers and Traders

The first Europeans to reach the Midwest were the French. French explorer Étienne Brûlé was cruising the shores of Lake Superior by 1622, and Jean Nicolet landed near what is now Green Bay in 1634. Better known are Marquette and Joliet, who were commissioned by the French government in 1673 to explore south of Wisconsin. The idea of creating a canal to connect Lake Michigan to the Illinois River (which would occur 150 years later) had its genesis during their expedition. By 1680, René-Robert Cavelier, Sieur de La Salle was beginning his extensive exploration of the region, from Canada to Texas. It was La Salle who named the interior of the continent Louisiana, in honor of King Louis XIV.

All this exploration led to an influx of French trappers and traders and the rise of the famous Voyageurs, who would carry goods through the continent's river systems to the Mississippi and the French port of New Orleans. It also led to conflict, as the nations of the Iroquois Confederacy, who were expanding their own fur trade to benefit the British, encountered French-backed tribes around the Great Lakes. But in another century, it would be the British the French would be fighting. The French and Indian War was actually just a small part of a widespread international conflict known elsewhere as the Seven Years War. Contrary to what the name suggests, this was a fight between the British and the French, though both sides had Native American allies.

The British won, and the land west of the Thirteen Colonies to the Mississippi River became British. The colonists rejoiced, as their cities were now overcrowded, farms weren't big enough to support families, and people were becoming desperate for more space. Desperate enough that a few had wandered into Ohio, despite facing hostile French and Native Americans. The only problem was that the King of England, George III, didn't want the colonists moving into the newly won territory. What's more, the King said anyone who had moved west had to return to the colonies. Colonists already unhappy with Britain saw this as one more reason, among many, to consider cutting ties with Great Britain. Declaration, Revolution, and then the Treaty of Paris, signed in 1783, officially granted the new United States its independence and granted the country all the land to the Mississippi River. This newly gained region, named the Northwest Territory, included the land that would become Ohio, Michigan, Indiana, Illinois, Wisconsin, and a bit of Minnesota.[5] (The region's name reflects the fact that it was north of the Ohio River. There was also a Southwest Territory, south of the river. The much smaller Southwest Territory was soon renamed Tennessee.)[6]

The newly formed United States government began passing laws for managing the Northwest Territory. The Land Ordinance of 1785 set out the requirement for surveying this territory. Surveyors would measure squares that were six miles to a side. These would be called townships. Each township was to be divided into 36 Sections of one-square-mile each, or 640 acres. These could be subdivided into 320-acre farms, which would be the smallest a farm could be. (Thomas Jefferson, whose dream was that the United States could become a nation of small family farms, later reduced that 320-acre minimum to 160 acres—which would become the size established sixty years later by the Homestead Act.)

Surveyors spread out across the Northwest Territory, dragging surveying chains (which are commonly found in museums covering the early history of the region). They would use standardized chains to make sure the measurements were precise—and their success is still visible to anyone flying over the Midwest, as the squares they marked out can clearly be seen. This ordinance also established the setting aside of land that had been promised as payment to soldiers who fought without pay during the American Revolution.[7]

Next up was the Northwest Ordinance, passed in 1787. This provided a government for the Northwest Territory, established how states could be formed, and how many states there could be (at least three and not more than five). It also protected civil liberties and outlawed slavery in the territory.[8]

Then, in 1803, Napoleon, still at war with Britain, needed money and offered to sell what was left of New France to the United States. Thomas Jefferson said yes. The Louisiana Purchase, which stretched to the Rocky Mountains, doubled the size of the young country. The northern part of this sweep of land became known as the New Northwest Territory and added the rest of the states now included in the Greater Midwest: Iowa, Missouri, Kansas, Nebraska, South and North Dakota, and most of the rest of Minnesota. Jefferson assigned Meriwether Lewis and William Clark the task of assembling a team to explore the new acquisition, and the following year, the Corps of Discovery set off on its two-year trek. Jefferson also started planning how to get the region settled. More explorers were sent out. New forts were built and French forts were taken over. In 1811, construction began on a wide, paved road that would make it easier for settlers to cross the country. Work on the National Road was temporarily interrupted by the War of 1812, sometimes called the second war for independence, when Britain swept down from Canada through the Midwest and tried to take back a country they had never really given up. The British headed east, where they met up with a larger British force. The Americans finally stopped them in Baltimore, where Francis Scott Key celebrated by writing "The Star-Spangled Banner." But while everyone celebrated, many recognized that the great stretch of open, undefended land created a weak point at the nation's back. The Northwest Territories, Old and New, needed to be settled as quickly as possible. And so the trickle of settlers turned into a torrent.

Pioneers and Settlers

The part of Jefferson's dream that was exceptional was not that people should farm. At the time, more than 80 percent of the population worldwide was farming. Before modern agriculture, for everyone to eat, just about everyone had to farm. Even lawyers and doctors usually had a farm on the side, even if just to feed their own families. The thing that was exceptional was the idea of anyone being able to *own* a farm. Because for much of history, most people farmed land that other people owned. Of course, not everyone wanted to own a farm. For them, there would be other jobs developing as the land opened up. But the first rush was for farmland. Hunger was a great motivator.

It was this promise of farming that drew people westward. Some traveled down the Ohio River. Some, the backwoodsmen, traveled on foot with little more than a backpack, a rifle, and a sack of seed corn. The initial wave of westward settlement came from the original states, especially New England and the Upland South, followed by the Mid-Atlantic states. People migrated at roughly the same latitudes from which they came, but with some overlap. In some cases, this was the first time New Englanders would come into contact with people from the Upland South, and the cultures were different enough to cause friction, especially over issues of slavery.

The first rush was into the original Northwest Territory, primarily because it was closer and because those first people to sneak into Ohio before the American Revolution had brought back stories of the wonder of the region. Plus, it was getting easier to reach this area. The Erie Canal opened in 1825, giving ships access to the Great Lakes. Over the next two decades, more canals were built, including several in Ohio and Illinois. The National Road had made its way as far as Vandalia, Illinois, by the 1830s. Then the recently invented steam locomotive was introduced, and the race was on to lay rails.

Inventions other than the train had an impact, too. John Deere's invention in 1837 of the self-cleaning steel plow made farming more attractive. And even though Cyrus McCormick had invented his reaper back East in 1831, it was when he moved his factory to Chicago in 1847 that the device found its real home on the surrounding prairies.

The thing that astonished, and sometimes almost overwhelmed, those who came was the size of the region and everything in it. No river in Europe could compare to the mighty Mississippi. Even more daunting was the land: it was so open and there was so much of it, especially on the aptly named

Great Plains. In the opening chapter of Willa Cather's classic book about the lives led by settlers on the Great Plains, *My Ántonia*, the main character comments on what greeted him as a newcomer traveling westward: "There seemed to be nothing to see, no fences, no creeks or trees, no hills or fields. If there was a road, I could not make it out in the faint starlight. There was nothing but land: not a country at all, but the material out of which countries are made."

Covered wagons still lumbered westward along rough trails, even after trains began to appear. The knowledge of those who had gone before was valued. The writings of Marquette and Joliet, Lewis and Clark, Zebulon Pike, and others were read. In 1859, Captain Randolph B. Marcy published a book that was to become a bestseller: *The Prairie Traveler*. It covered everything needed for crossing the plains, from packing to finding food, fixing your wagon to talking to Native Americans, caring for injured animals, and vastly more. Though Marcy had a solid career in the U.S. Army, it is this book for which he is remembered.

The year 1862 saw bills passed that created another huge jump in immigration to the region, both signed by Abraham Lincoln. One was for the funding of the first Transcontinental Railroad. The other was the Homestead Act. The Transcontinental Railroad would create thousands of jobs that would draw even more people to the Midwest (including thousands of Chinese workers, who settled in the region). The Homestead Act offered 160 acres of land to any head of household who would promise to live on and farm the land.

Trains, of course, helped move people more easily and more quickly, but that was not the only impact of the explosion of railroad building. In fact, the settlement of the Great Plains wasn't particularly great until the railways began to expand, not just because of the ease of transportation, but because the railway companies took an active part in populating the region. As they extended the train lines into the wilderness, railroad officials chose the locations for new towns on the Great Plains. Towns were spaced along the train lines at approximately eight- to ten-mile intervals.[9] The railroad companies had two ideas for earning back their rather considerable investment in building the railroads. The first was to encourage people to move to the area, riding the rails to get there. They ran publicity campaigns, both in

The Best-Selling Handbook for America's Pioneers

THE PRAIRIE TRAVELER

RANDOLPH B. MARCY
Captain, U.S. Army

INCLUDES
Routes · First Aid
Recommended Clothing, Shelter, Provisions
Wagon Maintenance and the Selection and Care of Horses
Information Concerning the Habits of Indians

This once best-selling book, authored by Army Captain Randolph B. Marcy, guided thousands of pioneers across the frontier in the mid-1800s. Based on Marcy's extensive travels in the west, it maps routes, shows pictures of landmarks, and offers a tremendous range of valuable information, including best foods to take along, caring for animals, repairing wagons, how to make a tent, and how to ford a river.

the U.S. and overseas. They even sent representatives to Europe to attract immigrants to this newly accessible farmland. (In the passage earlier from Willa Cather, the speaker is, in fact, on a train, heading out to newly opened land in Nebraska.) The second element of making their business profitable was to sell the land they owned around the rail lines. The land that had previously housed the huge work crews that laid the tracks would now be available to incoming settlers.[10]

The people who came were astonishingly varied, and the diversity would only increase as settlement continued. While the initial influx was from the eastern states, even larger numbers would come from overseas. The biggest wave would be the Germans: more than five million Germans poured into the Midwest over a few decades. (Worth remembering is the fact that the country of Germany did not exist in the early 1800s, so these people were Germanic tribes that had settled in Russia and Poland, as well as those from small German-speaking kingdoms and principalities such as Saxony, Hesse, Alsace, Austria, Bavaria, and so on—which is why in the Midwest German influence produced a rather varied range of specialties and traditions, and it's why settlers might be referred to as Russian Germans or Polish Germans—because a German from Russia and a German from Alsace, were not eating the same food, wearing the same clothes, or pursuing the same traditions. What they had in common was the German language.)

But while the Germans dominated, they were not alone. People flooded in from the British Isles, Scandinavia, Eastern Europe, and Southern Europe. The 1800s even saw immigration from Lebanon, as Lebanese Christians fled persecution, many of them settling in Ohio. And there were Chinese railroad workers fleeing the intolerance on the West Coast. Dozens of countries were represented, and in large enough numbers to create distinct communities. In fact, when Czech composer Antonín Dvorak got homesick while working in New York, he was sent to Iowa for comfort, because the Czech community was so substantial. Dvorak was comforted, and it was in Iowa that he finished his famous ninth symphony, *From the New World* (1893). Sometimes, a single group would settle in a community, such as the Cornish miners in Mineral Point, Wisconsin. But often, if there was a lot of work, the mix would be impressive. For example, in Minnesota's Iron Range, nearly two dozen different countries were represented. So, diversity was, from the beginning, one of the things that defined the Midwest.[11]

Becoming the Midwest

The original Northwest Territory became known as the Old Northwest Territory, once the Louisiana Purchase got dubbed the New Northwest Territory. But then these territories began to be divided into smaller territories and rapidly gained populations large enough to become states. Ohio was the first, obtaining statehood in 1803.

The Civil War became a defining time in the region. It was a time when the Great Plains were being opened up, but people were busy elsewhere, trying to preserve the Union and end slavery. The last state to join the Union before the war was Kansas (1861), and the first new state in the region after the war was Nebraska (1867). Migration had slowed slightly while the war continued, especially the movement of people from overseas, but after the Civil War, migration and immigration accelerated. Of course, post-emancipation, a lot of the migration was from the South. Large agricultural communities appeared seemingly overnight, including towns made up entirely of former slaves.[12] But as the region continued to grow and became more newsworthy, journalists and promoters of the region wanted something to call the area. "New Northwest Territory" and "Old Northwest Territory" weren't precise enough and were bordering on irrelevant.

The states that flanked the Civil War, Kansas and Nebraska, were pretty much the center of the country. However, it's not because they are midway between the two coasts that they earned the region the new name of Middle West. In the 1890s, Kansas and Nebraska were in the middle between the New Northwest Territory and the Southwest (Texas and Indian Territory, which would eventually become Oklahoma). It was a vertical middle.

Before long, journalists were using the name Middle West in stories about Kansas and Nebraska, describing the ideal of rural society that they saw reflected there. The people were hardworking, thrifty, and practical; the wide-open spaces seemed to have no end. The Middle West was contrasted with the East, which was now viewed as crowded and effete.

As the 1890s continued, the Middle West began to be redefined. If honest, hardworking, independent farmers, small towns, and endless cornfields were what identified the Middle West, those features could describe far more than just Kansas and Nebraska. People began to consider the "great interior region" outlined by Abraham Lincoln in an 1862 speech. Lincoln identified it as being "bounded east by the Alleghenies, north by the British dominions, west by the Rocky Mountains, and south by the line along which the culture of corn and cotton meets." He also stated that "this great interior region is naturally one of the most important in the world."

Slowly, the label "Middle West" spread outward to cover most of the "interior region" defined by Lincoln. Of course, as soon as it was defined, debates arose as to whether burgeoning industrial centers, such as Cleveland and Detroit, disqualified a state from association with the rural ideal. But the definition held. Then, in 1918, journalists began to compress the region's name, and the Middle West became the Midwest.[13]

There are other labels, of course: Corn Belt, Heartland. Corn Belt does not really equal Midwest, but it's close to being the same, as most of the Corn Belt is in the Midwest. And there was (and is) a lot of corn. Corn was the perfect crop for small farms, because it produces so prodigiously. It was an almost guaranteed success, and it was the only crop that fed both humans and livestock. Plus the early settlers from the East Coast had spent a couple of centuries falling in love with corn. So, corn was a key feature of many of the region's farms. The term Corn Belt actually started in Ohio, where the corn-livestock agricultural paradigm originated, and moved westward, as the term Middle West moved eastward. By 1880, Kansas and Nebraska were part of the Corn Belt. (Today, the label Corn Belt is morphing into Feed-Grains and Livestock Region,[14] because so much of the corn goes to feeding the abundant livestock. Does not roll off the tongue like Corn Belt, but it's more precise.)

Heartland, however, does describe the Midwest. It was the region that would grow up to feed the country—and, in time, much of the world. However, there were other reasons for calling it the Heartland. It would in time give us both the traits and the icons that would come to define our idea of "American." The Midwest was more egalitarian than the East.

It was this region that gave rise to rugged individualism, of necessity. If your nearest neighbor is a day's journey away, you figure out how to handle problems yourself. Hard work and patience were needed and, for those who survived, were rewarded. This—owning land and being independent—was the American Dream. Of course, this sunny view began to dim with time, as the nation became more industrialized and fewer and fewer people actually owned farms. (Today, farmers are down to about one percent of the population—though most are still on family farms that date back a century or more.) But in the late 1800s and early 1900s, the Midwest was viewed as being what America was supposed to be.[15]

However, getting back to Lincoln's quote, it is not just physically central to the nation; the Midwest is still the reason the country eats well and relatively inexpensively. It keeps the nation's lifeblood flowing. There is no other region so absolutely necessary for the continuation of life as we know it. It is still the heartland.

So Much, So Fast

The Midwest was settled faster than any other region in history. In addition to an explosion in population, it also saw a tremendous amount of innovation that contributed to life changing at a stunning speed. The 1800s began with Daniel Boone and ended with the Wright Brothers. Agriculture changed more in the last half of the 1800s than it had in the previous 4,000 years.[16] In eighty-two years, a massive region was transformed from unexplored territory to twelve settled states.

There are myriad examples that underscore the speed of change. One of my current favorites is Laura Ingalls and Frank Lloyd Wright. Hard to imagine anyone more associated with the frontier than Ingalls or more modern than Wright, and yet they were both born in Wisconsin only four months apart (1867). But the Ingalls family followed the frontier (as did many others, because land was always cheaper farther out), and Wright pursued the future. Or how about the fact that two Iowa boys, John Wayne and Wyatt Earp, met when Earp moved to Hollywood to be a consultant for directors making Westerns.

Of course, not everywhere grew at the same rate of speed, and not just because of distance, whether distance from the East or distance from one of the several lakes and rivers that made transportation easier. Work was a big consideration, especially among those who had little interest in farming. The beginning of a huge project, such as building the canals or the opening of a large mine, created a spike in settlement, as people rushed in to take newly available jobs. There were, in a way, multiple frontiers. As Frederick Jackson Turner, one of the first great historians of the Midwest, observes, "It is evident that the farming frontier of the Mississippi Valley presents different conditions from the mining frontier of the Rocky Mountains. The frontier reached by the Pacific Railroad, surveyed into rectangles, guarded by the United States Army, and recruited by the daily immigrant ship, moves forward at a swifter pace and in a different way than the frontier reached by the birch canoe or the pack horse."[17]

As a result, while there was speed, there were also odd juxtapositions and overlaps. Industry and agriculture surged, side by side and sometimes helping each other. For example, the rise of canned food and introduction of refrigerated train cars for shipping perishables not only made food more readily available nationwide, they also created more jobs, both on farms and in factories. The region remained wildly diverse and often contradictory. But more than anything, it was a region of opportunity and abundance, as well as of remarkable beauty.

By the twentieth century, the Midwest was well established and the United States as a whole had entered the modern age. The frontier was gone.[18] But that doesn't mean change would cease, for the region or the nation. World War I would mark something of a transition from the old to the new, and after this war (which, as was true of every U.S. war, saw many from the Midwest heading overseas), change would accelerate. While the region remained a blend of agricultural and industrial, it was still growing and changing. Everything from highway systems to electric lights became more ubiquitous. Inventions and innovations continued to be created. The groups that had originally settled the region would continue to flood into the area, but so would new groups. African Americans had always been part of the Midwest, but in the 1900s, the Great Migration would bring millions more to the region, as they abandoned the harsh reality they faced in the South. Mexico, Asia, and South America contributed to the growth of the region. So, the diversity of an always diverse region would continue to increase—but that is beyond the scope of this book. However, the time period that the book does cover gave us so much of what we have today, so many of the stories, institutions, and benefits. It is history we should know—but it is also, if we choose to visit, history we can enjoy.

CHAPTER 2

Witnessing History

Living-history venues, also sometimes called open-air museums, are places where historic buildings are paired with costumed "interpreters" who bring to life the day-to-day activities of an era or region. Interpreters may portray explorers, cowboys, farmers, blacksmiths, printers, weavers, soldiers, teachers, cooks, lumberjacks, shopkeepers, tinsmiths, sailors, or a whole range of other characters that can introduce you to the reality of a different time. Interpreters, along with everyone else working at a living-history venue, take history seriously and put a great deal of effort into making sure everything is accurate. As a result, while these places are a lot of fun, they are also great places to learn history.

One thing to keep in mind is that most living-history venues have hours that vary as the seasons change. So always check for a current listing of dates and times. Summer hours, when families are often traveling, are generally more extensive than spring and autumn, and some places may close entirely during the winter, or offer only an occasional festival during the off season, depending on how open to the elements they are.

Also, be aware that the day of the week can make a difference in your experience. Weekdays are usually quieter, which is great if you want to take photos with no crowds, if you want to talk with interpreters, or if you

Important and delightful elements of living-history venues are the costumed inter-preters. They are knowledgeable about the period and can share information, but they spend much of their time re-creating the activities of the era being preserved. Here, an interpreter at Sauder Village is busy in her kitchen, using a churn to make butter. Photo courtesy of Sauder Village.

like to read every sign. However, there is often more "action" on weekends, more events, more interpreters. Of course, part of this is because a bigger audience makes a bigger "show" more practical. However, it is also often because many volunteers who work at a venue (rather than the paid staff) have jobs during the week and are available only on their days off. Either way, weekends generally mean bigger crowds but more going on. Take this into consideration when making plans.

Do know that, though they represent the past, these venues do have modern conveniences, such as running water, restrooms, and safety equip-ment, and some are wheelchair accessible. So, you get all the cool stuff without the difficulties of the actual past.

But do make plans to visit these places. They are usually truly beautiful and are always interesting. They offer a remarkable way to "witness history" and discover the ways in which life has changed.

In Sauder Village, in addition to exploring historic buildings, visitors can try out historic means of transportation, such as this horse-drawn carriage. Photo courtesy of Sauder Village.

Sauder Village Living History Museum & Farm

Archbold, OH

When this destination was first recommended to me, I had wondered if there was any connection between this venue and the Sauder bookcases that line my office walls at home. The answer is "yes." Erie Sauder, born in 1904 and raised here in Archbold, after decades of working with wood, invented furniture that could be assembled by customers at home. He did very well. It was as Erie prepared for retirement that he began to act on his desire to tell the story of the region's history. And so began Historic Sauder Village. Today, at 235 acres, it is the largest living-history venue in Ohio.[1]

Exiting the Welcome Center, one steps into Ohio in the 1800s. The lovely, tree-shaded Village Green is circled by historic buildings where interpreters carve wood, make baskets, work with tin and copper, weave blankets, and spin wool—each one delighted to stop and explain his or her craft. (I particularly loved the woman spinning wool, as she was so tickled to demonstrate how, if there was a flaw in the wool, you could just break the yarn, remove the flaw, and then reattach the unspun wool to the yarn. "I've been spinning for many years," she chuckled, "and I never get tired of seeing that work.") The first building on the left, as one faces the Village Green, is the actual building where Erie Sauder, at age 16, built a lathe for turning wood. The thing that amused me here was that, in order to save energy, Sauder's mother only let him use the lathe when she was doing laundry, because the same engine that turned the lathe could also run the antique, wooden washing machine (and both lathe and washer were demonstrated).

Next stop beyond the Village Green's buildings is a large museum that offers impressive displays focused on Ohio history, the area's natural environment, rural life in the 1800s, and the tools and evolution of Midwestern agriculture. This is a lot more fun than it may sound from that description, as there are games, interactive activities, surprising collections, and remarkable ingenuity on all hands. In addition, there is a gorgeous collection of quilts, as well as everything you might need to make your own.

For me, among the most memorable items in the museum was the Council Oak carving. This handsome, one-ton sculpture shows friends Potawatomi Chief Winameg and Dresden Howard, who lived in this area in the early 1800s and were buried together under the Council Oak tree when they died. The massive oak stood nearby for nearly 300 years. When it became diseased in the early 1990s, rather than being destroyed, it was turned into this impressive carving.

Following the path away from the museum took me back into the world of vintage buildings and costumed interpreters doing demonstrations and telling tales. I stopped in the Natives and Newcomers area, which focuses on the life of Native Americans in Ohio in 1803, as well as the trappers and traders with whom they were interacting by this time. Then on to the Pioneer Settlement (1830s to 1870s), through the log schoolhouse and nearby jail, around and through the Peter Stuckey Farm (1837), and past the horse and buggy ride and depot for the train that circles the property. I also passed the Little Pioneers Homestead, which is designed specifically for children to enjoy.

I explored the water-powered grist mill (a mill being a necessity in a grain-growing region) and, as it was a warm day, happily visited the old-time ice cream parlor. Then back among the craft demonstrations and stores. While many of the demonstrations simply reflect life in the 1800s, a number of the crafts here employ very high-end artisans. There is an entire building (Burlington Glass Works) for glass blowing (and selling), where internationally lauded glass artist Mark Matthews creates stunning artwork. The basket weaver and potter were also creating collectible pieces. For more modest purchases, a sprawling General Store offers the sorts of souvenirs most commonly taken home—penny candy, books, reproductions of old toys, and so on.

I had arrived when the Village opened and left when it closed, and I still didn't see everything. (And they are currently in the process of adding more.)

Among the many things that make Sauder Village different from other living-history venues I've encountered is the degree to which it is equipped for longer visits. The property includes a campground, resort, playground, restaurant, and bakery. So, in addition to delighting those who love history, this could be the focus of a family holiday.

Historic Roscoe Village

Coshocton, OH

In the early 1800s, before trains offered a faster and more popular transportation option, boats were the easiest way to move people and goods. However, because there was not always a river or lake where it was needed, people dug canals. At Historic Roscoe Village, you can revisit one of the towns that grew up in the 1820s along the Ohio and Erie Canal—and even relive traveling by canal.

There is no charge for enjoying the shops, gardens, and restaurants of this charming town, with its tree-lined street and brick sidewalks, but if you want to explore the history, you need a ticket. So I headed for the red-brick colonial-style Visitor Center and Museum, which is conveniently right next to the main parking lot. There was so much of interest here that it took me more than an hour to get back outside. (And it would take longer if one had

At Historic Roscoe Village, the entire town is historic. Stores, restaurants, and a hotel are interspersed between buildings where interpreters re-create such activities as making brooms, running a printing press, and teaching school. Photo courtesy of Historic Roscoe Village.

children, as there are history-oriented craft projects available, such as tin punching, candle-dipping and weaving.)

In addition to an excellent movie about the building of canals, the museum offered dioramas of the Ohio and Erie Canal and explanations of the work that went into creating it. What an astonishing feat it was. The canal had to be dug. Then stone to line the canal had to be quarried in the nearby hills and transported to the site under construction. To compensate for uneven terrain, locks had to be put in every few miles. When a ravine needed to be crossed, an aqueduct had to be built wide enough for a canal boat to cross it. A stunning amount of work. And yet, in the 1800s, the rate of building was about 4–1/2 days per mile! Of course, the amount of work underscores the importance of the canals. They were the super-highways of the day.

The history of the town, of its restoration, and of the many carefully tended gardens, especially those around the Visitor Center, were also related. The restoration is of interest because of the family behind it. Edward Montgomery invented rubber-coated cotton gloves, which made him a fortune. He and his wife Frances decided to use that fortune to resurrect Roscoe Village, which had declined after the canal was replaced by the highway.

Eventually, I headed out through the gardens and into the village. First stop was the village smithy. It is always fun to see a blacksmith crafting something from hot bits of iron, and this smithy added lively conversation to his skillful manipulation of the forge, hammer, and anvil. At the next stop, a delightful woman who demonstrated an old printing press and then broom making (lovely brooms, too), told us that if you work here long enough, they'll train you for any of the tasks they need. She had even learned blacksmithing. Past the tollhouse and up to the doctor's office, to see the collection of medical equipment and then the doctor's house next door. Across the street, I explored the life-sized replica of a canal boat, this one "anchored" in one of the many gardens. Then to the Roscoe School, where a teacher was happy to explain what lessons would have been like in the 1800s. There was a craftsman's house and a museum that I didn't get to, as it was suddenly 4 o'clock, and the living-history aspect shuts down. Fortunately, all the shops and restaurants were still open, so I could explore for a while longer. There were so many clever and well-crafted items to peruse in the historic shops, and a café with a patio made for a pleasant end of the day.

Because it is a real town, as well as a living-history venue, Roscoe Village does not shut down when summer ends. If you're there during the Christmas holidays, you might have the opportunity to enjoy a lantern tour, a candle-lighting festival, and other holiday traditions. As with every destination, check the website for details.

Nearby: About two miles up the road, part of the canal has been preserved, and you can take a 40-minute ride in a traditional canal boat pulled by horses, traveling as you would have in the 1800s (though this activity occurs only during the summer). Also, a fairly easy walk from the Visitor Center, there are some surprisingly beautiful ruins of the old canal that are worth seeing, the great stones now green with moss and lichens but still standing imposingly in some places. A little farther along, an aqueduct that has been turned into a foot bridge brings home just how much work went into these canals.

Conner Prairie

Fishers, IN

In a quiet suburb of Indianapolis, just a few blocks off a busy street with all the strip malls one expects in Midwestern suburbs, I turned into a parking lot that was surrounded by trees. The attractive Welcome Center was inviting but gave no hint of what lay beyond. However, even in the Welcome Center, history soon became evident, with gift shop, discovery station, craft corner, and history-oriented play area for children. Then, on the other side of the building, I stepped into the past.

The first thing to command my attention was the massive hot-air balloon that re-creates the day in 1859 when Lafayette, Indiana, first saw a similar wonder. I watched the balloon lift into the air, but then, rather than standing in line for a ride, I continued on—into a more distant past. The first major themed area is the Lenape camp. The Lenape, or Delaware Indians, lived here from 1795 to 1820. Aside from exploring the wigwams and trading post, and examining the dugout canoe and other artifacts, it was here that I was first exposed to the surprisingly young interpreters that I would find all over Conner Prairie. There were adults, of course, but there were also teens and younger, all genuinely excited to be there and clearly skilled at their assigned tasks. "Want to try using the bow drill?" "Want to see how I can light a fire with a flint and a piece of steel?" Truly delightful. (The quality was not the surprise—everywhere I've gone, I have found enthusiastic and knowledgeable interpreters. It was their youth that surprised me. I would later learn that Conner Prairie has an extensive extracurricular Social Studies program for students ten to eighteen.[2] Wonderful.)

From the Lenape camp, I headed to the William Conner House. While every building here is authentic and original, this is the only building that sits on its original site. William is the Conner for whom Conner Prairie is named, as the venue sprawls across what was once his property. Built in 1823, when Indiana was still the frontier, the Conner House is one of the oldest brick

In the carpenter shop at Conner Prairie, an interpreter demonstrates working with wood to a visitor. Photo courtesy of Conner Prairie.

homes in the state, and the dates the Conner family lived here span the transition from territory to statehood. I learned about William Conner as I toured the handsome house—and his life was fascinating, from fur trader to state representative, married to the daughter of a Delaware chief, charter member of the Indiana Historical Society.

I moved next into the 1836 Prairie Town. Here, all the buildings one needs to have a viable town have been collected and are populated with interpreters. There are homes, a smithy, general store, schoolhouse, carpenter's shop, doctor's office, tavern, and more. Some of the interpreters in this section had to be artisans, as well, working at the potter's wheel, the carpenter's bench, the forge and anvil. The younger interpreters taught games in the yards or helped collect herbs for the doctor.

Finally, I turned toward the 1863 Civil War "Journey." Here, Union soldiers emerge from tents, the recently burned buildings smolder, and a train station and field hospital are busy. As always, there is much to explore. In one building, an excellent multimedia presentation re-creates a raid made on Indiana by the Confederates. In addition, there is a play area for young children who might need to expend a little energy.

Weary after hours of wandering, I caught the shuttle back to the Welcome Center, rather than walking back. I did feel that the Gift Shop deserved a little attention, and while there was much that was desirable, I bought only heritage popcorn and a CD of Thomas Jefferson's favorite fiddle music. Splendid day.

Naper Settlement

Naperville, IL

Unlike most living-history venues, Naper Settlement isn't hidden away from view. It's right in downtown Naperville. Walking along S. Webster St., looking over the fence, I could see the exteriors of many of the buildings. Still, it was like looking into a different world—and I could appreciate the advantage of having a place that is so accessible to surrounding schools and the nearby train station.

One enters the Naper Settlement through the Pre-Emption House, a re-creation of the 1834 tavern and hotel that was once a focal point of Naperville life. Just outside the door, I stepped onto the "Plank Road." Illinois was muddy in the 1800s. Before drainage systems were in place, wooden planks were used to create passable roads. One such early plank road connected Naperville to the rapidly growing city of Chicago.

I passed a sign about Naperville's current population that reminded me that, while most of the Naper Settlement focuses on the 1800s and into the early 1900s, it also works to connect the past to the present. So, even though the buildings are old, there is also information that brings the story up to today.

I walked along the path that took me past the fronts of all the buildings I'd seen from outside: blacksmith shop, print shop, stone carver's house, fire house, post office, log house, and meeting house. Each building offered interesting history and insights, either from information signs or from costumed interpreters.

Visiting midweek meant fewer interpreters, but it also meant fewer visitors, so I was able to talk quite extensively with the interpreters who were on hand. In the blacksmith shop, I learned the difference between a blacksmith and a farrier. A farrier cares for horse hooves, making and fitting shoes. A blacksmith fixes tools, plows, and other iron implements. However, in smaller towns, the blacksmith may be required to fill both roles. In the stone carver's house, I learned that Naperville is built on a bed of limestone, and quarrying was a major industry here in the 1800s.

Turning a corner, I caught sight of the charming children's play area, which includes reproductions of buildings (including a fort), a covered wagon, slides, and more. So, combined with the many children's programs this venue offers, it definitely accommodates the needs of families.

Continuing on, I passed other houses and a cluster of farm buildings, stopping next at the Copenhagen Schoolhouse, where a "teacher" was organizing vintage copies of McGuffey Readers. Copenhagen was a small town that in time became part of Naperville, but its name hints at the remarkable diversity of the town's settlers. Then on to the beautiful Martin Mitchell Mansion. It was this impressive Victorian home, built in 1883, that determined the location of Naper Settlement, as it was the donation to Naperville of this mansion and the surrounding land that made this venue possible. Everything else was relocated here.

Past the Century Memorial Chapel, built in 1864 (and still used for weddings), and back to the Pre-Emption House, where I descended to the lower level to explore exhibits covering even more of Naperville's fascinating history—which I'll leave for you to discover. But one fun tidbit to share: a lot of Germans settled here, and so of course there was a brewery. A young Adolph Coors worked here, at the local Stenger Brewery, before moving to Colorado. So, even though Naper Settlement is smaller than many of the venues included in this chapter, it is still filled with interesting and often unexpected bits of history.

Lincoln's New Salem

Petersburg, IL

Roughly 20 miles north of Springfield, Highway 123 cuts through dense forest, offering access to the winding road that leads to Lincoln's New Salem State Historic Site. Nestled in this wooded setting is a reconstruction of the

Lincoln's New Salem reflects the period during which Abraham Lincoln lived there, as well as the lives of those he knew. Photo by Cynthia Clampitt, used with permission of Lincoln's New Salem.

town in which Abraham Lincoln spent his early adulthood, including his first attempts at business. Ranged through the green "town" are twenty-three buildings, all built of logs, plus fences, wagons, wells, and other necessities of life. There are homes and barns and all the services a town would need— but they are not anonymous buildings, because we know who lived in each house and ran each business—including the two small stores that Lincoln and a partner ran, unsuccessfully.

The Welcome Center is a good place to start a visit. I appreciated the orientation video, which explains the history, the buildings, and the significance of this town's connection to Lincoln, who lived in New Salem from 1831 to 1837. Because New Salem is where Lincoln changed from a young man with no real focus to a lawyer and politician, but with some surprising "bumps" along the way. The tale was also laced with people who saw Lincoln's potential and offered work or guidance. But Lincoln's intelligence, wit, integrity, and passion for learning were the driving forces behind the change. The Welcome Center also has a nice collection of the equipment of life—spinning wheels, looms, butter churns, and so on. But I was eager to get into the "town." I had visited decades earlier with my family, and I was hoping I loved it as much now as I had then. (By the end, I think I loved it even more.)

The first two buildings were the home and shop of Henry Onstot, the town cooper. A gray-haired interpreter working in the shop perked up when a few people entered, launching into a little speech to explain what he does. "A cooper made barrels, buckets, and butter churns," he told us. He also explained that the reason this building is a reconstruction is that when Henry Onstot moved away, he took the logs with him. A cooper was a key figure in any town in the 1800s, because everything was shipped in barrels, from fine china to salt pork to rum. Of course, buckets and butter churns were also vital. Therefore, a good cooper would be kept busy.

In the Onstot residence next door, another interpreter was sitting by the fire. He explained that he was making ink from black walnuts. When I expressed interest in the town's history, he happily launched into details about the building, the people who once lived there, what life was like, and what crops were grown. It was delightful, and a good reminder that many interpreters are tremendously knowledgeable.

Continuing on, I wound through gardens and visited residences. After several homes, the blacksmith shop, a church, the wool house, and a doctor's office, I reached the Lincoln-Berry Store, the first of the two stores Lincoln owned here in town with partner William Berry. Shelves were filled with necessities for sale, including brandy and rye whiskey. I passed more residences, the local tavern (which in the 1800s, would be more like a rough bed and breakfast than a bar), the gristmill, and two more stores (including the second Lincoln-Berry operation). Surrounding everything were broad lawns, where wagons waited for riders and horses munched on grass. It was all so beautiful. I was euphoric by the time I left.

The kitchen at Kline Creek Farm has a "modern" stove, which was a big improvement over cooking in an open fireplace. The wood box on the left is filled with fuel for the stove. The large tub hanging on the wall is what bathtubs looked like in the 1800s. They were kept in the kitchen because that was where you could heat water for the bath. Photo by Cynthia Clampitt, used with permission of Forest Preserve District of DuPage County.

Kline Creek Farm

West Chicago, IL

Unlike many living-history venues, this is not a collection of buildings. It's a farm. The advantage to this is that one gets to see what life was like for much of the country in the 1890s—not just part of a life, such as a job, but everything, from plowing a field to setting the dining room table. The first time I visited Kline Creek Farm, it was for a corn festival, and in addition to hearing a talk about how harvesting was done, I actually had the pleasure of marching along rows of corn stalks, picking corn, husking it, and tossing it into a wagon drawn by horses—just as it would have happened in 1890 (though workers in the 1890s would have been much faster than I was). But that was just the beginning of the visit—and of what I learned.

Closer to the farmhouse, I watched interpreters teach children how to make corn-husk dolls. In the farmhouse, an interpreter offered an excellent tour, describing each room and how it was used. I learned that, on freezing winter days before central heating existed, servants might be asked to stand around the family in the dining room during dinner to add a little extra body heat. In the kitchen, another interpreter explained all the cooking tools, both unfamiliar and antique versions of ones still in use. He demonstrated lighting the large, cast-iron stove and then described the making of a treat that was popular at the time: crush popcorn and mix it with marshmallow—pretty much like the popular puffed-rice treats we make today. He also said that corn was often served for breakfast, with milk and sugar on it. (Worth noting: hot buttered popcorn wasn't introduced until the 1893 World's Fair.[3]) The interpreter also related that women of this time often wrote of the misery of their lives. Farming could make you independent and even lead to a degree of prosperity, but it was often lonely, with neighbors far away, and it was incredibly hard work.

House explored, I headed off to visit the garden (every house had one—all your herbs and most of your fruit and vegetables were home-grown), the barn (horses, wagons, and tools), and all the pens and huts for farm animals (cows, sheep, chickens). On that first visit, it was a crisp fall day with all the surrounding trees ablaze with color (the site is in the middle of a forest preserve, so there are a lot of trees). However, Kline Creek Farm is only a little more than twenty miles from where I live, so it's an easy trip—and a great way to introduce friends to living history. I get back regularly, especially when they have a special event (most recent visit was for their bee hives and honey collecting), so I can attest to the fact it is lovely throughout the year.

Shoal Creek Living History Museum

Kansas City, MO

Meandering through a housing development and around a golf course, it took me a while to find Shoal Creek. Upon arriving, I discovered that this handsome, 80-acre venue is different from the other entries in this chapter.

At Shoal Creek Living History Museum, historic buildings invite exploration. Photo by Cynthia Clampitt, used with permission.

It does offer 21 historic buildings, dating from 1807 to 1885. It shares the same goal as other venues, which is preserving the past. However, though it is opened all year, from dawn to dusk, it is not always staffed by docents or interpreters. It only really "comes alive" during events (usually on week-ends)—so depending on what you are hoping for, check their website to see what is happening.

When there are no events, there is no entry fee. You can wander at your leisure across the gently rolling terrain, among the wonderful vintage build-ings—but you can't go inside the buildings. However, there are large displays with photos of the interiors and information about the history of each building. When there are events, the buildings are open and the grounds are alive with costumed interpreters—and there is an entry fee. I was there on a non-event day, so I wandered and read signs.

All the buildings are handsome, but I loved the look of the 1824 Grist Mill. A mill would always be the heart of a community in a grain-growing region, and here, it is the center of the town. I also found the City Hall and Jail (1867) very interesting. Built in Missouri City, it was designed to accommodate prisoners on the lower level and the City Hall on the top level. Other buildings include private homes, cabins, general store, doctor's office, Crossroads Inn, and the Mt. Ararat Baptist Church, all beautifully situated.

Interesting buildings in a really lovely setting. Great for hiking and learning a bit if you're in the area. And I must congratulate them on finding a way of making the site available even when the "living" part is not possible. However, do check to find out the status of this venue before visiting, just so you know what to expect—especially if you're hoping to see it "alive."

The Henry Ford Museum/Greenfield Village

Dearborn, MI

The Henry Ford Museum of American Innovation is fabulous, and Greenfield Village is so remarkable it is essentially in a category of its own. Combined, these two form the largest indoor-outdoor museum complex in the world.

The complex reflects Henry Ford's passion for two very different aspects of history: everyday life and remarkable achievements. It is Ford's solution to the problem he had with history textbooks focusing so much on "guns or great speeches" while ignoring the things that made life possible, from agriculture to inventions. There is so much here, even after two trips to Dearborn, I can't help but think I've missed something.

I started in Greenfield Village, a venue that truly necessitates the use of the map that is offered when you buy your tickets. Here, the collection is not simply of representative buildings, but of historically important buildings: for example, the birthplace and bicycle shop of the Wright Brothers; the house where H. J. Heinz perfected his recipes (the company was started in the basement); Luther Burbank's birthplace; the homes of Noah Webster and Robert Frost; Thomas Edison's Menlo Park research complex; the farms of the Ford family and, because cars must have tires, the Firestones. A few places are reconstructions, such as the slave cabin of George Washington Carver, the original having been destroyed. But most buildings are orig-

A refurbished vintage Model T Ford is driven past the bicycle shop where the Wright Brothers worked on their dream of flying. These are just two of the iconically American pieces of history you can see at Greenfield Village. Photo courtesy of The Henry Ford Museum.

inal, and all provide ample background information, often in the form of an interpreter (sometimes taking on the persona of the original owner) or detailed signage, but occasionally with a recorded message.

The village is divided into districts, with houses and gardens lining streets like tidy neighborhoods. Depending on the district, the traffic on the streets might be a horse-drawn carriage or a Model T Ford (actual, refurbished, vintage Model Ts—available for rides). Costumed interpreters are as often farming the open land around the village as they are offering information to visitors. In the Liberty Craftworks district, the interpreters may be found carding wool, weaving, making pottery, blowing glass, working in the tin shop, or operating one of the saw mills, among other tasks. Not only are the crafts and skills demonstrated, but a good bit of history is also offered. For example, at the Glass Shop, I learned that glass blowing started with the

Phoenicians in about 50 B.C., and in the Tin Shop, I learned that when factories put tin smiths out of business (because tin cans were once all made by hand), many of them transferred their skills to creating the pipework needed for stoves and heating.

The Railroad Junction district offers a history of railroading, with a railroad turntable, roundhouse, coaling tower, and more. The Working Farms district, in addition to farms, has barns filled with collections of agricultural equipment and information about the development of agriculture in the Midwest—including some rather remarkable machines (check out the monstrously large steam traction machine). In one of the barns, I encountered a quote from Ford that I thought was particularly appropriate for the Midwest: "I believe that industry and agriculture are natural partners."

There are multiple places to dine, all reflecting history, including the large cafeteria named A Taste of History. I enjoyed the meal I had there, but I liked even more the Eagle Tavern, a nineteenth-century tavern where one dines communally at long tables (as would have been the norm back then). The menu is fun, and I was told it is seasonal. I ordered summer vegetable soup (particularly good), venison croquettes, and black-eyed pea salad, served with bread-and-butter pickles and corn bread. A family seated at the same table as I was had young children, and when they asked for straws, they were brought hollow pasta—because of course plastic hasn't been invented yet. Mrs. Fisher's Southern Cooking is an outdoor lunch stand that focuses on recipes from the cookbook, *What Mrs. Fisher Knows About Old Southern Cooking*, published in 1881 by formerly enslaved Abby Fisher (still in print).

All that is less than half of what is available. There are at least a hundred buildings, all of them interesting. Sprinkled amid the Americana, there are buildings that reflect other of Ford's interests, from a Swiss Chalet to a cluster of buildings from the Cotswolds. That may not seem like American history, but I felt that, to a certain extent, given that Ford could buy them and was able to get them here, that says something about his success. They became part of our history simply because Henry Ford was such a huge part of our history.

Next door to Greenfield Village is The Henry Ford Museum of American Innovation, an astonishing collection that covers the breakthroughs, inventions, and discoveries that created the modern world. The elegant, colonial-style, red-brick building is huge, with a floor plan that covers twelve acres. It actually looks rather like a college. As the name states, the collection includes a stunning array of inventions and innovations ranging across American history up to the present. Not too surprisingly, given Ford's career, there are a lot of exhibits related to transportation, with numerous cars, but also early planes and trains (including the oldest known surviving steam engine). Ford's fondness for farms is reflected in a significant collection of agricultural equipment. While much of the collection is twentieth-century, there is plenty from earlier centuries, such as George Washington's sleeping cot and cooking gear for use in the field and the chair in which Abraham Lincoln was sitting when he was shot.

I am a bit more in love with Greenfield Village, but The Henry Ford Museum is absolutely stunning and shouldn't be missed. To do justice to both Greenfield Village and the Henry Ford Museum, it would probably be wise to plan on spending two days, or more.

Nearby: Tours are also available to the Ford Rouge Factory and Benson Ford Research Center.

Living History Farms

Urbandale, IA

Just outside of Des Moines, close to Interstate 80, NW 111th Street leads off of Hickman Road to the welcome center for the Living History Farms—and access to two centuries of history. The word *farm* in the name is plural because there are three farms, one from 1700, one from 1850, and one from 1900. This distinct separation of eras is a large part of what creates this venue's identity. But first, after leaving the welcome center, one arrives in 1876, in the "town" of Walnut Hill.

In Walnut Hill, all the necessities of life are on hand, including houses, barns, a pharmacy, general store, bank, school, law office, millinery shop, church, cemetery, blacksmith, cabinetmaker, print shop, doctor's office, veterinary clinic, and broom maker. The costumed interpreters who populate the town introduce visitors to all these aspects of life, running the

On the 1900s Farm, at Iowa's Living History Farms, an interpreter drives a hay rake. The white farmhouse and red barns are visible in the background. The 1900s Farm is also known as the Horse-Powered farm, because farm equipment had advanced to the stage where the speed of horses could replace the plodding strength of oxen. Photo courtesy of the Living History Farms.

press, making brooms, and carrying on the other tasks of the time. They also stress the connection between town and farms—one could not survive without the other. And so the importance of the farms that lie ahead is established.

From Walnut Hill, a tractor-towed tram carries visitors to the first farm. In 1700, the farmers were Ioway, a North American Indian people who migrated from the Great Lakes area. The Ioway relied on hunting and agriculture, and both are represented here. Semipermanent lodges and a "traveling house" for the annual bison hunt can be explored. Gardens are green with maize, squash, and beans—the traditional "three sisters." Interpreters demonstrate farming techniques, tanning animal hides, and preparing food. The surrounding trees and tall grasses envelop the area snuggly enough that other time periods, whether our own or those ahead, cannot be seen.

A trail leads out of the Ioway farm (and there is a good bit of walking between farms, so wear comfortable shoes). Along the trail, a handrail acts as a timeline, with dates and information posted relating what is occurring in U.S. history. This offers context to events in the region. Of course, between

1700 and 1850, the Thirteen Colonies gained independence from Great Britain and the Louisiana Purchase expanded the new United States, adding, among other things, the territory that would become Iowa.

In 1850, Iowa, which became a state in 1846, was still on the frontier, and this farm reflects that, with a rough log cabin and barn, split-rail fences, and a rugged but promising life. Fields are planted and cottage gardens are thriving. Livestock has been introduced—and I was amused to learn that the reason chickens were allowed to wander through the house was that they are very good at keeping the cabin free of bugs. Here, interpreters spin wool, cook, plow, and take care of the other chores that make life possible, though always happily stopping to talk to visitors.

By 1900, farms were beginning to look like what most of us think of as farms, with white picket fences around tidy homes, broad yards, and red barns. Machines are beginning to appear that help with planting and harvesting. Most significant is the fact that farm equipment has advanced to a stage where the speed and agility of horses has replaced the plodding strength of oxen. The farmhouse is more comfortable and spacious than the log cabin. The kitchen now has an actual stove, rather than just a large fireplace, though wood is still the source of heat. Farms are larger and a farmer can feed more people. It is all becoming just a bit more familiar.

Even on an ordinary day, there is a tremendous amount to see and do at the Living History Farms. However, like most of these venues, they offer a range of special events and programs, from historic dinners to learning historic skills, so check the calendar on their website to discover additional things that might interest you.

Old World Wisconsin

Eagle, WI

Old World Wisconsin (OWW) is approached along a rural road flanked by the undulating, forested beauty of the Kettle Moraine area of southern Wisconsin. The parking lot and visitors' center are visible from the road, but the historic buildings are set well back from the road, among those surrounding trees.

Though explorers had arrived earlier, serious settlement of Wisconsin didn't start until the early 1800s, after the United States had won its independence and gained access to what was known at the time as the Northwest Territory. Enough settlers had arrived by 1848 for Wisconsin to obtain statehood. As with most of the Midwest, settlers came in waves. In Wisconsin, the first wave came from New England, with later waves coming from overseas. The varied settlement patterns and national origins are reflected in everything from Wisconsin's cuisine to its architecture.

As the state grew and modernized, log cabins and vintage stores were rescued, and more than sixty of these historic structures were brought here. Researchers did more than collect the old buildings, however; they documented their histories and the lives of those who built them and lived in them. So, when you go to OWW, you don't learn a general history of a typical settler's life; they can tell you exactly who owned the home, what region or country they were from, what they produced, and how they lived. In some cases, the original furnishings of the homes have been preserved. In cases where the original furnishings were not available, antiques that match the time period have been obtained. Either way, what you see is what it was like for the first settlers.

As would have been the case with early settlement, buildings are clustered by nationality of the original owners. You can visit settlements of Poles, Germans, Finns, Danes, Norwegians, and Yankees (New Englanders), as well as the Crossroads Village, where the shops and services that would support surrounding farms are situated.

Costumed interpreters carry out the tasks and activities of the time reflected by the buildings around them (1840s to 1910s). Visitors can watch a blacksmith form blazing-hot iron into useful objects at his shop, observe women preparing meals, or listen in as a teacher explains a lesson in the schoolhouse. Life as it was goes on as if nothing has changed—except that interpreters stop as visitors enter to relate how gadgets work or things are made.

Almost all buildings have large gardens, as people in early settlements had to grow almost everything they ate. The varieties of fences around those gardens are fascinating, showing both varied ethnicities and remarkable ingenuity, making the best of available materials. In addition, there are fields and farms where you can watch traditional types of farming or see early breeds of livestock. (The official Historic Farmer at OWW not only cares for the animals but is also responsible for knowing which heritage breeds would have been available.) On different weekends of the year, there are exhibitions ranging from early forms of baseball to harvesting the year's crops, from cooking to splitting wood, and much more.

Like so many of these open-air museums, Old World Wisconsin is remarkably beautiful, with the wonderfully preserved old buildings and their gardens nestled amid forests and ponds. Because of the size of the property (600 acres), there are open-air shuttles with regular stops in each of the communities, making it easy to get around. In addition, the large red barn visible from the parking lot houses a café, where lunches and beverages are available. Be advised, closed-toe shoes are a wise option, especially if you want to wander amid gardens or fields.

Heritage Hill State Park

Green Bay, WI

Sitting on a tree-lined street amid old suburbs, the Welcome Center for Heritage Hill gives little suggestion of what lies on the other side. Walk through the building, and you exit into a great, sprawling property that covers a history as sprawling as the land on which it sits. A greeter offered a tram ride to the bottom of the hill that rolls downward from the entryway, in essence going back through time, as distance is what separates time periods here—and I accepted the offer. At the bottom of the hill, and on the other side of a tunnel under the highway, one reaches the earliest dates represented. The first Europeans to reach northern Wisconsin were French (some debate whether the first to arrive was Brûlé in 1622 or Nicolet in 1634—but early), and French trappers and traders were soon to follow. The story at Heritage Hills starts with their arrival.

Pausing from his work in a log trading post, a trapper/interpreter related that trade brought Native American culture from the Stone Age to the Iron Age in one generation. Metal tools and cookware made almost everything easier, and they quickly replaced stone and wood implements. He also explained that when settlements were started, the tailor was usually the second person needed, after the blacksmith, because clothes were all still handmade. In this area, in addition to the trapper's cabin, I visited a maple-sugaring shack and "bark chapel" (a wigwam used as a small church), and watched a man doing the Black Ash weaving traditional among the Oneida.

I wound my way back up through the centuries. In the early courthouse, I was surprised by how much the setup looks like a modern courthouse. Where the path split, I went to the right and entered the Fort Howard section of the property. A large, white building atop a flower-covered hill turned out to be the hospital. The stockade and guardhouse were next, which gave me access to the entrances of the several buildings within the fort. First stop was the hospital, which offers many reminders of how far medicine has come since the 1830s. I also toured the schoolhouse (officers often brought wives and children with them when assignments were long and far from home), the company kitchen, the separate kitchen for the officers and their families, the post library, the guardroom for soldiers on guard duty (a place to rest without sleeping during a 24-hour shift), and the light prison. The officers' quarters were more specific: I saw Lt. Merrill's room, with mosquito netting over the bed, and the room of 2nd Lt. Randolph Barnes Marcy, who was joined by his wife and daughter in 1836. Marcy served with General McClellan during the Civil War, and Lt. Merrill was killed in the Mexican War. (Marcy was also the author of the best-selling book *The Prairie Traveler*, the guide for pioneers pictured in Chapter 1.)

The fort explored, I headed for the buildings on the other side of the broad lawn. At the Baird Law Offices (Baird became the first practicing attorney in Wisconsin in 1823), I learned a bit about the lawyer, but also learned about his half French/half Ottawa wife, who wrote a book about her life—a book that has been published and is available at Heritage Hill. In the blacksmith shop, I saw a cone-shaped device demonstrated that, though simple, was perfect for its job of sizing round objects, from finger rings to the hardware for harnesses.

Moving along to the late 1800s, I visited the Franklin Hose Co. #3 Volunteer Fire Department and then explored the Moravian church and an 1894 cheese factory, where a wagon full of milk cans stood close at hand. The 1872 Belgian Farm offered less familiar (to me) history. Belgians began moving to Wisconsin around 1853. The farmhouse was built right after the Great Fire of 1871 (not the one in Chicago; the much deadlier one that started in Peshtigo, WI, on the same night). Originally located in the area devastated by the fire, the wood farmhouse was constructed with a veneer of bricks, for protection. Inside, I particularly liked the blue stove in the kitchen and loved seeing the row of wooden shoes (sabots) in the mud room. Nearby, the long, log barn, with its central drive-through for un-loading hay, was especially handsome. (For those who like mysteries, I read that Kathleen Ernst used this Belgian Farm as the setting for her novel *The Lacemaker's Secret*.)

I passed the Tomb of the Unknown Solider (an unmarked grave found here of a soldier from the 1820s) on my way to Cotton House. This impos-ing, white-columned Greek Revival house was built in Green Bay in the 1840s. Its significance lies in its architecture and engineering, rather than the fame of the original owner, and the house is on the National Register of Historic Places.

After my long uphill climb through more than two centuries, I was ready to look for a drink of water, make a quick visit to the gift shop (I wanted to check out that book written in the 1820s by the lawyer's wife), and then head back to my car.

Forest History Center

Grand Rapids, MN

Often when we talk about what the Midwest provided the growing United States, the first thing to come to mind is food. That is not wrong, because the region certainly produced food abundantly. But it also produced stun-ning amounts of raw materials for building the nation's cities, with mines, quarries, and forests supplying the materials. Here, just outside of the "oth-er" Grand Rapids, the one at the headwaters of the Mississippi in Minnesota, the Forest History Center celebrates and re-creates the lumbering part of our past.

This is a heavily forested area, and one walks to the Welcome Center amid ferns, birches, and pines. The Welcome Center starts the visit well. There are wonderful displays about forestry, including a lot of kid-friendly

At the Forest History Center, the "barn boss" explains how teams of draft horses are used to move and load wood onto sleds. He also explains that teams don't just work together, they also live together. Photo by Cynthia Clampitt, used with permission of the Minnesota Historical Society.

elements. There is also a tremendous amount of information on everything from preserving forests to why earthworms (an introduced species) are a serious problem. There is a wonderful film of the last major log drive on the Little Fork River in 1937—a cold and dangerous endeavor that involves floating millions of logs down river to the saw mills, keeping them from creating log jams (and where the term *log jam* clearly came from). The film also showed the all-important wanigans, rafts that carried supplies and acted as camps and kitchens for the workers on the drive. The film said that a good cook did more to attract workers than anything else an employer could offer, so the wanigan with the cooking equipment would have been cherished.

In another room, a well-crafted multimedia presentation relates the events of the Cloquet Fire. This is a moving recounting of a shattering event; hundreds died and entire towns were gone, as well as much of the surrounding forest. The presentations and displays offered a remarkable introduction to forestry in this area. But then it was 12:30 and time to travel into the past.

Our guide, in the role of lumber camp employee, told us that it was now December 15, 1900, and it would be a 2-day walk to the logging camp (true at the time, but fortunately just about five minutes now). An order had been placed for six million board feet of lumber, which would be enough to build about 600 houses, she told us, so there was a lot of work ahead. All work was done in the winter, she related, for two reasons: farmers were available for work, and it was easier to move the logs on frozen ground—you could cover the road with water and then slide sleds loaded with logs on the ice.

We were taught a lot of lingo, which I enjoyed. It was explained that the word *wanigan*, which I'd heard in the movie, was an Indian word for *supply*. *The Push* was the boss, a *sky pilot* was a preacher, and an *ink slinger* was a clerk. There were tons of other fun terms, as well, from *swing dingle* to *swamp water* to *wind timbers*. We got to explore the housing for the lumberjacks (two men to a bunk, and lice could be a problem), the Carpenter's shop, the blacksmith's forge, the cookhouse, the barn, and more. The "barn boss" came out and showed us how the huge draft horses were worked, with horses that worked together always being stalled together. Two horses can pull a load of 20 tons—at least when the road has been covered in ice.

In addition to seeing demonstrations of many of the tasks that made up a lumberjack's day, another visitor and I were offered the chance to saw a log with a "modern" saw—a saw with a raking tooth, a post–Civil War invention that revolutionized lumbering. Then, in the wonderful kitchen and dining hall, we got to meet the cook. She explained what meals were like and what her job was. She made 30 pies and 24 loaves of bread every day—as well as all the staples of regular meals: beans, potatoes, and prunes at every meal, as well as meat. But for all this, the cook made more money than just about anyone else in camp except the boss—because as noted in the movie, a good cook made hiring easier.

Finally, a few of the costumed interpreters got together to teach us some of the songs and entertainments that would have filled the hours after dark that a lumberjack would have free. (They worked from "can see to can't see," which meant first light to sunset, which was not a long day in the winter, especially this far north.)

When we had seen all the buildings and had heard the tales the interpreters told, we were pointed in the direction of the river, where we could see and board one of the wanigans afloat by the river bank. Then we hiked back up the hill to the fire watchers' cabin and tower. The tower is 100 feet tall, or roughly ten stories, and it was once the only way to get an overview of the forest to look for smoke. (I passed on climbing the 126 steps to the top.) Then I hiked back to the Visitor Center, to see any displays I'd missed my first time through.

But what a remarkable adventure.

Old Cowtown Museum

Wichita, KS

Knowing that the state song of Kansas is "Home on the Range" may make it less of a surprise that the state would have a living-history venue that reflects a Wild West past. Early in Wichita's history, herds of cattle moving up the Chisholm Trail to the railhead earned the town the nickname of "Cowtown," and the city's living-history venue preserves that iconic past.

From the handsome welcome center, a path leads through time, coming first to the rugged cabin of an early settler and then on to a trapper's cabin, both filled with relics of their time and purposes. Continuing on, I turned a corner, and with a happy jolt of recognition, saw the "town." It is the quintessential street scene of countless Westerns, from movies to TV. It is perfect. However, though it looks like a movie set, Old Cowtown Museum is an accredited history museum. A few buildings are reproductions, when the originals were not in good enough shape to use, but the majority here are actual historic buildings from Wichita's earlier days. (Some of which I would later see in photographs at the Wichita Historical Museum.)

I strolled down wooden sidewalks amid the beautifully maintained old buildings, exploring each one. The shops and offices are filled with wonderful artifacts related to the original purpose of each building, including a music store, funeral parlor, clothier, art gallery, newspaper office, meat market, blacksmith shop, and more. Costumed interpreters shared tales and

The historic buildings at Old Cowtown Museum preserve the history of Wichita, known as Cowtown back in the days when Wyatt Earp was the local lawman. Photo by Cynthia Clampitt, used with permission.

carried out the tasks of the town, from running the printing press to keeping the jail to making iron implements—and even serving sarsaparilla in the Saloon. An early trading post and the homes of some of the early residents of Wichita are also perfectly preserved.

So much to learn about this place, this time period, these iconic characters from our past. Jesse Chisholm, the half Scottish–half Cherokee man who blazed the trail that bears his name, was illiterate but spoke 14 Indian languages. As a result, he was often called the prairie ambassador, as he could talk to almost any group. Chisholm's partner, buffalo hunter James Mead, became one of the founders of Wichita. However, it was William Greiffenstein who became known as the "Father of Wichita." Actually, there was a substantial Dutch and German presence in Wichita—enough that there was a *Turnverein* (German gymnasium club) Hall. And because the Tailor in town was German and Jewish, they never decorate his store for Christmas.

Knowing that there was an oyster craze in the mid-1800s that swept the nation (once trains loaded with ice could bring oysters from the coast), I was interested to see that even here, oyster dinners were advertised at the local hotel, and a sign announced the availability of oysters at the meat market. I knew even small towns in Illinois were consuming oysters, but it was a surprise to me to see that they were popular and available here, on what was at the time the frontier.

Wichita was "Cowtown" for a relatively short time—1872–1876—just as the era of the cowboy was relatively short, vividly memorable because of books and movies rather than because of a long history. In fact, by 1876 (the last year Wyatt Earp was the local lawman in Wichita), the cowboy era was pretty much over here. The area became more agrarian—a transition represented here by distance, with a lovely old farmstead about a block after the end of "town." An interpreter in the farmhouse was sewing on the front porch when I walked through, and she offered me a few historic recipes, which I was happy to have. In the yard, I was interested to see the sorghum press, as sorghum syrup became a popular sweetener in free states in the mid-1800s as antislavery forces looked for something that would replace the sugar that depended so heavily on slave labor.

Then back from the farm through town and to the Welcome Center. Before leaving, I stopped to take a photo of the bronze Remington statue that graces the entrance—four cowboys on horseback, pistols in the air, clearly headed for fun in Cowtown. And Cowtown was fun—and a fabulously worthwhile place to explore the reality behind the iconic images of the American West.

Nearby: A short distance away is the **Mid-America All-Indian Center**. A docent at the center told me that there are 60 to 70 different tribes in Wichita, and this center is a popular gathering place. While there is a small amount of history, the focus is on more recent Native American accomplishments, with the goal of reminding people that Native Americans aren't gone. I felt that the artwork alone made it worth a visit. Definitely watch the video on artist Blackbear Bosin. And head out the back door and walk to the river, where the impressive Keeper of the Plains statue overlooks Wichita.

Stuhr Museum of the Prairie Pioneer

Grand Island, NE

When I turned off the highway at the entrance for the Stuhr Museum, the long driveway was heading toward something that looked like a white palace on an island. Once I had a map of the property, I learned that this was the Stuhr Building, the location of art galleries and fascinating items of local history. However, guided by the map, I continued on, past the train engine with passenger car and caboose, and down a side road toward Railroad Town. I parked the car and set off on foot. (Worth noting, features here are far enough apart that driving is often the most reasonable option, and the map shows parking spots near major sights.)

Railroad Town is the re-creation of one of the towns built by the railroad companies in the 1890s to support the influx of immigrants moving to the region to start farms (the immigrants having been drawn to the area by ads placed in European newspapers by the railroad companies). The town was so perfectly laid out, with a main street and residential areas, that it had the feeling of a real town. It helped that all the buildings were originals.

The costumed interpreters were numerous and knowledgeable. Two women were busy making hats in the millinery shop. The tinsmith stopped his work to chat, relating among other things that all the tools in his shop came from a single tinsmithing family (this used to be a vital craft in all communities). Two men were working in the blacksmith shop, one a trainee and the other an actual working farrier (someone who specifically makes the things needed for horses—in his case, he actually makes corrective horseshoes for horses with leg problems). Randy Dack has been a blacksmith for 40 years and has been at the museum for 23 years—though he still does specialty work all over the state. I was delighted to learn that some of these skills are not simply being preserved but are still needed. Randy pointed out (because he says everyone asks) that while a blacksmith in 1890 had to make just about everything, he didn't have to make nails—those were being commercially produced by that time.

Train station, fire department, horse stable, bank. The veterinary hospital looked ready for surgery. The Glade Mill, a flour mill, had large flour packers for filling sacks and a hefty sewing machine for closing the sacks.

Railroad Town at Stuhr Museum of the Prairie Pioneer uses historic buildings to re-create one of the towns the railroad companies created in the 1890s. Photo courtesy of Stuhr Museum.

In the elegant, Victorian Lesher house, the interpreter opened what looked like a built-in cupboard; it was a dumb waiter for bringing butter and milk up from the basement. In the telephone exchange, the interpreter explained that the little weaving project she was working on dated back to the Vikings. In the Stolley house, I learned that the house—with no running water or electricity—was lived in until the 1960s and then donated to Stuhr. That's only part of what I explored in Railroad Town, as there is much to see. Then I headed back to my car and started around the big "loop" that took me to the rural schoolhouse, rural church, 1890s farmstead, and Pawnee earth lodge. Between these stops there are broad expanses of prairie flowers and the Stuhr wetland.

I continued on to the 1860s log "road ranche." (The "e" in *ranche* is not a typo, though I have not yet found an origin for this word—but this is not the only place it appeared, as this was a common business, especially in Nebraska, in the 1800s.) A road ranche was a place where those traveling the trails could stop to spend the night, get feed for their animals, supplies for themselves, possibly get a horse shod, or whatever else might be needed to keep them going. There were road ranches all along the trails leading west across Nebraska. The ranche at Stuhr offered handsome, rustic storage buildings, horse barn, guest accommodations, and a well—all things that would improve one's chances of surviving a long journey. This collection of log buildings was surrounded by trees, and one of the other things I learned at Stuhr was that all the trees are relatively new. The Great Plains didn't have any shade trees—plains being by definition places with no trees. (I would learn later, at the Stuhr Building, that 150,000 trees had been planted in Hall County, where the Stuhr Museum is located, by 1872.) It is hard to even imagine how daunting it must have been for the earliest immigrants to just look across endless miles of tall grass.

My final stop was the Stuhr Building. The ground floor offers art galleries and the second floor focuses on history. Among the things I learned is that Hall County in the late 1800s had a successful African American physician (Dr. Charles Flippin, born in Ohio in 1868, the son of freed slaves). I also learned that by the 1890s, Grand Island (the town where Stuhr is located) was producing beet sugar at a prodigious rate—2,110,000 lbs. in 1892. Displays included many of the things associated with the evolution of life in the 1800s—covered wagon, printing press, early telephone switchboard, radio—up into the early 1900s, with medical equipment and hair perma-nenting machines. I smiled as I returned to the first floor of this elegant, gleaming white building, where fountains and openness, as well as a nice gift shop, made for a surprisingly modern end to a historic day.

Of course, all this wonderful history doesn't just happen on its own. Historians, archivists, researchers, and others scrutinize the available evidence to ensure that information and re-creations are accurate. One such dedicated individual is Kay Cynova, whose job it is to make sure Stuhr Museum and all its interpreters reflect reality. Here she shares a few details of that job.

Is That Authentic?

Authenticity. I have been teased about how passionate I can be about authenticity at Stuhr Museum. "Passionate" may even be too gentle a word in my case, as I can get quite rabid about authenticity. I have had the undeniable pleasure of being in charge of authenticity at Stuhr—especially in historic areas—for quite some time now, and for me, making sure that we interpret our artifacts correctly, that we present programs, interpretations, and classes in an honest manner, that we have the most recent research to back up the artifacts and the stories that we talk about, is one of the best jobs in the world in my book. Close to that, helping others to become excited about the past, sharing the knowledge that I have learned over the years—even if it is just a tidbit—is so much fun! There is so much to learn and so much to share and only so much time to do it.

Where does one start to make and keep a whole museum or even single site authentic? Most of it begins with knowing our site and our mission and from there conducting research on the location, structures, people, material culture, and activities attached to the site. We are fortunate at Stuhr to have an archive that contains substantial documentation on area history and genealogy, books on material culture, newspapers, and thousands of photographs and glass plate negatives that are glimpses of a moment in the past, and I get to consult these items whenever I have questions about an artifact or an activity or a person. Our resources do not stop there, because the Nebraska State Historical Society is a wonderful support service that is easily accessible for any site in the region. In addition, through organizations such as ALHFAM,[4] I have taken workshops in many of the tasks that were a part of everyday life, such as cooking on a coal-fired stove or learning how to make bacon.

Granted, we are only human, and sometimes there are slips—but visitors are quick to point things out if they think something might not be authentic, such as a garden hose laying on the ground. But that is why we are so careful—it only takes one thing being wrong, one statement with mixed truths for those visitors to question your site's credibility. The whole reason for maintaining authenticity at any site, to do the very best job of presenting accurate stories, to do the very best job of interpreting an artifact or a building or a person, is not for our sakes but for our visitors.

Levels of authenticity change over time, and in many cases, there are reasons—primarily for the safety of our visitors and our staff—that we cannot be 100 percent authentic. That is why there is a red box hiding a fire extinguisher in all the buildings. However, we work hard to blend these things in so that you can for just a moment believe that you are visiting a nineteenth-century home or business. We periodically revisit research to help us maintain a level of authenticity that keeps on track, and sometimes when we do, we learn new things. This spring, I had the opportunity to do just that. At times it can seem as if you have exhausted all the resources available on a given subject, but often taking a new look at old information will reveal something previously missed. Revisiting records on a number of our buildings revealed information that had previously been overlooked—and it was exciting information! And now we pass it on, sharing first with the interpreters who work in our sites, and finally with our visitors. We will keep looking, so that we can share everything we find with all who visit with us.

Kay Cynova is the Director of Interpretive Resources at the Stuhr Museum of the Prairie Pioneer in Grand Island, Nebraska, and has had the joy of being able to work at Stuhr for over 30 years.

CHAPTER 3

Perusing History

This chapter focuses on a selection of museums, historic homes, frontier forts, archaeological sites, and vintage places that don't feature a living-history element. Some offer tours and some are self-guided, but all offer the chance to learn more about the region's or nation's history.

Large cities generally offer the largest museums, as urban histories cover either more territory or more people. State capitals are usually home to state museums. Of course, cities also often offer a great deal more to explore, including numerous smaller museums. However, there are museums everywhere. It would be impossible to list them all. I couldn't even include every museum I've visited. However, I have seen all those included here, usually sought out because they seemed particularly iconic, impressive, or unusual in some way, but also sometimes serendipitous discoveries. I simply hope to give you an idea of why it is worthwhile to look around when you hit the road—and encourage you to look up all the possible museums or historic sites any place you visit.

Be aware that any venue, including museums, can change. New events or discoveries and new administrators or technologies can have an impact on what needs to be shown and how it is displayed. Of course, a large city museum with multiple exhibits is more likely to change than a small, local museum or one that focuses on a single aspect of history. In fact, big museums often have entire areas dedicated to temporary exhibits, though even the "permanent" exhibits are sometimes updated. So be aware that, in some cases, what is described here may have been altered at some point. But it's unlikely that a museum will be less great for having been updated.

There are so many places to enjoy, including a surprising number of delightful options in small towns that you might not otherwise visit. Almost anywhere you go in the Midwest, there will be something that reflects the past. I simply hope the following inspires you to keep an eye out for history, wherever your travels take you.

National Underground Railroad Freedom Center
Cincinnati, OH

This is a really remarkable museum that recounts a hard history (one that, sadly, stretches into the present) in a beautiful, moving, and even-handed manner. It does not pull punches, but it offers enough hope and heroism to make the story uplifting. The imposing museum faces the Ohio River, a one-time dividing line between slave states and free. On entering, I was directed to the elevator, as the permanent exhibits begin on the third floor.

The largest exhibit on this floor, "From Slavery to Freedom," focuses on the three centuries of the European and American slave trade. The history of slavery unfolded around me as I followed the winding path through the exhibit. There were display cases filled with artifacts, photographs, and excellent information signs, but also life-size re-creations of cabins, trading ports, trees, and people. One element I appreciated was that, as I moved through the exhibit, each era was set off by different music. For example, as I browsed through the section on the battle against slavery in the British Empire, the music playing was "Amazing Grace," a song written by former slave trader John Newton, who inspired William Wilberforce to lead the fight to end slavery. There were individual histories of enslaved people, but also stories of African Americans free even before the American Revolution, whose numbers grew in New England and the Mid-Atlantic states as abolitionist sentiment grew. Also addressed was the impact of settlement on Native Americans in these regions. The growing influence of abolitionists parallels the rise of the Underground Railroad. The exhibit carries the story

Splendid displays in the "From Slavery to Freedom" exhibit at the National Underground Railroad Freedom Center bring alive the story of slavery and the fight to end it. Photo by Farshid Assassi/Assassi Productions, courtesy of the National Underground Railroad Freedom Center.

through the Civil War and Reconstruction. I can't imagine this exhibit not touching anyone who sees it.

Also on the third floor is the exhibit "Invisible: Slavery Today." This looks at the many places in the world where slavery still exists, with suggested ways to oppose it. The second floor offers "Escape," an interactive introduction to the Underground Railroad. This exhibit is designed to be family friendly and includes such activities as teaching code words and songs from the period. In addition, on this floor, there is a slave pen found on a farm in Kentucky and brought to the museum. The theater on this floor offers a film narrated by Oprah Winfrey about two of the key "conductors" on the Underground Railroad. Before leaving the second floor, I enjoyed the view of the Ohio River afforded by the balcony.

In addition to permanent exhibits, special traveling exhibitions are frequently on offer. Also, for those who want to dig deeper, there is a library and family research center on the fourth floor.

Rutherford B. Hayes Presidential Library & Museums

Fremont, OH

Rutherford B. Hayes was the 19th President of the United States (1877–1881), but he was the first one for whom a library and museum was built. To be honest, its being the first is what drew me to this museum. It turned out to be both a lovely destination and a far more interesting history than I expected. And the museum was not the only first associated with Hayes. He was also the first U.S. President to take the oath of office inside the White House and was the first to travel to the West Coast during his term in office (with William Tecumseh Sherman as his guide). He began the now-traditional Easter Egg Roll on the White House lawn. And he was the only one of the presidents who served in the Civil War to be wounded five times.

The museum, along with the family home, is on the Spiegel Grove estate. The home, in which five generations of the Hayes family lived, was built by Sardis Birchard, Hayes's uncle. The "B" in Rutherford B. Hayes is for Birchard. Birchard named the estate Spiegel, which is "mirror" in German, because of the natural reflecting pools on the property. The impressive, 31-room red-brick mansion, built in 1863, is adjacent to the museum, which was opened in 1916, more than two decades after President Hayes had passed away. The museum is handsome but looks rather like a cross between a government building and a mausoleum.

I was happy to discover that the museum covered local history and national events, as well as the Hayes presidency. I also learned from one docent that it is a popular place for genealogy research. Here are a few of the things I learned.

The town of Fremont is on the Sandusky River, which, along with the Scioto River, provided a canoe route between Lake Erie and the Ohio River long before Europeans came to the area (though with a portage of a few miles). Fort Sandusky, also known as Fort Stephenson, survived the War of 1812 and grew into Fremont.

Hayes trained as a lawyer but loved literature and was a member of a literary society. He promoted the creation of Ohio State University under the Morrill Act, and, as a member of the board of directors, urged a broad course of study, not just agriculture. His wife, Lucy Webb Hayes, was the first co-ed at Ohio Wesleyan College.

Rutherford was known as Rud to friends and family. James Garfield, who followed Rud as U.S. President, said that Rud was "so pristine" that no nickname could be pinned on him. Before being elected President, he was elected to Congress (even while still fighting in the Civil War), and then was elected as Ohio's Governor (1875).

A dedicated abolitionist, Hayes worked to free African Americans before the Civil War, fought in the Civil War, and then worked to protect the rights of African Americans after the Civil War. But his love of equality did not stop there. He vetoed a bill passed by Congress to limit Chinese immigration, and he removed corrupt officials from Indian Agencies. He hoped that education and keeping Native Americans away from white influence could help improve the lives of indigenous people (however, a man of his age, he considered "civilizing" Native Americans an important goal of education). He also created a policy for handling the still-dicey relationship with the southern states, titled "Peace and National Unity," to try to further reduce tensions as Reconstruction began to wind down.

Other than information, there were excellent displays throughout the museum. There was part of the Hayes Tavern, which had been run by Rud's grandfather in Brattleboro, Vermont, before the family migrated to Ohio. The White House carriage from his presidency (a Brewster landau) was there, as well as an old fire truck and belongings his children had once loved. One display was of items from Johnson's Island, a Union POW camp in Lake Erie. And downstairs, there was an impressive weapon collection created by Rud's second son, Webb C. Hayes.

But there is so much more to see and learn. For me, another affirmation that there is great history everywhere.

National Road & Zane Grey Museum
Norwich, OH

As I drove along Interstate 70, en route to the National Road Museum, I was struck by how daunting a task it would have been to build a road across this undulating landscape 200 years ago—and how daunting it would be to travel without that road. Reaching the exit for Norwich, I turned north to where a sign and an old truss bridge marked the entrance to the museum's driveway. Green fields edged with trees spread before me as I pulled into a parking area bordered by antique road-building equipment and granite mile markers that once stood along the National Road.

I knew a bit about the National Road: envisioned by George Washington and Thomas Jefferson; first federally funded interstate highway; often called "the road that built the nation." I was about to learn more.

Officially named the Cumberland Road, because it began in Cumberland, Maryland, this would be the means of opening up the Northwest Territory. With funding approved in 1806 and signed into law by Jefferson, the building began in 1811 (with a pause for the War of 1812). Workers carved a path 66 feet wide across newly minted states, ending in Vandalia, one-time capital of Illinois, in 1837. But even before it was completed, traffic surged, as people escaped the over-crowded cities of the East Coast for the promise of farmland and a future.

Upon entering the museum, the first thing to catch my attention was a massive Conestoga wagon. This was the tractor-trailer of its day, capable of carrying six tons of freight. Impressive. Because I love word origins, I appreciated the sign that related that old boots and shoes were often used to cover metal brakes on the wagons, which is why we call the pads that make today's braking systems work "brake shoes."

Though the largest vehicle on display, the Conestoga wagon is not the only one. Another favorite was the stagecoach that had sled runners, though it could have the runners switched for wheels when the weather changed. However, the real heart of the museum is the 136-foot-long diorama that wraps around the room. It presents both a timeline and the route of the National Road, with the first trees being felled and land being leveled in Maryland and developing as it spread westward, with travelers, houses, bridges, hotels, stagecoaches, and by the end of the road, cars and gas stations appearing as time passed.

I learned that toll houses began to appear in 1833, as the project began to rely on the states to fund the road's continuation. While the toll houses gathered funds, they also gathered information, which reflected not only the numbers headed west, but also, in time, a tremendous flow of livestock (which were charged tolls) moving east, as open land in the Midwest made it possible to feed the increasingly hungry cities on the coast.

The diorama is remarkably rich in detail and information, and you probably want to allow yourself at least an hour to take it in. Look for the unusual Y bridge—Amelia Earhart (a Midwesterner) used it as a landmark. Note how things changed as railroads entered the picture. Admire how the road was paved. Marvel at how much the world changed between 1811 and 1837. There's so much of interest here, but I want to leave plenty for you to discover when you visit.

Once roads began to get numbers, the National Road became Route 40. While Route 40 would in time extend far beyond the end of the National Road, there are still sections of the road that are part of the nation's first interstate highway.

Finishing the National Road, I headed for the corner of the building that showcases memorabilia of local author Zane Grey. Grey was born in 1872 in nearby Zanesville, named for Grey's great-grandfather, Ebenezer Zane, who founded the town in 1797. (And that's a whole other interesting bit of history.) Grey wanted to write, but his father insisted he train as a dentist. Dad even tore up Grey's first book. Grey practiced dentistry in New York, but he hated both his career and the city. In 1904, he abandoned both, heading west to pursue his love of writing. He wrote more than 80 novels about the American West and is credited with essentially creating a new literary genre, the Western. More about Grey and his life, including a stint as a semiprofessional baseball player, can be perused in the museum.

The connection between Zane Grey and the National Road is that the road reached Zanesville in 1826. Zanesville was briefly Ohio's state capital and is still the location of the aforementioned Y bridge.

Johnny Appleseed Museum

Urbana, OH

It is a testament to the impact of John Chapman (1774–1845), better known as Johnny Appleseed, that a museum exists—because Chapman rather famously owned very little (other than a place to grow apple tree saplings), and thus there was not much for anyone to collect. This museum, housed in historic Brown Hall on the Urbana University campus, has the largest collection in the world of memorabilia and written information about Johnny Appleseed, and yet it barely fills two rooms. The interactive displays are interesting, offering insights into Chapman's impact and his importance. Among the things to be viewed are a cider press used to make cider from apples planted by Chapman (cider being the reason apples were grown at that time), photos of monuments and markers, informational panels that detail Chapman's remarkable life, an excerpt from the well-known Disney cartoon of the Johnny Appleseed legend, and a wide range of publications for the serious student to peruse. However, among the things that impressed me most were the quotes about Chapman—not just what was said but who said it, such as General William Tecumseh Sherman, who said Chapman would never be forgotten, and Sam Houston, who called him "one of the most useful citizens of the world." At a time when establishing a homestead required the planting of 50 apple trees, someone selling healthy apple seedlings would, indeed, be useful.

This is probably not a museum you'd visit unless you had an interest in this remarkable character. However, if you are interested, it offers, in addition to insights, information on other related destinations, from Chapman's burial site in Fort Wayne, IN, to the historical markers and significant locations that line the Johnny Appleseed Memorial Byway. But whether you visit or not, it is good to be reminded that there were quirky individuals in our history who were able to create a lasting legacy.

Food historian Lucy Long has a special interest in regional history, culture, and food. I leave commentary on Chapman's impact to her.

The Real Johnny Appleseed

Johnny Appleseed is well known as an American legend, but residents of the eastern Midwest celebrate him as their own real-life local hero. I didn't know this until I moved to northwest Ohio from the east coast and discovered that he had been a living person, John Chapman. Historical events and museums frequently mentioned him, and Johnny Appleseed reenactors made appearances at schools and festivals. Other residents proudly talked about him, pointing out that he planted apple trees throughout this area in the early part of the 1800s, a time when western Ohio was still the frontier and apple orchards were a symbol of civilization. My own children played "Johnny Appleseed," pretending to talk to animals and using him as an excuse to go barefoot and wear pots on their heads.

John Chapman was indeed a real person. Although he was born in Massachusetts in 1774, he moved to central Ohio around the turn of the century. His occupation of traveling fruit-tree salesman was a common and respectable one, and his Swedenborgian religion was one of a number of utopian, pacifist Protestant sects. He promoted peaceful coexistence with nature, a belief he put into practice by growing apple trees from seeds and establishing his own orchards. In the early 1810s, he purchased land with his brother in Mansfield, Ohio, and lived there until around 1833, continuing to sell his trees. In 1834 he settled in Fort Wayne, Indiana, where he established more apple orchards and remained until his death in 1845.

Chapman seems to have been somewhat quirky, but popular culture portrayals have turned him into a caricature. Most of these show him as a kind-hearted eccentric who liked to commune with nature, talk to animals, go barefoot, and wear his cooking pot as a hat. The 1948 Walt Disney film, for example, introduced him nationally, but he remains misunderstood and under-appreciated. A 2016 bestselling novel set in northwest Ohio, Tracy Chevalier's At the Edge of the Orchard, includes him as a major figure, but emphasizes his role in selling saplings for trees producing apples for hard cider.

The eastern Midwest, however, treats him as a significant historical figure. A number of his trees and orchards were well known and documented, and those sites are today treated as historical landmarks. His gravesite is now a monument on a hill in the Johnny Appleseed Park in Fort Wayne, Indiana. Open to the public, the park holds an annual festival commemorating Chapman that features arts and crafts, food, drama, music, and children's games thought to represent his time period.

What shines through in these celebrations is a very different perception of Johnny Appleseed, one who represents Midwestern qualities and ideals—pioneer spirit, individuality, independence, ingenuity, and down-home-ness. And the apples he planted are seen as "all American," appropriate for an area many think of as the "Heart of America." Perhaps most importantly, though, Johnny Appleseed is a hero they can call their own.

Lucy M. Long *directs the Center for Food and Culture (www.foodand culture.org) and teaches American studies, ethnic studies, folklore, and nutrition at Bowling Green State University in Ohio. Her many publications include* Regional American Food Culture *(2009),* The Food and Folklore Reader *(2015), and* Ethnic American Cooking *(2016).*

Tippecanoe Battlefield and Museum

Battle Ground, IN

An 85-foot marble obelisk in a lovely park, remarkably green when I was there, shows where the Battle of Tippecanoe took place. Across the parking lot from the park's entrance is the museum that details what occurred, who was involved, and what it meant for the country. The story left me with the question: How might U.S. history have been different if more Native Americans had listened to Tecumseh, rather than to his twisted, alcoholic brother, Tenskwatawa, also known as The Prophet?

That Tecumseh was highly respected is most famously reflected in the middle name of one of the Civil War's great generals, William Tecumseh Sherman. This small but excellent museum does a good job of demonstrating why Tecumseh deserved this respect, using both his own words and the words of those who knew him.

The main focus of the museum is the Battle of Tippecanoe, which took place on November 7, 1811. The story is told through artifacts, video, a fiber-optic map, and other exhibits. Tecumseh had carefully built a powerful confederacy of tribes and had arranged a meeting to negotiate on behalf of Native Americans. But then, just before that meeting, The Prophet convinced a large number of warriors that he could cast a spell that would keep them from being hurt by bullets, and then led them on a surprise raid in the middle of the night. So, Tecumseh never got to carry out his wise and well-reasoned plan.

For what seems to be a relatively minor battle, Tippecanoe was significant—both because of those involved (including future president William Henry Harrison), and because of the events surrounding it (the War of 1812 would begin seven months later).

The museum probably requires only an hour to see everything, but allow yourself extra time for the gift shop, at least if you like to read. There are reproductions of historic toys and clothing, but the most daunting part of the store for me was the selection of books. I can't remember having ever seen a better collection of titles on U.S. history.

The History Center

Fort Wayne, IN

I was reminded of two important facts at the History Center in Fort Wayne. First, that places with "fort" in the name generally started out as actual military forts, rather than as settlements or towns. Second, that the importance and success of a place can change fairly dramatically with time.

As is often the case, I was returning home from a research trip and had looked for someplace to break up a long drive. Fort Wayne's museum, and the history it shared, turned out to be a very happy discovery. The building that houses the museum is, itself, historic. Constructed in 1893, it was originally Fort Wayne's City Hall.

This is not a huge museum, but it is rich in important details. Exhibits carry the area's story from prehistory through Native Americans in this area when Europeans arrived (the Miami). One display commemorates the building of a fort by Revolutionary War hero General Anthony Wayne (the fort was dedicated on October 22, 1794, now considered Fort Wayne's "birthday"). The story then moves through the stages that turned the city into a transportation hub and industrial powerhouse, and on to more recent developments, including some significant inventions and nationally known entrepreneurs.

Situated at the junction of three rivers, the site was a natural crossroads and had been the focus of trade when the Miami made their home here. Commerce would increase as more people arrived. The Wabash and Erie Canal (1830s), like canals elsewhere, made transportation easier and swifter—though the canal would, within a couple of decades, lose its primacy to the railroads. Ironically, the first steam locomotive to arrive in Fort Wayne arrived by canal in 1854. But the railroad brought more than transportation—it brought jobs. The Bass Foundry and Machine Co., a huge and vital supplier of parts for trains (wheels, boilers, and so on) had more than 1,100 employees by the 1890s. Fort Wayne was soon linked by rail to every major city in the U.S., and more than 200 trains passed through every day.

Signage in the museum is excellent and offers a lot of information. Check out the sword given by George Washington to the Miami chief Little Turtle, General Wayne's camp bed, details on how surveying was done (the results of which are still evident if one is flying over the Midwest), photographs of foundry workers and train engines, the original self-measuring gas pump, the huge brass steam whistle used at the International Harvester factory, and more.

Nearby: The historic Barr Street Market, adjacent to The History Center, is the oldest public space in Fort Wayne, dating back to 1837. On Saturdays from May to September, it is the location of the city's Farmers' Market. An internet search will turn up several other worthwhile sites in Fort Wayne, including the burial site of Johnny Appleseed, if you are following that trail.

Barker Mansion

Michigan City, IN

I'm always fascinated to discover people who have had a huge impact on the region but who never make it into textbooks. Among these were the Barkers of Michigan City. In 1855, John Barker bought a one-third interest in the town's first railcar factory. In time, Barker's son, John H. Barker, joined the company. Dad retired in 1869 and the remaining partner sold his shares to John H. The Barkers and their associates built a booming business and the most complete factory of its time. They developed an innovative style of mass production that would later be adopted and refined by Henry Ford and renamed the assembly line. By 1907, they had 3,500 employees and produced 15,000 train cars a year. Needless to say, at a time when trains moved just about everything from freight to food to military troops (especially during the Civil War), a company producing this many train cars was exceedingly important, both to the region and to the nation as a whole.

So that's how the Barkers made their money. How they spent it was largely on charity, but they also built a handsome mansion that is definitely worth visiting. Built in 1857 and expanded in 1905, this 38-room, English manor–style house is a treasure trove of period furnishing, antiques, art objects, and cutting-edge technologies that are pretty impressive even now. When John H. and his wife both died in 1909, their orphaned daughter, Catherine, who was fourteen at the time, was one of the wealthiest women

Barker Mansion is lovely, but the history of the Barker family is even more interesting than their house. Photo by Cynthia Clampitt.

in the world. Despite these deaths and other tragedies in the Barker family story, it was wonderful to learn about their far-reaching charitable work—and particularly delightful to learn that John H. Barker's grandchildren are still involved with the preservation of the mansion.

This is a spectacular house—and ninety percent of the furnishings are original. So you can really see both the taste and interests of the Barker family. Tiffany lamps, Frank Lloyd Wright windows, gorgeous wood paneling everywhere, Chippendale furniture, Dresden china, Italian marble. Elegant, Old World, but also modern. The butler's pantry has gas warming ovens, to keep things warm between the kitchen and dining room. Barker installed a central vacuum system that was powered by engines at the factory. Bathrooms throughout are remarkable, including one where the shower has holes the length of the pipe, so you could shower without getting your hair wet. Even the servants' quarters had nice bathrooms. On the third floor, originally a ballroom, there are displays of personal artifacts from the Barkers, including pianos, gloves, and souvenirs from their travels. Also on the third floor are a classroom, teacher's quarters, and a children's playroom.

A couple of things mentioned but not shown: Barker had a tunnel from the back of the house to the factory, so no weather could keep him from getting to work. John H. also looked out for his workers, laying train tracks near the factory, to make it easy for workers to get to work. He also gave workers free wood to heat their homes. Brilliance, sorrow, and virtue—an all-around remarkable story.

You can reach Michigan City by an exit off Interstate 94, but I think taking Route 12, known in northern Indiana as the Dunes Highway, is vastly more scenic, and it didn't add a lot of time to the drive. While a self-guided tour of the mansion is a possibility, I recommend taking the guided tour, because there are many things one might not notice if they were not pointed out. There is no difference in cost between the two options.

J. H. Hawes Grain Elevator Museum

Atlanta, IL

The clean, rustic lines and high, barn-red walls of the J. H. Hawes Grain Elevator Museum in Atlanta, Illinois, may not look very revolutionary, but grain elevators changed everything. The Hawes Museum, which sources date to 1903 or 1904, is the only fully restored wooden grain elevator in Illinois. With a train car pulled up to the side of the old grain elevator, this museum offers the opportunity to explore developments that transformed the Midwest—and the world.

Prior to the development of grain elevators in the mid-1800s, grain was sewn by hand into two-bushel sacks that had to be lifted, carried, loaded, and unloaded. Moving all those sacks required stunning amounts of labor—and a lot of laborers. But then the grain elevator came along. Dump the grain in a wagon, weigh the wagon, dump the grain in the grain elevator. Once the grain is unloaded, conveyor belts carry it up and deposit it in tall, vertical bins. When someone buys the grain, push a button, and gravity unloads the bin into a wagon, train car, or boat that can carry the grain to its next destination.

The blank façade does not give away the revolutionary nature of the grain elevator. The train car at the side of the building represents a powerful partnership that changed the world. Photo by Cynthia Clampitt, used with permission.

At the Hawes Museum, start where the wagons did—at the scale house. Here, a fully loaded wagon would stop on the scale's large platform, to determine its weight. Weighing it full and then empty let you know how much grain had been delivered.

Step inside the scale house to see record books, weights, and measuring devices for recording deliveries. At the Hawes Museum, the original scale house, which did not survive the passage of time, has been replaced by a small building from Chicago with its own remarkable history. This small wooden structure was the original headquarters for the two brothers from Germany, Frederick and Louis Rueckheim, who invented Cracker Jack. Documentation about the Cracker Jack Company is posted inside the building, along with a photo of the building in its original location.

Once the grain was weighed, the horses would pull the wagon into the grain elevator. Inside, a lever was pulled that opened a trap door and tilted the wagon, dumping all the grain into the bin below. A tilted wagon and permanently open trap door show visitors both the process and the destination of the grain. Then look up to see the remarkable interior structure, with its long conveyor belts that move the grain into storage. In the building next door, the engine that drove these belts is on display—because the leap from horses to steam engines made the process even more efficient.

That might not sound like a big deal, but it was huge. Massive amounts of grain could be handled easily and swiftly. A large grain elevator could move grain at a rate of 24,000 bushels per hour. As engines to power the elevators improved, so did the speed and efficiency with which they worked. It transformed the way the world processed farm products. And while trucks have replaced wagons and scales and grain elevators are larger, this is still essentially how grain elevators work today.

The signage at the Hawes Museum is excellent, offering details on every element of the museum, so self-guided visits are easy and informative.

Nearby: The Hawes Museum is just one block from a well-maintained section of Route 66, which passes through the charming center of the small town of Atlanta. Nearby, the Atlanta Museum is housed in another of the town's historic buildings, upstairs from the old-fashioned Palms Grill Café. As is true in most of Central Illinois, local history here includes Abraham Lincoln.

Chinese American Museum

Chicago, IL

In the early 1870s, Chinese immigrants, mostly Cantonese, arrived in Chicago. Unwelcome in California, they crossed the continent, primarily as laborers on the Transcontinental Railroad. Once the first arrivals had settled in, others followed. While the Midwest was more welcoming than the West Coast, there were still many obstacles to overcome. Most of the arriving Chinese spread out across the city, opening small businesses. Still, enough stayed together that, by the 1880s, a thriving Chinatown had grown up near Clark and Van Buren, in the heart of what would come to be known as the Loop. Needing more space, and lower rents, the Chinese community began to relocate, finally moving Chinatown to its current location in 1912. All of Chinatown is worth exploring—and worth dining in. But look for the Chinese American Museum if you want to learn more about the experiences of Chinese immigrants in the American Midwest.

Large, stone guardian lions flank the entrance of the museum. Inside, the first floor features temporary exhibits focused on aspects of Chinese American culture or showcasing traveling collections. The second floor is home to the permanent exhibit, *From Great Wall to Great Lakes: Chinese Immigration to the Midwest*. Displays offer items brought from China, as well as things that reflect life in the U.S. There is also a worthwhile video titled *My Chinatown: Stories from Within*.

This little museum is lovingly and thoughtfully curated, and despite sad losses due to a fire in 2008, there is much to see, from large dragons to tiny shoes for bound feet, furniture to food, cherished traditions to new lifestyles. Most importantly, the museum offers valuable insight into a piece of Midwestern history that doesn't always get considered: the Chinese experience in the region. Then, when you have seen all the museum has to offer, you still have Chinatown to explore.

Joliet Area Historical Museum

Joliet, IL

For many years, if one thought of Joliet at all, it was more than likely the great, Gothic 1858 correctional center that came to mind. However, though one can now tour the retired Joliet Prison, it would be a pity not to get beyond that iconic edifice and examine a bit more of the city's remarkable history. Fortunately, the Joliet Area Historical Museum does a great job of showcasing the things that made Joliet important—and interesting.

Joliet was named in 1845 for French-Canadian explorer Louis Joliet, who visited this site in 1673, when the Midwest was still being called New France. Almost as soon as the town was named, it began to contribute to the explosive growth of the Midwest. Limestone quarries earned it the nickname "Stone City," but mines and iron and steel works soon saw that moniker expanded to "The City of Stone and Steel." However, the museum focuses on all aspects of Joliet history, from early Native American artifacts to the space program (aerospace engineer John Houbolt, who led the team that designed the lunar orbit rendezvous plan, grew up here).

The museum is cleverly designed to make elements of history come alive. I climbed into a reproduction of an early trolley to watch a movie of riding through early Joliet. I wandered past displays showcasing local businesses of the past, walls of glorious stained glass, and displays of period clothing. I learned that, at one time, more horseshoes were made in Joliet than anywhere else in the world. I also found out that Dairy Queen started here.

I love the way the main floor is divided up, with partial walls that look like they are in the process of being built of local limestone. Joliet limestone was, in the mid-1800s, a remarkably valuable commodity, used to build everything from the Chicago Water Tower to the main staircase of the White House. But Stone City was also producing steel, and the Joliet Iron and Steel company was among the world's leading makers of steel rails and rods. This made Joliet the largest employer in this area, and thousands of newly arrived immigrants from southeastern Europe found work here. Displays are enhanced by great audio-visual content and touch-screen computers.

Upstairs, one exhibit honors those who served in wars ranging from the Civil War through World War II. Another exhibit traces Houbolt's work—where a window in the floor looks down to the first floor, re-creating the view of North America from space. So, a really dandy museum that highlights, among other things, the developments that contributed to the explosive growth of the Midwest in the 1800s.

Nearby: Joliet Correctional Center is now available to be toured, the ruins of one of the great iron and steel processors can be explored in Iron Works Park, and the Slovenian Heritage Museum commemorates one of the groups that settled this area. From a slightly more recent period, but still worthwhile if you're in town, the glorious 1926 Rialto Square Theater, called by some one of the country's most beautiful theaters, offers tours, if you're not there for a performance. Also, Route 66 passes through Joliet.

John Deere Pavilion

Moline, IL

One of the most significant inventions in the early history of the Midwest was the self-cleaning steel plow invented by John Deere. Before this plow was created in 1837, settlers trying to plow the prairies had to stop frequently to clean the sticky prairie soil off their iron plows. Stopping occasionally may not seem like a big deal today, but consider the fact that, in plowing just one acre, a farmer would have walked ten miles. Stopping all the time to clean the plow made for a long day.

The John Deere Pavilion in Moline is a great place to explore just how much things changed after that. There is a display of the types of farming implements used in the early 1800s (and for thousands of years before that), as well as the story of John Deere and his plow. Leading away from this display is a collection of early tractors. The term *tractor* was first recorded in 1896—just four years after an Iowa blacksmith named John Froelich created what would become the prototypical farming tractor. John Deere had begun working on developing tractors, but when Froelich's Waterloo Boy tractor proved to be a great success, John Deere bought the company. (You can see an early John Deere Waterloo Boy in the photo.) Tractors revolutionized farming—though cost initially kept them from being rapidly adopted.

At the John Deere Pavilion, in addition to modern machines, the early history of agriculture is on display, including the farming tools with which we began the 1800s, the famous John Deere plow, and the invention of tractors. Photo courtesy of John Deere Attractions.

However, as prices came down, horses were slowly replaced by these more powerful and versatile machines.

While the history at the John Deere Pavilion is wonderful, many people, including youngsters, will also be delighted with the modern equipment, some of which looks like it's part of the space program. Knowledgeable docents make all aspects of the visit educational. And the Pavilion offers a stunning reminder of just how far we've come in less than 200 years.

Nearby: John Deere World Headquarters are also located in Moline and can be toured. In addition, not exactly near (in Dixon, 72 miles away), is the John Deere Historic Site, which offers tours of the Deere Family Home, built in 1836, and a re-creation of the blacksmith shop in which Deere created his revolutionary plow.

Arabia Steamboat Museum

Kansas City, MO

This museum is home to the largest collection of pre–Civil War merchandise in existence. It is also where you can learn about determination and discovery, because it represents the vision of a small group of people who wanted to find a lost ship.

On September 5, 1856, the Arabia Steamboat was traveling along the Missouri River when it hit a snag—a partially submerged tree that pierced the hull of the boat. The boat sank, but the water was not deep, so all the passengers made it to shore. However, when the crew returned the next day to salvage the considerable cargo, the boat was gone. It had settled on quicksand and, overnight, had vanished. Jump ahead 132 years to a group of Kansas City businessmen determined to find the missing boat. The river had changed course, so the boat, while 45 feet underground, was no longer under the river.

Entering the imposing, glass-fronted museum, I headed for the gift shop to buy a ticket for the next available tour. An incline led me down to a theater where the tour begins with a movie about the finding of the steamboat, the 1988–89 excavation, and the remarkable logistics of salvaging and storing materials that had been underground for so long. The businessmen who found the boat had to dig down to the wreck, keep groundwater from refilling the hole as they worked, salvage the cargo (200 tons of it), and then refill the hole and have the farm that stood above the wreck restored in time for spring planting! At the end of the film, a member of one of the families involved in the salvage entered the theater and answered questions and shared a few additional details, including the fact that hundreds of ships sank on the Missouri River. It was, in the 1800s, one of the most dangerous shipping routes in the world, and the average life expectancy of a boat was five years. He also noted that the foods from the ship were perfectly preserved and the champagne was still carbonated.

Then into the collection. There is almost no way that any description can do this justice. It was stunning. In fact, so much merchandise was lost with the sinking that the town for which it was headed, Logan, Nebraska, was abandoned, as this was to be everything they needed. There are personal items that escaping passengers left behind, such as brooches, coffee mugs, and decorative items, but the bulk of the collection was merchandise intended for sale. This included everything one would need to set people up in life: sets of china and medical kits, buttons and keys, rifles and wagon wheels, canned sardines and bottled pickles, buckets, doorknobs, pocket knives, boots, shoes, cutlery, coats, furniture, cook pots, mill stones, spools of thread, flower vases, tools for multiple trades—and dozens and dozens of items in each category of goods. One exhibit is the reconstruction of a comfortable room completely furnished and decorated with salvaged items. In the middle of the main room, there is a counter where one can actually watch people still at work, cleaning and preserving items that have not yet moved into the main collection.

There are also some pieces of the steamboat itself that have been salvaged and preserved, including the paddle wheel. But it is the staggering collection of merchandise that really drives home what a stunning loss this would have been in 1856, as well as what an incredible find it was in 1988.

Stay tuned: The businessmen who found the Arabia continue to look for other boats that sank along the Missouri River. They have now located the Malta, which sank in 1841. So the story continues—and the museum may grow.

Patee House Museum

St. Joseph, MO

As I approached the handsome, four-story, red-brick Patee House, which opened in 1858, it was easy to believe that this was, as it was once advertised, the "Finest hotel west of the Mississippi." Today, it houses a museum, and a sign out front relates that *True West* magazine rated it "One of America's Top Ten Western Museums." It was, in fact, fabulous.

With a history as remarkable as anything in its collections, Patee House has been designated a National Landmark. It was built in anticipation of the Hannibal to St. Joseph Railroad, which first arrived on February 14, 1859. Abraham Lincoln's first visit was in 1859. In 1860, the men who established the Pony Express made their headquarters on the first floor. In 1861, a young Mark Twain bought stagecoach tickets for himself and his brother

Though the stables for the Pony Express were down the street, headquarters for the operation were at the Patee House Hotel. When the hotel became a museum, it preserved the headquarters. On the left is a mochila, the padlocked leather letter carrier that was draped over a rider's saddle. The price of postage, $5 per half-ounce, emphasizes how vital this service was. Photo by Cynthia Clampitt, used with permission of Patee House Museum.

at the office in the lobby. When the Civil War began, it housed the office of the Provost Marshal for the Union Army. After the war, the hotel's grand ballroom became the courtroom where Confederate officers were tried. In 1882, Jesse James's wife and children stayed here after the famous outlaw was murdered nearby. So, the hotel has seen a fair bit of drama.

The Pony Express headquarters and the stagecoach ticket office are both there, fully restored. The lobby is filled with glass cases displaying interesting memorabilia from the hotel's dramatic history. I examined it all, and then I headed into the museum proper. Wow. It would be impossible to relate everything the museum holds and all I learned while there, but here are a few highlights. An entire street from the 1800s has been re-created, with a post office, dentist, drugstore, barbershop, bank, ice-cream parlor, mortician, and more. Each "building" is connected to a bit of local history. For example, the jail offers the full story of the arrest of outlaws Robert and Charles Ford, who murdered Jesse James.

In the center of the hotel, there is an actual train engine—the one that once ran between Hannibal and St. Joseph. It is surrounded by cars and old fire engines. I learned here that Studebaker, before the company made cars, made carriages here in St. Joseph. A train station, a full-size carousel, and a beautifully restored 1854 saloon finished off the first floor. Then I went upstairs.

On the second floor, the Grand Ballroom was filled with antique furniture and musical instruments. Private dining room, displays of famous visitors, Native American artifacts, old phones, switchboards, antique radios, horse-drawn hearse, carriages, and covered wagons filled all available space. A wonderful display about the Buffalo Soldiers included a life-size camp site, with soldier, horse, and tent, along with photographs, paintings, and extensive history of the famous African American cavalrymen.

The third floor displayed the hotel rooms of the 1860s, from basic to decidedly upscale. Then down the stairs and out the back door.

Worth noting: to engage children, there is a game running through the museum—something of a treasure hunt, where they are asked to identify what does not belong in an exhibit.

Nearby: In fact, just outside the back door of the museum: the Jesse James House. James moved into this little cottage with his wife Zerelda and two small children on Christmas Eve 1881. It was here that, on April 3, 1882, he was murdered.

Pony Express National Museum

St. Joseph, MO

People had used horses to help them deliver messages in the past—but never over distances or at speeds like this. The Pony Express would cover a distance of 1,800 wild, rugged miles and do it in 10 days. It was such a remarkable feat that, even though the telegraph would soon replace it, the service and its riders would remain legendary. And it started here, in St. Joseph, Missouri. On April 3, 1860, the first rider left the stable that now makes up the front of the Pony Express National Museum.

After I got my ticket, the sight of a mounted rider and a man at the stable door about to open it caught my eye. Titled "A Moment in Time," the life-size figures re-create that final moment before the stable door was thrown open and the first rider burst out to the cheers of the gathered crowd. It was tempting to head for the display and straight into the museum, but I'm glad I stopped first and watched the movie about Pony Express history. The 13-minue film explained so much about what I would see in the rest of the museum. Plus, it's exciting to see great riding.

In the part of the building that was a stable, I saw the blacksmith shop, horse stalls, and tack room. But then the building opened up into the newer section. Displays, maps, and information signs offered details about the Great Plains, the Salt Lake Desert, mail routes, and why St. Joseph was selected as the starting point. The center of the room held life-size replicas of a covered wagon pulled by oxen and a relay station, where riders would dine and sleep before continuing on. Nearby rested saddles and a mochila, the leather pouch that held the mail for the riders. Dioramas re-created the route and related the difficulties faced by the riders. The importance of the service and danger faced by riders were reflected in the pay scale: $50 to $150 per ride, at a time when the average skilled laborer earned roughly $1.60 a day.[1]

There is a considerable amount of information about the riders them-selves, both in the main exhibit area and in the Hall of Riders. In addition to identifying 232 of the riders who rode for the Pony Express, the Hall offers lots of "lift and learn" displays, which are fun for all, but particularly good for kids. Included are "What did they eat?" displays for each part of the route—and they ate surprisingly well. I also enjoyed the "after the express" information about all who had significant careers later (Buffalo Bill was a rider!). A surprising number of riders lived into their 70s and 80s.

What a remarkable piece of history. And what a great job they've done recalling it all. But then it was time to move on. I passed the wonderful children's play area (period toys and clothes) and through the very nice gift shop on my way out. Finally, out the front door, I turned right and walked two blocks to the Patee House Museum (see previous entry).

Nearby: The St. Joseph Fire Museum offers a collection of historic firefighting equipment dating back as far as 1865, when the city's fire department was founded. My favorite part was the fence around the yard: fire hydrants connected by hoses.

Washington Historical Society Museum

Washington, MO

I had a couple of free days between speaking engagements in Missouri, so I used the time to follow up on recommendations made by one of my hosts. Washington, a town of 14,000, would remind me that the world is filled with places that are more interesting than one expects.

Walking in the front door, I got a surprise. Hanging by a display about a local hero, an Army Air Corps bomber pilot from World War II, they had a short snorter. It was only the second one I'd ever seen, the other one having been my father's. My dad was also in the Army Air Corps (ancestor of the Air Force) during World War II, and I learned here that these mementos of time in the service were specific to the Army Air Corps. To make a short snorter, you tape together paper money from every country in which you serve, and then have your friends and fellow fliers sign it. The bills/notes are rolled tightly and kept in one's pocket, to be handy when another friend was made and needed to sign. Granted, this is outside the time frame I've chosen for most of this book, but it delighted me to see this reminder of my father. It also underscored one other benefit to small museums—you never know when you might be surprised by something that actually touches your own life.

Though this was not a large museum, it was big enough to consume a couple of hours. The collection is beautifully and lovingly organized—and Washington had a history that surpassed my expectations. The region became part of the U.S. with the Louisiana Purchase and, once settlers began to come, trade on the Missouri River made Washington prosperous.

The museum highlights the important role the river played in local and national history—a huge impact, in fact, as the Missouri, almost as long as the Mississippi, was *the* major highway of its day. The museum also features everything else of interest in the region, from Native American artifacts to natural history, wars to decorative arts.

This area was largely settled by Germans, so German influence was much in evidence. Two elements of German culture in Missouri in the 1800s were particularly noteworthy: *Turn Verein* and zithers. *Turn Verein* means, essentially, "gymnastics club." Old films show precision teams doing synchronized exercises. Displays are filled with equipment and photos of members, and info cards explain a bit of the history. Founded in 1859, the Washington Turn Verein took a break during the Civil War, but then started up again. This was not a local movement, but rather an international phenomenon. From 1878 to 1897, Washington, MO, was the Turn Verein Headquarters for the entire United States.

Zithers were upstairs. Austrian-born Franz Schwarzer, who had studied the zither after college, arrived in the U.S. in 1866 and in Washington in 1867. An excellent video revealed the remarkable climb by Schwarzer from local artisan to the best zither maker in the world, with a gold medal from the international competition in Austria. There were examples of his glorious work all around the room. During his very productive career, Schwarzer made approximately 11,000 zithers! (If you're not certain what a zither sounds like, search for the soundtrack of the movie *The Third Man*.)

Neither Turn Verein nor zithers may draw you to Washington, but if you're nearby, I do recommend this museum. However, whether or not you see it, it is a good reminder that today's big cities were not always the only important ones.

Nearby: A few blocks closer to the Missouri River is another place that made Washington important worldwide: The Missouri Meerschaum Company, the oldest and largest corncob pipe manufacturer in the world. This is where Mark Twain and Rudyard Kipling got their pipes, as did, a bit later, everyone from Norman Rockwell to General Macarthur. Not a museum at all, but rather still a busy manufacturing plant (making roughly 800,000 corncob pipes per year), they do have a shop—and a lot of history. It's not a place to linger, but it's fun to see examples of so iconic a bit of Americana.

Brucemore

Cedar Rapids, IA

Three families are associated with the splendid, Queen Anne mansion that is now known as Brucemore. Meatpacker T. M. Sinclair and Company, opened in 1871 in Cedar Rapids, quickly grew to be the largest employer in the area and one of the biggest in the world. When T. M. died in an accident in 1881, his brother-in-law, Charles, kept the business going, while his widow Caroline watched the children and, from 1884–1886, directed the construction of the mansion. The company continued to thrive, in time becoming Wilson & Company and then Farmstead Foods. However, long before that, in 1906, Caroline had traded homes with the Douglas family, another of the great industrialists to build the town.

Cedar Rapids sits on the Cedar River at a point that has, as the name suggests, rapids. As was true almost everywhere in the 1800s, rapids were a source of power for running machines, particularly mills. George Bruce Douglas had founded a company that took advantage of that water power: Douglas and Stewart Mill, which in time joined with other mills to form Quaker Oats.

The love for the arts of the Douglas family, especially the women, is reflected throughout the house, from a mural of Wagner's Ring Cycle in the grand entry hall to the hiring of Grant Wood to decorate a sleeping porch on the 2nd floor. Irene Douglas bound books as a hobby, and the library is filled with her superb handiwork. Rooms are filled with furniture that actually belonged to the families who lived here, largely because family members are still in the area. All four floors hold items of interest, from rooms for entertaining to bedrooms to organ pipes on the third floor (the pipe organ console is on the first floor). The party room in the basement was added by the last of the three families to live here, the Halls. Howard Hall married Margaret Douglas and moved to Brucemore in 1937. Hall wanted a place to entertain clients, so he transformed the basement into two "playrooms"—the Tahitian

Room, a re-created island experience, and the Grizzly Bar, a bar with a bear skin on the floor. (My guide told me that, because of the paintings of scantily clad Tahitian girls, they don't show these rooms to very young children.)

Elegant furnishings on all floors are pleasing, but it is the stories of the families who lived here that are the most fun. Because school groups do tour, there are interactive elements, including digital displays, that engage younger visitors.

The mansion is beautiful, but so are the grounds, which cover 26 acres. Among the trees, lawns, and flower gardens, there are interesting elements worth noting. The bookbindery that kept Irene busy is still there. The pet cemetery includes a statue of one of their many German shepherds. There are duplex homes that once housed the families of servants. The carriage house is now the visitors center. The cutting garden is now used by Iowa First to raise food. There are information signs all over the property describing gardens and outbuildings. Oh—and outside the house, look up—every chimney is different.

The Halls, like the families before them, were great philanthropists. The legacy of loving the arts lives on in the use of the grounds for performances of the Orchestra of Iowa. And, in 1981, the Halls donated the entire property to the National Trust, for the community to enjoy.

National Czech and Slovak Museum & Library

Cedar Rapids, IA

A surprisingly large percentage of those who came to work in the growing industries of Cedar Rapids were from Eastern Europe, and that is commemorated in this impressive museum, which is a Smithsonian Affiliate. Much of the building is taken up with lecture halls and a research library, but there are also large exhibit areas.

This museum features two permanent exhibit and two temporary exhibits. The main permanent exhibit is "Faces of Freedom." This begins with quotes and recordings about freedom, escaping communism, and what one is willing to risk to make dreams come true, and then moves on to a timeline of the complex history of the part of Eastern Europe that includes the homelands of Czech and Slovak people during various reigns of conquerors and invaders. A digital interactive map makes it possible to see where different groups have settled in the U.S.—and not just Europeans. There are displays on the struggle for freedom back home, and a re-creation of the interior of a ship bound for the U.S., bunk beds piled high with battered luggage. Displays highlight the arts and culture of the Czechs and Slovaks, including great composers, authors, artists, and artisans. The display of traditional costumes is splendid—dozens of life-size mannequins, adults and children, in brilliant native dress, all on a revolving platform, so you can see them from multiple angles. Nearby, a console allows you to press buttons to hear different Czech and Slovak music, from classical to folk to pop.

Next, head outside to view the immigrant house, an actual house that the Seeger family lived in from 1890 to the 1980s. It's small: a living room that doubled as a sleeping room for the adults, a large kitchen, and a small attic area where the children slept. But it is remarkably attractive and comfortable, due to the care the family put into the décor, especially the beautiful woodwork.

The temporary exhibits are generally more contemporary, but when I was there, I enjoyed being reminded, in an exhibit on robots, that we get the word *robot* from the Czech *robota*, meaning "compulsory labor." The word was first used in the meaning we have for it today in a 1920 SciFi play by Czech writer Karel Capek: *Rossum's Universal Robots*, about a factory creating artificial people.

At some point, do try to see the video about when they moved the museum to its current location after it was nearly destroyed by a flood. It is an impressive demonstration of technology and community spirit combined to rescue a cultural icon. There may also be movies about the temporary exhibits. And there is a delightful gift shop with lots of books, should you wish to learn more.

Nearby: About two blocks from the museum is the part of town where the tremendous influx of Czech, Slovak, and Moravian immigrants settled. Near the Cedar River, along 16th Street, is an area known as the Czech Village. This is mostly a place where Czech and Slovak immigrants settled, and as a result, there are places that cater to their needs. The sidewalks have inlaid stones that identify important elements of Czech culture, from King Wenceslas to houbi/morel mushrooms, and there is a bandstand in the center of town where people gather for various festivals. If you stop at the Sykora Bakery, which was built in 1900, you can find a range of Czech, Slovak, and Moravian pastries and foods to eat there or take home. (The rye bread is memorable.)

Dubuque Shot Tower

Dubuque, IA

Physics made shot towers popular back when muskets and black powder were still common. A drop of liquid falling through the air, given enough distance, will become a sphere. This is true of raindrops, but it is also true of molten lead. Pour the molten lead through a grate of a specific size, and allow it to fall far enough, and it becomes a sphere. If it falls into a bucket of water at the bottom of that drop and hardens, it remains a sphere. Shot could be made much faster this way than the older method of molding individual lead balls. In fact, the shot tower in Dubuque was capable of producing as much as eight tons of lead balls per day, though it rarely worked at full capacity.[2]

Modern rifles don't use shot, so shot towers ceased being useful. Today, only a handful remain in the nation. The Dubuque shot tower was constructed in 1856 and was in use until 1881. For the next thirty years after its retirement as a shot tower, it was used as a fire lookout tower. Today, it is a locally cherished monument and is on the National Register of Historic Places. It is not actually a place to tour, but rather a place to see because of its rarity. There is an information panel at the base that tells more of its history and illustrates the making of shot in the tower.

Worth noting is that it can be a little difficult to find. Best bet is to simply head for the Port of Dubuque, along the Mississippi River, and follow the signs—but don't let the circuitous route stop you.

Nearby: The shot tower is highlighted here because it is both iconic and rare. However, there are other things to see in the area that will make the diversion to the Port of Dubuque worthwhile, most notably the National Mississippi River Museum and Aquarium, which you actually pass en route to the shot tower.

Shot towers took advantage of the physics of liquids to turn molten lead into shot for muskets. This shot tower in Dubuque, Iowa, is one of only a handful that remain in the U.S. Photo by Cynthia Clampitt.

Buffalo Bill Museum

LeClaire, IA

LeClaire is a small town that hugs the Mississippi River and straddles I-80 north of the Quad Cities. The downtown area boasts some wonderful architecture dating to the mid-1800s, which made it the perfect location for the TV show "American Pickers." However, its more long-standing claim to fame is that it was the birthplace of William Cody, better known as Buffalo Bill. The town's main street, Cody Road, follows the curve of the river, but in town, a bend in the river creates a little more space behind the town's boutiques, hotels, and restaurants, making the very short Front Street possible. Here, you have access to riverboats, great views across the mighty Mississippi, and the Buffalo Bill Museum.

Despite its name, the museum is not just about Buffalo Bill—something that is evident as soon as you see the large, red paddle wheel out front and the story-high glass wall that offers a view of a riverboat. In fact, the museum covers several key elements of life in the 1800s, from living on the frontier to relying on the river. The boat visible from outside is a full-size, stern-wheeler riverboat: the Lone Star, the only surviving wooden-hulled vessel of its style. It is important enough in its own right to be designated a National Historic Landmark. (And you can actually climb aboard and explore the old boat.)

At the opposite end of the museum (which is spread across two buildings) there is a full-size, re-created one-room schoolhouse. Between the classroom and the riverboat, the museum is divided into topics and time periods, from prehistory to the twentieth century.

One section is, not surprisingly, dedicated to Buffalo Bill. Photos, maps, displays, and signs carry the story from early boyhood, through frontier life and the Civil War, to international fame. A photo of Buffalo Bill with Wild Bill Hickock was a good reminder that, on the sparsely populated frontier, characters as remarkable as these two would meet. But Cody was not the only famous person from Iowa, and signs and photos detail the lives of other famous Iowans, including Wyatt Earp, John Wayne, Bix Beiderbecke, and Herbert Hoover.

One display that particularly interested me, as a food historian, was of ice-harvesting equipment. When food transportation from the Midwest was growing, ice was the key to keeping meat fresh, and tons of ice were sawed out of rivers and lakes across the region to "refrigerate" warehouses, train cars, and even early home iceboxes.

Documents, clothing, tools, antique furniture, household items, models, and more contribute to the stories of Native Americans, homesteaders, settlers, and life on the Mississippi. Some exhibits offer audio narratives. All children are invited to play "find and seek" in the museum, with a prize for those who participate, and for children ages 3 to 8 (accompanied by an adult) there is a special room that offers activities ranging from a dress-up area to a riverboat pilot's wheel to a garden.

Not a huge museum, but a surprising amount of history for its size. Well worth a stop if you're traveling through the Quad Cities area.

Herbert Hoover Museum and Boyhood Home

West Branch, IA

Most grade-school textbooks say little more about Hoover than he got elected U.S. President just before the worldwide economic collapse we know as the Great Depression. So, imagine my surprise when, while traveling in Western Australia, someone started telling me about how Hoover saved the koala. "He was working here as a mining engineer. A real wizard at that. But he was not happy about how the huge demand for koala fur in Europe and the U.S. was destroying the koala population. As soon as he had the chance, Hoover stopped the trade."[3]

Hoover was suddenly of much greater interest to me, so during a trip across Iowa, I headed for his museum and boyhood home, where I learned that Hoover had a remarkable life even before being elected president of the United States. Born in a tiny cabin in Iowa (located behind the museum), his early childhood was happy. His father was a successful blacksmith who made farm equipment, but he died when Herbert (or "Bert," as he was known then) was just six years old. Bert's mom died three years later. The orphaned Bert was put on a train and sent to Oregon to live with a maternal

Herbert Hoover was born in this tiny cottage in Iowa. His father was a blacksmith who worked in the building visible in the background. Photo by Cynthia Clampitt.

uncle. In 1891, at age 17, he became the youngest member of the freshman class at the newly opened Stanford University in California. He quickly distinguished himself as a student and then as a geologist after college. In 1897, he headed for Australia, to the big gold-mining areas out West. He did an impressive job and his men soon called him "The Chief," a name that stuck with him for the rest of his life. He became known internationally as the "doctor of sick mines," and this led to a lot of travel and considerable prosperity. At age 24, newly married, he headed for China, to help develop coal mines. When Hoover and his wife, Lou, got trapped in China by the Boxer Rebellion (1900), Hoover organized relief efforts for the many foreigners trapped with him in Tientsin. Organizing disaster relief turned out to be a recurring theme in Hoover's life. But I'll leave the continuation of that story to food historian Rae Eighmey. (And I'll let the museum reveal the rest of his life to you.)

Herbert Hoover's Midwestern Roots Supported International Rescues

Herbert Hoover's essential humanity began at the dinner table. That's what I think anyway. He described his Iowa childhood where the memories of delicious foods overlaid the struggles of difficult times. Food changed Herbert Hoover. And as a person who writes about food and history, that's one thing that drew me to him.

When he was six, he knew economic hardship following the death of his blacksmith father. His mother found work as a schoolteacher, but still the former president recalled powerfully the delight of generous childhood dinners at the home of his Aunt Millie. Christmas sweets were simply popcorn balls made with sorghum along with the walnuts and hickory nuts Hoover and his brother picked in the fall.

Hoover told stories of youthful fishing and hunting adventures that ended with the plucking and campfire cooking of prairie chickens with "wondrous flavor" surpassing, in his adult opinion, that of the Ritz. He was captivated by the "mystery of growing crops."

Hoover was keenly aware of the power of food—as nourishment for the soul as well as for the body. And in 1915 his choice to leave his career as an internationally known and highly successful metallurgical engineer was propelled by the calling to rescue the starving people of Belgium and northern France. When World War I broke out in August 1914, Hoover and his wife were trapped in England, as were thousands of other travelers. He quickly discovered that his organizational expertise could not only help fellow Americans get back home, but he could help relieve the food pressure during the first years of the war.

When Congress voted to enter the conflict in April 1917, Hoover brought his understanding and skills back home. He undertook what may be his most important public service accomplishment—guiding the nation and our allies through the social upheaval of World War I. His success depended upon the insight that he expressed to President Woodrow Wilson in the spring of 1917, that "Food will win the war."

He mobilized an all-volunteer effort that inspired and encouraged the spirit of American ingenuity and volunteerism. During the eighteen months of food conservation efforts, tens of millions of American homemakers and professional cooks "Hooverized" their dishes to align with the requested restrictions that eliminated wheat and meat from all but three of the twenty-one regular weekly meals.

Hoover did not accept any pay for his war-relief and food-conservation efforts. Nor did he accept a presidential salary. His reward can be seen in the statistics of success where tens of millions of tons of food made its way from American farms to European tables. And in the thousands of flour sacks that grateful Belgians and French embroidered, or painted, and sent as a tribute to Hoover's efforts and America's generosity.

Rae Katherine Eighmey is the author of, among other books, Food Will Win the War.

Oneida Nation Museum

Oneida, WI

The Oneida Nation Museum near Green Bay is a small museum, but it is packed with information, in part thanks to the clever use of technology. The museum starts with an explanation of how the Oneida Nation fit into the Six Nations (the nations that accepted the law of peace proposed by Hiawatha, also known as the Iroquois Confederacy). There are two other bands of Oneida besides the Wisconsin band, in New York and in Canada.

Near a display of headdresses that identify each of the Six Nations, there is a computer that interprets the symbols created with "wampum," purple and white clamshell beads that the nations of the confederacy wove into belts that preserved history and laws, established authority, or sent messages to other nations. From here, the museum follows the chronology of Oneida history. A section of the interior of a traditional longhouse offers many hands-on items for kids to enjoy. An interactive exhibit relates the

Lacrosse is a team sport that is still played today. Imagine playing hockey at eye level. It was created by Native Americans and was an important part of their culture. In lacrosse, a ball is moved toward a goal using sticks with nets at the end, like those shown in this display at the Oneida Nation Museum. Photo courtesy of the Oneida Nation Museum, Oneida, Wisconsin.

importance of the game of lacrosse, which played a role in the law of peace. Touch screens and interactive displays relate the significance of different animals, as well as the Oneida move to Wisconsin in the 1820s. I was surprised to learn that there were Oneida Code Talkers during World War II, since all the stories I'd heard previously had been of Navajo Code Talkers. Different art forms important in the Oneida culture are displayed, and what handsome work it was: lace, baskets, beadwork.

As is the case with most Native American cultures, warriors are valued, and Oneida experience, from helping George Washington to those Code Talkers, is highlighted. There is even an interactive veterans database. Wonderfully worthwhile museum.

Nearby: Also part of the Oneida Nation, but not part of the museum, is a full-size, reconstructed Oneida longhouse, operated by Oneida Nation Tourism. Surprisingly impressive structure.

Civil War Museum

Kenosha, WI

It may seem odd to some to have a Civil War museum in Wisconsin, and yet without the involvement of the states of the Upper Middle West, the Civil War would have had an entirely different outcome. This museum makes it clear why. But as wonderful as the information is, the presentation of it is stunning. This Smithsonian Affiliate Museum offers more than just a collection of artifacts, though there are plenty of those. There are also life-size dioramas throughout, from towns to battlefields, from the buildup to the war to the aftermath. The main exhibit area on the ground floor is titled "The Fiery Trial," and in the center of this area, there is a 360-degree movie that shows just how fiery the trail was. The title of the film, "Seeing the Elephant," refers to a tale from the 1820s of a farmer who read about an elephant and was eager to see one. When he did find an elephant, it resulted in personal loss "But at least I've seen an elephant." The saying "Seeing the elephant" became a popular catchphrase in the mid-1800s for gaining knowledge through often risky experience, and this was how many volunteers initially approached the conflict—curious to see what the war was like, eager to distinguish themselves—and no idea what horrors lay ahead. The movie is stirring, moving, horrifying, tragic, but beautifully crafted.

Surrounding the elevated platform where the movie is shown, there are display cases that detail the contributions of each of the states of the Upper Midwest: Iowa, Indiana, Illinois, Michigan, Minnesota, Ohio, Wisconsin. But here, as elsewhere throughout the museum, the stories are not abstract. There are photographs of and letters from specific people, which makes it more poignant. At several spots around the museum, there are panels labeled "12 Tales of Real People," which name individuals from the region and relate the part each one played. On a re-creation of the deck of a paddle boat, the statues all begin "talking" as you approach, introducing themselves by name and relating their reasons for being on the boat: a widow taking her husband's body home, a free African American soldier from Michigan going home after losing an arm in battle and wondering how he will continue to work as a carpenter, two little boys going to live with relatives after their father is killed, and so on—ten in all. And all spoke of Lincoln's recent death.

In the pre-war section, the benches of a meeting house face a lectern, where the speaker comes to life on a screen—an actor re-creating one of the powerful speeches delivered by Frederick Douglass. During the war, Abraham Lincoln meets with General McClellan in a battlefield tent. Horses pull wagons, supplies are gathered, weapons are readied. Soldiers gather and head for the war. We learn that nearly three-quarters of a million young men from the Upper Midwest volunteered, and they fought in every major theater of the war. There were also hundreds of women who went, mainly as nurses and caregivers, but roughly 400 enlisted and served in the ranks as men. But even that doesn't fully explain the impact of the region. From the great meat-processing plants to the fields of grain, the mines supplying minerals to the forests supplying wood, the Middle West, as it was then known, supplied the materials needed to keep the soldiers and the war effort going. Michigan alone produced more than 6,000 tons of copper per year, for everything from belt buckles to cannons.

Newspapers changed because of the war, as people were demanding more than just local news. And much of the information in the exhibits is presented as front-page reports. Swords, canteens, a model of an iron-clad riverboat, medical equipment, uniforms, and mementos from loved ones fill display cases. Turn a corner, and there is someone looking in a window, loading a wagon, resting outside a hospital, firing a cannon. The windows of a train car light up with a full-length video of the passing countryside. While nothing is ever really "just like being there," this museum comes close to creating the sense of urgency, energy, and hardship of the war and of the events surrounding it.

When I finally tore myself away from the main exhibit, I headed upstairs. The Veterans Gallery honors those who served in every conflict from the American Revolution to the Gulf Wars. Life-size statues unite the different eras, with Civil War soldiers huddled around a campfire and soldiers from other eras standing around the room. Next stop was the temporary exhibit area. While this area changes regularly, the excellent presentation about the formation of Wisconsin's 1st Cavalry suggests that this will always be an interesting exhibit. In the main hall, there is also information about current efforts to excavate notorious Camp Douglas, a POW camp located in Chicago. Finally, to refresh the mind after so much intense information, the view of Lake Michigan from the second-floor patio is splendid.

Nearby: Next door to the Civil War Museum is the Kenosha Public Museum, which includes everything from archaeology to the fine arts. "The Wisconsin Story" is an exhibit that covers the state's prehistory, from geology and a locally excavated woolly mammoth to early Native Americans. A short distance away is the Southport Light Station Museum, a restored 1860s lighthouse keeper's residence and a lighthouse built in 1866. Just around the corner from the lighthouse is the Kenosha History Center, with collections that range from the early days of Kenosha to vintage Ramblers, cars that were built in Kenosha beginning in 1900.

Cooks, Books, and Bandages

Following soldiers to the sites of battles was not the only way women contributed during the Civil War. While working on my book *Midwest Maize*, I learned that the 1860s saw the rise of charity cookbooks, collections of local recipes that gave women another way to help the war effort. Members of church groups, ladies' aid societies, and various clubs collected recipes from everyone in the community, found advertisers to cover the cost of publishing, and then sold the cookbooks to raise money to buy bandages and other supplies for soldiers. This was successful enough that the community cookbook as fundraiser continued long after the war ended.

This pale golden stone construction is common throughout the Cornish community of Mineral Point. Here, the smaller of the two buildings is Pendarvis and the larger is Trelawny—both named for families in Cornwall. Photo by Cynthia Clampitt.

Pendarvis

Mineral Point, WI

Pendarvis is actually just one building in a cluster of handsome stone buildings, each with its own name (it is flanked by Trelawny and Polperro), but it is the one that is famous, because it is the one where interest in preserving the Cornish culture and architecture of Mineral Point was kickstarted. Pendarvis is the name one finds listed by the Wisconsin Historical Society, though all of Mineral Point is on the National Register of Historic Places (and was the first city in Wisconsin to be so listed).

In 1827, when Mineral Point was settled, Wisconsin was still a territory. The discovery of rich mineral deposits, primarily lead and zinc, drew a flood of miners from Cornwall, England, throughout the 1830s. The miners built

Mineral Point into a prosperous Cornish town of tidy, golden buildings. But with the advent of the California Gold Rush in 1848, many experienced miners left, and the town began a slow decline. Fortunately, in the 1930s, Bob Neal, who was of Cornish descent, and his partner Edgar Hellum decided the area should be saved. They began restoring Pendarvis, a building on Shake Rag Street, turning it into a restaurant. Pendarvis became a destination, and income funded restoration of the buildings on either side of Pendarvis. As noted earlier, this also drew attention to the beauty and history of the area, and others began to get involved. But Pendarvis is the place that became a destination.

At the Welcome Center, I signed up for the guided tour. While exploring Pendarvis and Trelawny, the focus was on the history of the restoration and the restaurant. It was in Polperro that the region's mining history came to the fore. This building was filled with old mining equipment, photographs of Cornish miners, and information about life in the 1830s.

Nearby: Within a long block of Pendarvis, Shake Rag Street ends in the heart of Mineral Point. Built in what is known as the "driftless area," an area the Ice Age glaciers skipped, the town is surprisingly hilly. Historic, pale-gold-stone buildings line the streets, many filled with crafts, art, gifts, and the artisans producing them. Not far from where Shake Rag joins Commerce Street is the Mineral Point Railroad Museum. My guide at Pendarvis told me that it is easy to find Cornish pasties here, as there is still a lot of Cornish influence, and there is a Cornish Fest in September. She also mentioned that within roughly 20 miles, there are a couple of historic mines that are open to visitors.

Mill City Museum

Minneapolis, MN

In 1680, a Belgian missionary named Louis Hennepin, who had recently parted company with French explorer Robert de La Salle, was captured by Sioux Indians. Accompanying his captors on a hunting trip, Hennepin reached a waterfall on the Mississippi River, which he named the Falls of St. Anthony. All this took place in the area known at the time as New France. It

The modern Mill City Museum was built inside the ruins of the old 1880 mill that exploded. Photo by Cynthia Clampitt, used with permission of Minnesota Historical Society.

would be another 120 years before the Louisiana Purchase would make the area part of the United States. By the mid-1800s, a village began to grow on the west side of the falls. When the village was incorporated in 1867, the name chosen combined the Sioux word *minne*, which means "water," with the Greek *polis*, which means "city." The falls retained the name Hennepin had given them, and the county where they are located was given the name of the Belgian missionary. Because it was the Falls of St. Anthony, in the heart of Minneapolis, that would make the city successful—and lead to its having the nickname of Mill City.

Mills need power to operate, and a nice, wide waterfall was just the sort of power source needed to run a variety of mills. Sawmills took advantage of some of that power, but it was flour mills that truly made Minneapolis Mill City. And it was the remarkably dangerous act of making flour that led to this museum being so unusual. Grinding grain into flour puts a lot of dust into the air, and flour dust is actually explosive. The Mill City Museum is built inside the ruins of what was once the largest flour mill in the world— until the flour dust exploded.

The ruins of the Washburn "A" Mill (1880) contrast nicely with the glass-and-steel construction of the museum (2003). And the museum offers a remarkable history of a city that for half a century milled more flour than anywhere else in the world. So many familiar names grew up in Minneapolis: Gold Medal Flour, Pillsbury, General Mills. The presentations are as interesting as the information. For example, there is a "show" in the Flour Tower that is essentially a huge elevator that carries viewers through the mill's history as it climbs the eight stories inside the wheat tower. Following the show, I perused the vintage equipment and exhibits that detailed the conversion of crop to consumer good, finding that not only was the signage excellent, but the docents were very knowledgeable. Some interesting facts I learned: the road in front of the mill used to be wood, the stone bridge now for pedestrians used to carry a train, and the millers in town founded the Art Institute here. A sadder fact was that, before filters were installed, breathing the flour dust led to something called "miller's cough." I'm glad to know that the bag of flour I buy now is no longer exacting such a price from the producers. Finally, on the top floor, I exited onto the observation deck, which offered a great view of the city, river, rapids, and ruins.

Nearby: At the back of the museum is Mill Ruins Park, and along the river, overlooking the falls, there are information signs about the nature and beauty of the falls, as well as of the engineering that went into utilizing them. On the other side of the river, you can tour the Pillsbury "A" Mill (which is notable among mills not only for its size, but also for having never exploded). Converted to artists' lofts, the building still offers a look at how the operation functioned during the heyday of flour production.

This is the portrayal of the Mille Lacs Ojibwe summer camp in the Four Seasons Room at the Mille Lacs Indian Museum. Photo by David Turner, courtesy of Minnesota Historical Society.

Mille Lacs Indian Museum

Onamia, MN

If you are traveling north on Highway 169 and you see a building with a large sign saying Trading Post, you are within a few yards of the museum. If you see a casino to your left, you have just passed the museum and need to turn around.

The Mille Lacs Indian Museum is on land belonging to the Mille Lacs band of Ojibwe, on the shores of the impressively large Mille Lacs Lake. The museum is owned by the Minnesota Historical Society, but the Ojibwe helped build it and had a say in what was displayed.

In the spacious lobby of the museum there is an open area, where, I was told, exhibits change regularly. When I visited, it was a display of jingle dresses, which originated here, on the Mille Lacs reservation, in 1919, so 100 years ago. Just beyond this, a timeline begins, with events progressing as the timeline follows the curve of the wall. It starts in 1750, which is roughly when the Ojibwe made this area home. The first item on the timeline notes that the Mdewakanton Dakota were in the area at the time, and there were battles. It then relates, "While some people believe the Dakota left the area voluntarily, most agree they were driven out around 1750 after a decisive battle with the Ojibwe."

The timeline continues through many events, treaties, councils, and developments, up to the present—because, as is the case at many Native American museums, while describing the past is important, it is also important to make it clear that Native Americans are still around, and that they are still active members of society.

I perused displays on food—corn, hazelnuts, Jerusalem artichoke, and the vital Manoomin, or wild rice. Legend holds that a prophet told the Ojibwe to move west until they found a place where food grew on water, and wild rice was identified as the realization of that prophecy (and is still an important food source for the Ojibwe).

Displays, videos, and dioramas show how life adjusted and adapted, while still retaining much tradition. Quill work became beadwork, once glass beads were available. A video shows Ojibwe playing the traditional game of lacrosse and the adopted game of baseball. Another shows dancers at modern-day powwows, along with displays of the gorgeous attire worn by traditional dancers.

The Ojibwe call themselves the Anishinaabeg, which means "the people" or "the original people." Interestingly, the signs that include quotes from Ojibwe sources are in Ojibwe, which is still spoken in this area (but translations are included for visitors). I followed the curve of the room around the museum, watching as the culture altered through the centuries. There is a wall of veterans from twentieth-century wars, because they still respect warriors. There are also lots of photos of children, so younger visitors can identify.

But then it was announced that the Four Seasons room would be opening, and I headed there. This room holds a life-size re-creation of scenes around Mille Lacs 200 years ago, divided into the four seasons of the year. Each season required a different camp. One thing that made this display special is that local Ojibwe modeled for the mannequins, so all the figures in this room represent real people. The four seasons/camps are spring/sugar-bush camp (maple-sugar harvesting and making); summer/fishing camp; fall/wild-rice camp; and winter, in a protected hollow with access to hunting. There was much hunting and ice fishing in the winter, and killing a snow rabbit was a rite of passage for young boys. A recording of Ojibwe elders was played, so we could hear the language. A remarkable place, with so much detail. One of the things the guide told me was that there are thirteen stuffed animals in the room, and kids love looking for them. The guide emphasized that maple sugar and wild rice are still important in Ojibwe culture, and also related that most Ojibwe have both a native name and a Western-style name, for drivers' licenses and such. Fascinating to see how what is important in different eras has been preserved.

Nearby: The sprawling Trading Post next door is not just a gift shop—though there is a great gift shop and bookstore there. It also offers Minnesota's largest collection of Native American arts and crafts. The woman behind the counter told me that it is also still a trading post, working to support local artisans.

Kansas Museum of History

Topeka, KS

The angular, modern exterior of the museum, while handsome, did not suggest history to me. Then I stepped inside. What a treat this place proved to be.

As is true of many museums, there was a temporary exhibit, and I entered that first. While this will have changed by the time you read this, it was a good reminder that temporary exhibits can be impressive. Because it offered an important historic event or person from each of the 105 counties of Kansas, it was also a good reminder that there is almost nowhere you can go that doesn't have some bit of interesting and even significant history. For example, Dr. Brewster Higley, who lived in Smith County, was probably a good doctor, but he is best known for a poem he published in 1872 titled "My

Western Home." Friend Daniel Kelley set the poem to music, and it became widely known as "Home on the Range," now the state song of Kansas. There were 104 other stories of rough-and-tumble towns, of striking oil, of poets and innkeepers, of the world's first female mayor, and of Native Americans and African Americans.

Then I entered the main museum. Wow! Displays are big and impressive: a full-size wigwam, full-size covered wagon, full-size bison, and an actual engine and a few cars from the famed Atchison, Topeka, and Santa Fe train line. Educational, of course, but combined with all the stuff that can be touched or explored, also very kid friendly. The narrative begins with Native American culture and flows into early (1600s and 1700s) Spanish and French explorers and trappers and eventual waves of pioneers that swept in during the mid-1800s, then on through the Civil War, and up to the present.

The way things are presented was a constant delight. There are certainly display cases and information signs, but there are a lot of wonderful surprises, too. For example, I noticed out of the corner of my eye a woman leaning against a balcony railing, admiring a vintage airplane hanging nearby, and then I realized it was a mannequin of Kansan Amelia Earhart. I also learned that salt mining in Kansas (vital in a world without refrigeration) began in the 1860s, and in the late 1800s, mussel shells from the Neosho River were a major source of "pearl" buttons.

Familiar names and events are on all sides: "Bleeding Kansas," John Brown, the Underground Railroad, Dodge City, cattle drives, Wild Bill Hickock, Dwight Eisenhower, Fred Harvey, Carrie Nation, Clyde Cessna, Pizza Hut, White Castle, James Naismith (inventor of basketball), and so much more. Fascinating to see how much American history, including our notions of the Wild West, is really Kansas history.

There is so much more I could share, but I'll leave something for you to discover. Impressive place.

Nearby: The Kansas State Capitol is, like most state capitols, imposing, but the big draw here is a series of famous murals by John Steuart Curry, most notably the once-controversial painting of abolitionist John Brown.

African American Museum

Wichita, KS

To a greater extent than perhaps any other Midwestern state, African Americans were a key element of Kansas history. The people settling the Kansas Territory wanted to create a free state. Neighboring slave state Missouri wanted to ensure that, if Kansas became a state, it would be a slave state. This led to armed conflict even before the Civil War. The most famous of the conflicts was in 1856, when abolitionist John Brown violently retaliated against a pro-slavery mob that had plundered Lawrence, KS. So was born the name "Bleeding Kansas."

But Kansas was safe for African Americans, both those escaping slavery and those already free, and they came. Then, after the Civil War, there was a major influx. These African Americans became known as Exodusters. A number of all-African American towns were created, of which only Nicodemus remains. The famous Buffalo Soldiers were brought together at Fort Leavenworth, KS, to form the 9th and 10th Cavalry.

Knowing this history, I wanted to visit The Kansas African American Museum (TKAAM), to learn more. The building that houses the museum is, itself, on the National Register of Historic Places. Built in 1917, the Calvary Baptist Church became a cornerstone of the city's African American community. When it ceased to operate as a church, it was seen as the ideal location for commemorating African American history.

I had the great good fortune to have as my guide Dr. Lona Reeves, the museum's education director. We started on the ground floor, which is mostly reserved for events and temporary exhibits. However, the walls are hung with artwork by contemporary African American artists, and at the back, there are displays of artifacts—mostly wonderful wooden carvings—from Africa. Then we headed to the second floor. Here, photographs and biographies are hung all the way around the perimeter.

Because so many African Americans came to Kansas, among those biographies there was a remarkable range of famous people who were born in or moved to or lived in Kansas at some point. Hattie McDaniel, who was the first African American to win an Oscar, was born in Wichita. George Washington Carver moved to Kansas at age 13. Photographer and first

African American Hollywood director Gordon Parks was born in Kansas, as was musician Charlie "Bird" Parker. Famously associated with Harlem, Langston Hughes lived in Lawrence, KS, for many years. Gwendolyn Brooks was born in Topeka, KS. It was lovely seeing so many remarkable accomplishments memorialized.

There were also many things that were new to me. I learned that Ronald Waters helped stage the first successful sit-in—which was done in Wichita well before the more famous one that occurred in North Carolina. (The downside of remoteness is that heroic actions may not get noticed by major media.) Buffalo Soldier Ruben Waller was born into slavery, gained his freedom, had a successful military career, and lived to 105. Oscar Micheaux, the first African American movie maker, produced a movie in answer to the racist film *Birth of a Nation*. One of my favorite surprises was Junius Groves, who was an agricultural scientist and entrepreneur who had become known as "the potato king of the world" by 1902, and who became one of the wealthiest African Americans in the U.S. But these are just a few of the many inspiring stories.

I knew that there had been many African American cowboys during the days of the cattle drives, as well as a few lawmen. In particular, I'd read about the legendary Bass Reeves, the tall, fearless lawman who arrested more than 3,000 outlaws during his career as a deputy U.S. marshal. Consequently, I was delighted when my guide Lona Reeves stopped in front of a photo of Bass Reeves and told me he was a relative.

My tour concluded with an introduction to the Kansas African American History Trail project. Hoping to get more people, including African Americans, interested in this history, museums and historic sites on the "trail" issue "passports," which get stamped each time you visit a new location. I now have my History Trail passport with the first stamp on it.

Wichita-Sedgwick County Historical Museum

Wichita, KS

For me, this was the perfect museum to see the day after I visited the Old Cowtown Museum (see Chapter 2). Wichita came into existence in 1865, after the Civil War, and never existed in a time without photography. As a

The Wichita-Sedgwick County Historical Museum is located in the heart of Wichita, in a building that used to be the Wichita City Hall. Photo by Cynthia Clampitt.

result, at this museum, I could see early photos of some of the buildings now at Old Cowtown, in their original settings as the town was being born. It underscored the connection between displays and history.

The museum is housed in what was once the Wichita City Hall. The imposing building, opened in 1892, makes it clear that the city's founders had a great sense of Wichita's potential importance—which was not unreasonable, given that Wichita in 1890 was the fastest-growing city in the U.S. Reflecting the building's past, "Mayor's Office" is still stenciled in gold on one of the windows, and inside, the mayor's office has been reproduced as it was in the late 1800s.

This museum is the perfect place to get a sense of the trajectory of Wichita's history. I found it tremendously worthwhile, as it pulls everything together. Names famous from books and TV were placed in context. Bat

Masterson grew up near Wichita and Wyatt Earp was a lawman here. And there was another Buffalo Bill. William Mathewson had earned the name well before William Cody did. Mathewson was an explorer, hunter, and Indian scout who, later in life, once he'd settled in Wichita, was able to host Cody's Wild West Show on his land.

Displays and presentations flowed from explorers and early founders well into the twentieth century. Wyatt Earp (who preferred words to guns), grasshopper plagues ("darkened the sky like a storm"), and Billy the Kid (whose mother and stepfather helped found Wichita) transitioned into the Victorian era (and there is an entire, splendidly furnished Victorian cottage reproduced on one floor). Eventually transitioning into the twentieth century, displays moved on to the Jones car company (with a video of how they got the car into the building), Clyde Cessna building a plane in Wichita in 1916, the advent of the soda fountain, and, in 1932 in Wichita, the first public performance on an electric guitar.

This is just skimming the surface. I had many pages of notes by the time I left. All history pleases me, but this was particularly fun history, as it was so filled with familiar American icons.

Nebraska History Museum

Lincoln, NE

This museum was recommended to me by a friend who teaches at the university in Lincoln, and who knows my love of history. She even recommended the guide I should have, and Jack was waiting for me when I arrived. He guided me enthusiastically through the excellent displays, which cover 10,000 years of Nebraska history. I won't even try to share everything I learned, but here are a few highlights:

- Of the many Native American groups that were here when Europeans arrived (Pawnee, Omaha, Ponca, Oto, Ioway, Sac, Winnebago, Cheyenne, and Arapaho), about half were moved to other states and about half adapted and are still living in Nebraska today. The Omaha and Winnebago still have annual powwows.

- The Pawnee were one of the largest groups in the area, and the Skidi Pawnee was the largest Pawnee group. The Skidi brought Aztec astronomy with them when they moved north from Mexico. They grew four different colors of corn: red, blue, yellow, and white.
- Fort Atkinson, from 1819–1820, was the westernmost military post in the U.S. and had the first bowling alley in Nebraska. This fort was never involved in fighting, so they started farming and brought the first European women to the plains.
- In roughly 1840–1850, approximately 450,000 people crossed Nebraska on the Platte River Road, on the way west.
- The Homestead Act led to rapid settlement in the 1860s, and in 1867, Nebraska had a population large enough to become a state. Because so much of this settlement occurred after the invention of photography, we have a wonderful record of what life looked like for those who arrived.
- Dr. Susan LaFlesche Picotte, an Omaha, was the first Native American to become a doctor, graduating in 1889 at the top of her class from the Women's Medical College of Pennsylvania, one of the first medical schools to accept women.
- Because Nebraska is 1500 miles from both East and West Coasts, it was popular during World War II for military plants. Forty percent of all ammo used during WW II was made here, as were bombers and depth charges.
- During World War II, approximately 12,000 German and Italian POWs were located here. Many of the POWs happily worked on local farms, in place of the farmers who had gone off to war.
- The production of butter and cream was an easy way for women on farms to make extra money. It would be collected each day by local creameries. One creamery, in Beatrice, did exceedingly well, and eventually relocated to Chicago, becoming the huge food conglomerate Beatrice Foods.

That is just a fraction of what I learned, but I hope it is enough to make you want to visit and learn more.

Nearby: The Nebraska State Capitol is just a few blocks away. It was the first statehouse in the country to adopt a design that dramatically departed from the prototypical form of the nation's Capitol and use an office tower. It is interesting to see how elements of Nebraska history and life have been worked into the design, not just in obvious ways, such as large murals and statues, but also in more subtle ways, such as brass light fixtures that incorporate images of wheat and corn.

Durham Museum

Omaha, NE

Even before I got to the collection, the building had made an impression. The Durham is housed in Omaha's former Union Station—a gloriously Art Deco structure that is even more astonishing inside than out. The Main Waiting Room is 160 feet long by 72 feet wide, with 60-foot ceilings, soaring windows, and 13-foot-tall chandeliers. Adding to the delight of this impressive room is the presence of "talking statues," bronze figures in small groups that reflect the people who used the station, but with recordings playing that express the likely conversations of the soldiers, families, a salesman, a young couple, and more. Seats and ticket windows are all still in place, though behind the ticket windows one now finds a gift shop. But the 1931 soda fountain at the end of the hall is still handsome—and still serves sodas and phosphates (and, I was happy to find, also has very good coffee).

Heading through the doors that once led to train platforms, I enjoyed displays about the building, rail travel and how it changed over the years, and people important in the area's history. And then I headed to the much larger lower level, to explore the bulk of the exhibits. The Baright Home and Family Gallery explores the development of life in the region. The narrative flows from the open prairies and the Omaha Indians who once lived here, with displays surrounding a full-size tepee and an earth lodge. It moves on to a worker's cottage of the 1880s, and then to a prosperous home of the 1940s, all wonderfully re-creating these periods.

One display looks at the impact of the dominant ethnic groups here, which, in the late 1800s and early 1900s, were (in alphabetical order) African, Chinese, Czech, Danish, English, German, Greek, Irish, Italian, Jewish,

Lithuanian, Mexican, Polish, Scottish, Swedish, and Welsh. (A fairly standard level of diversity for the Midwest.) Notable companies and individuals are highlighted. Bekins Moving and Storage started in Omaha, and one of its early trucks is on hand. Mutual of Omaha is there, of course, with a short, worthwhile movie about the early days of the city. I encountered Dr. Susan LaFlesche Picotte, whom I'd "met" at the museum in Lincoln. Born in 1865, she was the first Native American woman to graduate from medical school. And Father Flanagan founded Boys Town not far from here.

There are great displays on early immigration and a splendid diorama of the 1898 Omaha World's Fair, aka the Trans-Mississippi Exposition. This being a train station, there are a couple of trains running the full length of the building, available for exploration. There are also model trains, a reproduction of a 1915 grocery store, and a streetcar. Temporary exhibits and photography displays were also excellent.

I then headed to the Byron Reed Gallery, which houses a stunning collection of coins, currency, documents, books, maps, and more, all willed to Omaha when Reed died in 1891. The collection includes coins from Ancient Greece, Rome, and Egypt up to the late 1800s. The thing I found most interesting, and surprising, was the revelation that, until 1857, because coins used to be made of valuable metals (gold and silver), people across the country would accept just about any currency as payment. A scale was displayed that would at that time have been used to simply weigh the amount of gold or silver one was offering, regardless of which country had minted the coins. Then, in 1857, using foreign currency was outlawed in the U.S.

Remarkable. And there was so much more.

Eating History: Runza and Bierocks

Unlike many special ethnic foods with historic backgrounds, if you are in Nebraska, you don't have to look too hard to find a Runza. In fact, there is an entire chain of restaurants called Runza, with more than eighty locations. The Runza is a small loaf of soft bread filled with beef, onion, and cabbage (though there are now many variations). The restaurant chain dates back to 1949, founded in Lincoln, Nebraska, but the Runza itself was introduced into the Midwest in the 1800s by German-Russian settlers.

However, the Runza is not the only meat-stuffed bread specialty in the Midwest. Talk about Runza, and someone is almost certain to mention Bierocks, found commonly in Kansas, which are round instead of rectangular, but are otherwise similar in both ingredients and history. But if you're in Nebraska and see a sign saying Runza, you might want to stop and try it. I recommend the Original, with beef, onion, and cabbage, for your first Runza. It's a tasty bit of history.

Fort Clark State Historic Site

Stanton, ND

This is a fascinating site, but, unless you're an archaeologist, it's not one where you need to allow a lot of time. It is considered one of the most important archaeological sites in North Dakota, offering insights into both Native American culture and a once-thriving international fur trade. A combination of archaeological features, reconstructions, and information signs amid a broad expanse of lushly grassy terrain make the site worth a visit, nonetheless.

The initial settlement here was built by the Mandan in 1822. As at other Mandan sites, the women grew beans, corn, squash, and sunflowers, but here, men grew tobacco, as well as following the more traditional pursuit of hunting bison. Not too surprisingly, the Mandan here were also great traders. As a result, in order to facilitate trade with the Mandan, James Kipp of the American Fur Company built a small fort here in 1830. Of more lasting importance than the tremendous success of the trade was the fact that the head trader at the fort, Francis Chardon, kept a journal of life at the fort. As a result, we have details of life, trade items, river travel, the various tribes, and smallpox and cholera epidemics.

Though Lewis and Clark and the Corps of Discovery had passed through this area in 1804 and 1806, the fort was not named as a result of that endeavor. Rather, while it was named for that same William Clark, it was in his capacity as Superintendent of Indian Affairs for the Louisiana Territory.

A self-guided tour is all that is offered: hiking along gravel paths that connect markers, information signs, and the few buildings that were reconstructed by the Civilian Conservation Corps (CCC) in the 1930s. I learned that the fort became a popular stopping point for travelers in the area, including Swiss artist Karl Bodmer (who left us some wonderful images of the Native Americans in the region), Prince Maximilian of Neuwied (now part of Germany), and American ornithologist and naturalist John James Audubon.

Among the interesting informational signs was a large map showing the routes and extent of the fur trade. This sign also listed the trade goods that came from Europe and the countries from which each came: tools from England, wine from Spain, mirrors and clay pipes from Germany, and more. Remarkable to realize how extensive world trade was even then. Another sign related the many different people and languages, both Native American and European, that could be heard at the fort, related who the workers were, what they did (interpreters, clerks, blacksmiths, carpenters, and more) and how much they earned (top pay for managers could be more than $1,000 a year), and spoke of the lives of wives and children who lived at the fort. The sign by the reconstructed stone shelter explained the work and purpose of the CCC.

Knife River Indian Villages National Historic Site

Stanton, ND

The Interpretive Center at Knife River relates the fascinating history of this area and, just outside, offers a re-created earth lodge. The nearby "village" is actually a field of craters where the many earth lodges of the village once stood. Archaeological evidence indicates that this area of the upper Missouri River was occupied by various groups of Native Americans for more than 11,000 years. The Hidatsa, the people here when Europeans arrived, appear to have lived in the Knife River area for 500 years or more.

Starting at the Interpretive Center, I found myself again taking copious notes, as there was so much to learn. The area takes its name from the flint found here. Knife River flint was considered the best flint on the continent—a valuable commodity at a time when everything with a sharp edge was made from flint. This flint became one of the area's first major export items.

Through trade, the Hidatsa got horses from the Spanish in the Southwest and guns from the French and English in the Northeast. Other groups would eventually get these goods, but Knife River is the first place that had both. Trade was, in fact, the reason that the Hidatsa had semi-permanent settlements—because if you want to build a successful trade network, people have to know where to find you.

As with the Mandan, the Hidatsa economy was based largely on buffalo hunting and agriculture. Each family had a "garden" for growing food, with each garden being roughly the size of one to three football fields. The Hidatsa and Mandan recognized private ownership, with women owning the earth lodges and families owning gardens. It was the gardens that made a settled existence possible. They grew corn (favoring green corn), beans, squash, and sunflowers. (And if you want to know how they did it, the book written in the mid-1800s by Buffalo Bird Woman about Hidatsa gardening is still in print!)

Both groups did more than survive, they thrived—enough that they actually enjoyed leisure time and devised games. One game they played, Tchung-kee, was also played by the neighboring Mandan, as well as by groups in Wisconsin and along the Mississippi River, linking the Hidatsa with others (I'm guessing trading partners). The game involved rolling a small (two or three inches) stone ring across the playing area, while competitors tried to toss a pole (the tchung-kee) in an attempt to spear the ring through the center.

Because of proximity and related cultures, the Hidatsa and Mandan, along with the Arikara, became known as the Three Affiliated Tribes.

Also recounted in the museum is the story of Oscar Will, a plant breeder who arrived in North Dakota in 1881 at the age of 26. Because of his active interest in traditional crops and traditional wisdom about growing them, Hidatsa, Mandan, and Arikara individuals shared corn, squash, and bean seeds with him. Decades of experimentation and breeding led to new and improved varieties, many of which are still available. The still-popular Great Northern Bean is one of Will's creations (bred from Hidatsa seeds).

Heading outside, I visited the earth lodge. This one was larger than ones I'd seen previously, created for a larger family, but also with room for a couple of horses. Owned by women, earth lodges were also built by women, with an older woman supervising. It generally took seven to ten days to build. This lodge was more extensively furnished than ones I'd seen previously, with several beds, food storage platform, shrine, fire pit, dolls, painted buffalo hide, and much more. Really wonderful. Then I strolled over to the "village," which is a sea of circular indentations in the lush grass. Fortunately, posted information signs include aerial photos that make the extent, size, and position of the indentations more discernible. This general area is where Sacagawea was living when she first met explorers Lewis and Clark.

CHAPTER 4

Exploring History

While some museums may require just as much time as the places described in this chapter, the locations that follow involve multiple buildings or might be both indoors and outdoors. They are places to wander and explore. In some cases, you may only need a couple of hours to see one of these venues, but in several cases, you might need a full day or even more than one day to see everything. Occasionally, related venues are a short drive apart. While all this is true of the living-history venues in Chapter 2, as well, these are places that don't fit in that category.

Of course, it could be said that all major cities fall into the "exploring" category, but since that's a given, they are not included here. This is a sampling of the numerous historic towns, large-scale collections, or multifaceted venues in the region that offer opportunities for a bit more wandering.

Bishop Hill, IL

People coming to the United States to escape religious persecution is something of a recurring theme in the nation's history. In 1846, a group of Swedish immigrants, led by Erik Jansson, established a settlement in northwestern Illinois, naming it for Jansson's birthplace, Biskopskulla, which, translated, means Bishop Hill. The group had left Sweden because their beliefs did not match those of the Church of Sweden, and they established a community here where they could build new lives. The colony prospered, first through farming and then through the production of furniture, wagons, fine linens, brooms, and pottery. As with all communities of humans, problems arose and changes occurred over time, but Bishop Hill never lost its sense of being Swedish. And it preserved the wonderful buildings created during the initial decades of settlement, as well as the crafts that helped them prosper. Because of that preservation of the past, the entire town of Bishop Hill has been designated as both a state historic site and a national historic landmark.

Also because of that preservation, Bishop Hill is a delightful place to visit and explore the past. The barn-like 1848 Colony Church was the village's first permanent building, and it is open to visitors. Definitely don't miss the handsome 1854 Steeple Building, which houses the Bishop Hill Heritage Museum. (Check out the broom-making machine.) This is the most central museum, but there are others, including the Bishop Hill Museum and Henry County Museum. You can also visit the Colony School, Colony Blacksmith Shop, Colony Carpenter Shop, and Dairy Building, among others. The beautifully kept vintage homes can be admired, as well, but not entered. People still live there, and so these houses are, as the map in town notes, for "Walk-by viewing only."

The Twinflower Inn, originally constructed in 1855 as a hospital, and the Gallery Inn, built in 1856, are now lovely B&Bs, should you wish to spend the night, but are handsome and historic enough to be worth seeing even if you simply drive by. The Colony Store (1853), on the broad, shady village green, kitty-corner from the Steeple Building, is filled with Swedish delights, from gifts to comestibles, and has a record of visitors, a surprising number of whom come from Sweden to see how things turned out. There are other vintage buildings, as well as shops selling traditional crafts, a bakery, and a couple of places to eat. I have become particularly fond of P. L. Johnson's, originally built as Bishop Hill's hardware store. Just off the village green, this building is half gift shop and half Swedish café. My favorite menu items thus far are their fresh-baked Swedish rye bread, the cream of spinach soup, and any salad with their lingonberry vinaigrette. Cabbage rolls are good, too. And, if you know anything about the Swedes, you won't be surprised that they have good coffee.

Bishop Hill is a very small town, only about six blocks in any direction, so you can spin through fairly quickly—see a couple of museums, drive around looking at old buildings, pick up a gift at the Colony Store, and move on. But it is also a really serene place, with abundant open space, trees, and charm—a lovely place to relax and enjoy everything at a leisurely place.

Cahokia Mounds

Collinsville, IL

There are more surprises here than you might guess, starting with the fact that Cahokia was not built by the Cahokia. The area was named by the French for the Native Americans the French met in this area in the 1600s, centuries after Cahokia had been abandoned by the Mississippian mound builders who created this once important city.

Cahokia is a State Historic Site but is also a UNESCO World Heritage Site. The first settlement in the area began in roughly A.D. 700. By 1250, the population of Cahokia was roughly the same as that of London (15–20,000), though spread over a larger area. The site has preserved more than 70 of the mounds out of roughly 120, including the impressive Monks Mound, the largest prehistoric earthen structure in North America. Monks Mound, which resembles an Aztec pyramid in form, is 100 feet high and covers more than fourteen acres. It overlooks a forty-acre central plaza. A walking trail leads around this plaza and among the many mounds, with information signs naming and explaining the features. While climbing on most mounds is not allowed, there are stairs up Monks Mound, offering the chance of an overview of the site.

After exploring the mounds, I headed for the wonderful museum, which details Cahokia's history and the lives of the people who lived there. Central to the museum is a life-size, walk-through diorama of a residential area of Cahokia, where children play and adults work amid the bark and prairie grass houses, storage structures, and tools of everyday life. The rest of the museum offers well-documented displays of pottery, weapons, statues, a

William Iseminger, retired Site Assistant Manager for Cahokia Mounds, painted this depiction of Cahokia at its height. It clearly illustrates the centrality of Monks Mound, but it also shows the stockade that surrounded the center of the city, as well as "Woodhenge" on the left. The original painting is in the Cahokia Museum. Photo courtesy of Cahokia Mounds State Historic Site.

700-year-old canoe, and vastly more. An excellent movie supplies context for what is in the displays and elaborates on the culture of Cahokia. Maps and trade items show how widely they traded. There is a considerable amount of information on food, since that was one of the keys to this civilization. While hunting, fishing, and foraging were still part of supplying food, agriculture, particularly the growing of corn, made it possible to support more people with less work. So, as was true for the Maya and Aztecs, it was agriculture that made a large city possible. Unfortunately, overhunting and the resultant lack of protein in the diet were among the problems that some think might have contributed to the decline of Cahokia.

A lack of protein was not the only problem the city faced. One display shows some of the archaeological evidence of urban stress in Cahokia. Crowded living conditions (4,000 people per square mile!), pollution, and poor sanitation had the same impact as in so many other cities, including increases in disease. So it's not just modern cities that lead to urban stress.

By roughly 1350, Cahokia had been abandoned. There are many solid theories about why everyone left, including the depletion of natural resources. But since the mid-1300s were the beginning of the Little Ice Age, I can't help but wonder if dropping temperatures had something to do with it.

After a few happy hours in the museum I headed for the final stop at Cahokia: Woodhenge. About half a mile from the museum, and on the other side of Collinsville Road, archaeologists found evidence of several large circles of posts that aligned with both Monks Mound and the sunrise. One of these circles has been reconstructed, and it offers one last opportunity to wonder about the people who settled this area so long ago.

The Grove

Glenview, IL

The Grove is one of those places where, once you've been there, you can't imagine why everyone doesn't know about it and about the remarkable Kennicott family who created it. Seriously, the Kennicott impact on the U.S. has been close to epic.

The Grove is both a National Historic Landmark and a 145-acre nature preserve that was settled in 1836 by Dr. John Kennicott. Kennicott was, in addition to being a physician, a naturalist, horticulturalist, and visionary. He was the main promoter of something originally known as the Illinois Idea, but which became known as the Land Grant Act, or Morrill Act. This enabled states to create universities. He helped start the Illinois State Fair and ran it for three years. He started a magazine called *The Prairie Farmer*. And never slowed down on seeing patients in the large area his practice covered. Despite all this, his son Robert accomplished so much, his story often eclipses that of his father. Robert was the first Illinois state naturalist. He founded the Chicago Academy of Science. The Smithsonian, where he sent his many discoveries, still reveres Robert Kennicott. When Robert went to Alaska, his writings about the plants, animals, and resources led to the purchase of Alaska. All that, and he died by the age of thirty.

On top of that, the Kennicotts protected this beautiful wooded preserve, where they made their home. The Kennicott house, which the family moved into after twenty years in a log cabin, is a definite must-see, even if you can't take in everything at The Grove. Inside the 1856 Gothic Revival building, a guide in period costume takes visitors through the many rooms, including Dr. Kennicott's office, explaining what life for the Kennicotts was like. The snake on the dining room table (dead) helps illustrate how focused on nature and education the Kennicotts were. The Kennicotts still living in the area made it possible to fill in gaps in the narrative, as well as supplying family heirlooms.

The Grove Interpretive Center is probably the best place to start, as knowledgeable staff can tell you about all there is to see at The Grove. In addition to assistance with your visit, the center offers live displays of creatures indigenous to The Grove. The winding trails through the woods invite exploration. Many come simply to enjoy the beauty of nature here. However, the trails can lead you to several other buildings. The Grove Schoolhouse is a re-creation of the original, which was designed by Dr. John Kennicott (who believed that girls should be just as educated as boys). The Kennicott Archives are worth visiting, though you will need to arrange a tour. The "reading room" is gorgeous, with vaulted ceiling, inlaid stone floors, walls hung with family portraits, and windows etched to show some of the creatures the Kennicotts studied.

This area was important to Native Americans prior to the Kennicotts' arrival, and the Glenview Park District, which owns and operates the property, has re-created a Native American Village, where they regularly hold programs for school children. Also located at The Grove is the slightly more recent Redfield Estate (1929), but this is reserved primarily for weddings and other events.

Fortunately, the Interpretive Center carries books, and I found one about John Kennicott and one about his children, to augment all that I learned at The Grove—because how could I not want to know more? Reading that two of Robert's siblings had founded Kennicott Brothers, a wholesale florist (carrying on the horticulture tradition), I looked the company up. Still in business, and still headed by a Kennicott.

Lockport, IL, and the I&M Canal

In the United States, the Erie Canal was the giant of the age of canals—but it was just the start of the nation's canal building. Of the canals constructed in the Midwest, while each was vitally important in the area it reached, the one with the biggest impact was the Illinois and Michigan, or I&M, Canal. The name of this canal, as well as the source of its importance, came from the bodies of water it connected—the Illinois River and Lake Michigan. The Illinois River runs into the Mississippi River, so by connecting Lake Michigan with the Illinois River, shipping vessels on the Great Lakes—including those that reached the Great Lakes from the Atlantic Ocean via the Erie Canal— had access to much of the heartland and could travel all the way to the Gulf of Mexico.

The ninety-six-mile-long I&M Canal did more than create dramatically improved shipping. It also created opportunities along the route of the canal. There are more than a dozen cities that exist because of the canal, and Chicago would never have grown so fast, in population and commerce, without the I&M. Both the idea and the path of the canal were actually suggested roughly 150 years earlier by Père Louis Joliet, who explored the area with Jacques Marquette in 1673. Joliet thought a canal could be created across the relatively short distance between lake and river, but it would be a while before there were enough people on the continent to realize Joliet's vision.

Eventually, there were enough workers, and enough motivation, to make the canal happen. Lockport, Illinois, was established in 1837 as headquarters for construction and administration of the I&M Canal. The canal was an instant success, with tons of agricultural products moving toward Chicago and settlers headed out into the region. Today, though the canal has long been retired, Lockport is still a destination that offers a lot of history.

The canal itself is a good place to start. There is a walking path that runs along it, with occasional silhouette statues of characters one might have seen in the 1840s. (These statues, and related information signs, are not limited to Lockport, appearing at other key sites along the canal.) Between 8th and 9th Streets, you'll come to Lincoln Landing, where a statue of Abraham Lincoln contemplates the canal. (Lincoln, who first traveled on the canal in 1848, was enthusiastic in his support of the project.) The large, limestone

The Gaylord Building was originally part of a warehouse complex for storing construction materials. The taller section now houses the I&M Museum. The park in front of the buildings is called Lincoln's Landing. Photo by Cynthia Clampitt.

building at the end of 9th Street is the Gaylord Building. The building, which is now owned by the National Trust for Historic Preservation, was constructed in 1838. However, it got its current name from the local merchant who bought it in 1878. Originally, it was a warehouse complex that offered office space and also stored construction materials for building the canal. Today, the tall part of the Gaylord Building houses the I&M Canal Museum. The lower, warehouse part of the building has been repurposed and now houses the excellent Public Landing Restaurant (wood beamed ceiling, stone walls—all wonderfully historic, so good for more than just the food).

Inside the I&M Canal Museum, an exhibit on the ground floor titled *Illinois Passage: Connecting the Continent* considers the impact of the Illinois & Michigan Canal on the development of northeastern Illinois. It includes artifacts, historic photos, and excellent signage that relate the importance to Illinois of this canal.

A block farther up 8th, on the corner of State Street, is an old white clap-board house, the one-time home of the canal superintendent, which now contains the Will County Historical Museum. This offers a more general look at life in this area, from Native Americans up through the Civil War, with medical tools, office machinery, agricultural equipment, fiber arts, wedding dresses, and photos of the armies of immigrant workers who built the canal.

Strolling along the canal in the direction of 2nd Street, you come to Heritage Village. Owned and operated by the Will County Historical Society, this site offers a collection of historic buildings from around Will County. The half-dozen historic buildings are not open (unless you've booked the site for an event), but they are still worth seeing. I was amused by the small, wooden Mokena Calaboose (Jail), built in 1881. The Symerton Train Depot (also 1881) was the most handsome building, I thought, while the Wells Corner One-Room School House (1856) was almost touching in its simplicity. The shaded setting, with the canal close at hand, made the site most attractive.

Depending on how caught up you are by the history of the I&M Canal, there are other places to see the canal besides Lockport. I have a friend who bicycled its entire 96-mile length. The one other I&M site I've visited so far is in LaSalle, about 50 miles west. This is the site of Lock 16. Here, the canal is still wide enough for boats to comfortably negotiate the waters, and canal boat rides with costumed interpreters are offered. (Stop at the Lock 16 Visitor Center up the hill from the bridge to buy tickets.)

Springfield, IL

While statues, historic markers, and more commemorate Lincoln in places all over Central Illinois (including the town of Lincoln, the only town in the U.S. named for Lincoln *before* he was president), the greatest concentration in Illinois of Lincoln memorabilia must be Springfield. However, though Lincoln is a key reason for visiting Springfield, that is not all the town offers.

Springfield and Central Illinois
African American History Museum

This small but lovingly developed museum is located a short distance from the Lincoln Monument and Tomb. I was offered, and happily accepted, a guide, which added considerably to my understanding of what was presented. The large main room of the museum is divided into sections that focus on general African American history, Illinois-specific history, and Springfield history. There were blacks in Illinois before there was a United States. More than a century before the Thirteen Colonies revolted against Britain, the French had introduced slavery into what would become Illinois. A few displays focus on this early history, offering details about the French *Code Noir*, or Black Code, French-Canadian slaveholder Pierre Menard, and the freeborn Jean Baptist Point Du Sable, the half French-half Haitian trader who settled in what would become Chicago with his Potawatomi wife in the 1770s. Other displays move up through the post-Revolution attempts by the newly created United States to prohibit slavery in the Northwest Territory, early African American schools in Illinois, and, in the 1800s, early African American pioneers—many with descendants in Springfield today. Displays along the walls show the old families that settled, built, and still reside in Springfield. My guide said that members of these old families are seen as being essentially the aristocrats of Springfield's African American community. This history was both heart-rending and heroic.

Abraham Lincoln Presidential Library and Museum

This splendid museum opened in 2005. One might wonder why it took so long to create a museum that focuses on our 16th President, but the first step into The Plaza, the grand entryway to the museum's exhibits, makes it instantly clear that it was worth the wait. Lincoln's life unfolds around us, from a life-size figure of young Lincoln in front of a log cabin through his early career, to the life-size figures of Lincoln and his family standing in front of a nearly life-size façade of the White House, through the Civil War, and finally to his death bed. Dioramas re-create the drama and issues of Lincoln's day in remarkable detail. Even events one knows well gain new power. Interactive touch screens throughout offer additional insight and details to the surrounding displays. Live theatrical presentations bring events to life and a youth activity area (Mrs. Lincoln's Attic) helps engage a wider audience. The museum's Treasures Gallery features changing exhibits of the rarest and most precious artifacts connected to Lincoln. And there are abundant technical approaches to learning, from an "Ask Mr. Lincoln" feature, where visitors can select a question and then view the filmed response, to the special-effects presentation "Ghosts of the Library." In addition, staff members in the Gateway area, near the Museum Store, will happily share information about the many other Lincoln-related sites one can visit around Central Illinois. Truly a remarkable museum and a must-see for anyone interested in Lincoln and this important period of our history.

Lincoln Home

For seventeen years, Abraham and Mary Lincoln lived in this house, which has been open to the public since 1887. The twelve-room, Greek Revival house has been restored to its appearance during the time Lincoln was running for the presidency: 1860. A National Historic Site, the house is part of the National Park Service, so when you tour, your guide will be a park ranger—and my experience has always been that park rangers are remarkably knowledgeable about any historic area they represent, so I was not surprised to have an excellent guide here. The furnishings and decorations in the Lincoln Home are handsome, though more homey in the family areas than in the areas where guests would have been welcomed. There are lovely touches (a top hat on the hat rack, a pile of books waiting to be read) to underscore that this is a place that the Lincolns lived, ate, and raised children. Overall, while there are formal touches, it seems as comfortable and honest as one would expect from Abraham Lincoln. The tour takes in nine rooms (including a child's room and the kitchen), the backyard, and the outbuildings.

Also in Springfield: The Lincoln Monument and Tomb, Dana Thomas House (designed by Frank Lloyd Wright), Old State Capitol, State Museum (geology, dinosaurs, and an overview of settlement in the state), Illinois State Capitol, Elijah Iles House (town's oldest home).

Before we leave Lincoln behind, food historian Rae Eighmey offers insight into a more personal aspect of Abraham Lincoln.

Discovering Abraham Lincoln

I find myself captivated by the everyday details of Abraham Lincoln's life. The foods he ate and helped prepare put flesh on the bones of his history.

It is said that the kitchen is the heart of the home. For me, kitchens and the cooking that goes on within them, are the key ingredients for understanding history and the people who have lived it. At Abraham Lincoln's Boyhood Home, a National Park Service site located outside of the aptly named Lincoln City, Indiana, an hour west of Louisville, Kentucky, I was moved by the bronze castings made from the original cabin sill plates unearthed during the 1930s by a crew from the Work's Progress Administration. The deep hearth, also cast in bronze, forms one end of the small plot. I could easily picture the young Abraham and his sister Sarah cooking their meals when their father Thomas traveled back to Kentucky.

Yes, Abraham Lincoln cooked. He made the meals for this step-brother, cousin, and their employer on the trip down the Mississippi. They set off in 1821 to sell farm products—apples, corn, hogs—from central Illinois to the New Orleans markets. Abe was twenty-one and seeking adventure.

But it is in the Springfield kitchen with the efficient, state-of-the-art, cast-iron stove where I can readily identify with Lincoln's life. Mary loved the Royal Oak stove so much that she wanted to take it to the White House. That is until she learned that they had people to do the cooking for them. During the years of his Springfield law practice, Lincoln ended his day by fetching the family cow from the community grazing pasture in the center of town. Then he would put on a blue apron and help his wife prepare the meals for their sons. No doubt Fido, the unkempt dog, would be underfoot.

Lincoln was a gracious host in the White House. He spooned foods from family-style serving dishes saying: "You must try some of this." Plain foods were his favorites. But, overcome by official responsibilities, he would skip meals. Mary invited guests—old friends—to stop by for a nine o'clock breakfast to force Abraham to take a break from work. At lunch he would simply eat an apple and drink a glass of milk. And in the darkest days of the Civil War, Mary asked the staff cook if she could prepare an "old fashioned chicken fricassee" to tempt her husband's appetite.

It was the Midwest that shaped Lincoln. And it is from the cultural richness of the sites dedicated to him in the Midwest that we can understand the flavors of his life.

Rae Katherine Eighmey is the author of, among other books, Abraham Lincoln in the Kitchen: A Culinary View of Lincoln's Life and Times.

Illinois Railway Museum

Union, IL

In the mid-1800s, trains changed everything. Suddenly, people could travel and goods could be moved faster than ever before. Not just in the U.S., but everywhere. The impact on the expanding Midwest in particular was tremendous, largely because the distances were so much greater. Trains made travel easier and opened areas that at one time seemed too distant. They also increased economic opportunities, from bringing luxuries inland to supplying raw materials and food to East Coast cities. As a result, many states have good train museums—but the Illinois Railway Museum is the nation's largest. Stations, signals, train cars, engines (including some that have been loaned to studios for movies), platforms, streetcars, and miles of track give the visitor access to a broad history of trains in the U.S.

From its start in 1953, when ten men each contributed $100 to buy their first train, the museum has grown to cover 100 acres. It is home to more than 450 pieces of historic railway and transit equipment, much of it in the museum's thirteen massive storage barns. The museum covers a wide spectrum of railway history, but the oldest items date to the mid-1800s, when trains first appeared in the Midwest. (And to put that date in context, a

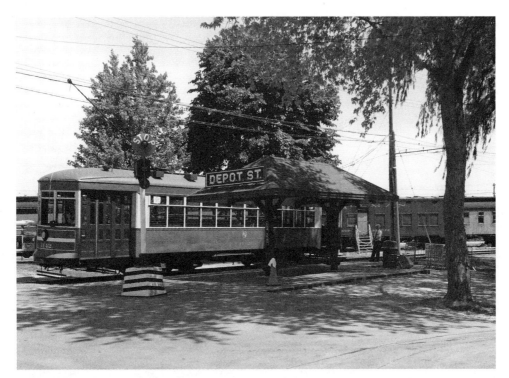

In addition to an astonishing array of train engines and train cars, the Illinois Railway Museum is also home to a considerable number of other elements of transportation history, including streetcars (some, like the one shown here, offering rides), depots, and crossing signals. Photo by Cynthia Clampitt, used with permission.

steam locomotive capable of pulling cars did not exist until the early 1800s.) In addition to vehicles, there are displays ranging from how trains work to how travelers were fed.

The main train depot on site was built in 1851 for the Galena and Chicago Union Railroad. Locomotives fill the yards, as well as the barns. There are also trams, trolleys, streetcars—plus tracks that enable the museum to offer rides. Some trains can be boarded and explored. Barn 3 holds Pullman sleeping cars, splendid private cars, dining cars, train kitchens. Barn 7 houses streetcars and trolleys, including a horse-drawn streetcar dating to 1859. Barn 8 has cars from the Chicago "L" starting from 1898. In Barn 9, the giants reside: massive transcontinental monsters.

That's just a sampling of what this museum offers. Even for those who are casually interested, this museum can fill a couple of hours. For the true train enthusiast, it will likely take much longer. And before you go, check their website for special events, because these offer even more opportunities to enjoy the historic trains.

Like many not-for-profit organizations, the Illinois Railway Museum depends on donations—but here, donations can qualify you for the "Take the Throttle" program. You can be trained as an engineer and actually get to operate one of the trains—or two trains (diesel and electric) for a slightly larger donation. Of course, they're also always glad to welcome new volunteers.

Nearby: Just over one mile away is the McHenry County Historical Museum. A log cabin dating to 1843 stands in front of the collection of buildings (which includes an 1895 schoolhouse) that make up this seasonal museum. Inside, explore elements of Northern Illinois history, including an old milk truck, an intimidating jail cell, spinning wheels, photographs, and many other artifacts that represent life in the rural Midwest. Not a destination museum, unless you live in McHenry County, but a fun additional stop if you've driven all the way to the railway museum.

Arrow Rock, MO

A peaceful, meandering drive took me through historic Blackwater, past a Lewis and Clark Trail marker (not uncommon this close to the Missouri River), and finally into Arrow Rock State Historic Site. The once busy town of Arrow Rock was established in 1829 at the intersection of the Missouri River and the Santa Fe Trail—so definitely a high-traffic spot back then. The entire village is a National Historic Landmark.

The village is something of a blend of American West and Colonial, with verandas and red brick in abundance. I loved the drainage ditches along the road—all lined with large rocks, with little bridges from street to sidewalk. Main Street is part of the Santa Fe Trail and is lined on one side with shops.

One major disappointment was finding that there had been a fire at the J. Huston Tavern. Opened in 1834, this is the oldest dining establishment in Missouri. I walked around the handsome, two-story, red-brick building and peeked through an open door at the ongoing restoration, but there was no chance of dining.

At the Friends of Arrow Rock office, on Main Street, I was asked if I'd like to take the town tour. My guide, Sue, was delightful. As she guided the little golf cart tram around town, she unleashed a torrent of wonderful details about past and present. Each place we saw was interesting, but a few were particularly noteworthy.

Dr. John Sappington, the inventor of quinine pills, made his home here. Much of the Midwest was plagued by malaria in the 1800s, and this life-saving invention was a massive success for the doctor. Sappington's home is now a museum. Nearby was the home of the great American artist George Caleb Bingham. I suspect his painting *Daniel Boone Escorting Settlers through the Cumberland Gap* is most widely recognized, as it often appears in history textbooks. I think my favorite, however, is *The Jolly Flatboatmen*. I learned from Sue that Bingham used local people as models for his paintings, and descendants who visit recognize their relatives in the paintings. The item that Sue pointed out on the John P. Sites Gun Shop is that, since not everyone could read in the 1800s, his sign was a rifle mounted high on the side of the building. (She also mentioned that Sites was a model for one of Bingham's works, a painting of a shooting contest.) Today, guns created by Sites are collector's items.

The Lyceum Theater was a surprise. Built in 1872 as a church, it has been transformed into a 413-seat performing arts center. Though the population of Arrow Rock is 55, Sue assured me that the quality of the productions here attracts people from all over the region and regularly fills all 413 seats.

The 1881 Black History Museum reflects the history of African Americans in Arrow Rock. Freed slaves worked and purchased homes here and established their own church—Brown's Chapel, which stands only about a block from the museum.

Too many other things to include details of them all, but I also saw the stone jail (Calaboose), the Courthouse, Boardwalk Storefronts, the Big Spring, and handsome homes—some of them converted into B&Bs (which Sue assured me are very nice). The walking-tour map I'd found on the Arrow Rock website made it easy to return to things I wanted to see, once I was again on my own. However, Sue had told me I should try to get to the Visitor Center, about half a mile up the road, so I headed there before everything closed. I'm glad I did, as the Arrow Rock Visitor Center offered good background information on Arrow Rock, George Caleb Bingham, and how things in the area got their names. Arrow Rock, not surprisingly, refers to the nearby bluffs that supplied flint to Native Americans for arrows and knives for millennia.

Nearby: Arrow Rock is in Saline County, so named because of the abundance of salt springs. Four miles from Arrow Rock is Boone's Lick State Historic Site. Here, Daniel Boone's sons had a successful salt processing business. Outdoor signs and exhibits relate how salt became big business in this area.

Hannibal, MO

Just the name Hannibal, Missouri, resonates for those of us who are fans of Samuel Clemens, aka Mark Twain. And a visit to Twain's boyhood home is rewarded with just as much visual delight and fun information as one might hope. The Historic Downtown of Hannibal hugs the Mississippi River and offers multiple Twain-related opportunities, starting with Hill Street, an entire block of buildings related to Twain, but also including an interpretive center, drug store, art gallery, gift shop, and more.

Hill Street

Lining this single block, you find Samuel Clemens's boyhood home, "Becky Thatcher's" house (actually the home of Laura Hawkins, but she was the inspiration for Becky Thatcher), and the office of Judge Clemens (Sam's dad was a justice of the peace). These can be seen from the lovely, brick-paved street, but for a small fee, you can go inside and see pictures and hear stories. You also gain access to the garden behind "Tom Sawyer's Fence," which offers information but also leads to the cabin of Tom Blankenship, who was the inspiration for Huckleberry Finn. Missouri was a slave state, and Samuel became friends with a slave known as Uncle Dan'l, who became Jim in the Tom Sawyer and Huck Finn tales—and helped shape Twain's antislavery views. Samuel's father, described as stern but of "splendid common sense," died when Samuel was twelve, and just around the corner, Grant's Drug Store is where he passed away from pneumonia. Samuel was taken out of school and apprenticed to a local printer, but by his teens, he

The white clapboard building in the middle of this photo was the boyhood home of Samuel Clemens, better known as Mark Twain. Photo by Cynthia Clampitt.

was ready for adventure and on his way west—though he would later return to pilot riverboats (1857–1861).

Museum

A couple of blocks from Hill Street is the Mark Twain Museum. This museum offers more insight into the transition from Clemens to Twain, and also has a lot of features that should delight younger visitors. Here, Twain's adventures and books come alive with movie clips and recordings paired with mock-ups of caves, a stagecoach, a raft by the riverbank, and more. The mezzanine level features a replica of a steamboat pilot house. Here, visitors can gaze out on the mighty Mississippi, grasp the great wooden pilot's wheel, ring the bell or pull the cord for the steamboat whistle. The top floor gallery displays fifteen Norman Rockwell paintings originally created to illustrate special editions of *Tom Sawyer* and *Huckleberry Finn*.

On the Mississippi: Keep an eye on the river when you visit Hannibal, as steamboats still stop here. You might even consider one of the steamboat day tours offered at Hannibal.

Other Twain-related places in Hannibal: Small but significant is Jim's Journey: The Huck Finn Freedom Center, an African American history museum that honors Daniel "Uncle Dan'l" Quarles. Readers today may not realize that Twain's Jim represents the first time an African American appeared in literature as fully human, rather than as a caricature. Then, a bit downstream, there are the Mark Twain Caves, where you can take a one-hour tour of the cave systems that inspired one of Tom Sawyer's adventures.

Nearby: Across the river and a short distance north of Hannibal is the city of Quincy, IL. Begun in 1825, it was once the second largest city in Illinois. Its proximity to Missouri before the Civil War made it an important part of the Underground Railroad, and it was the location of one of the Lincoln-Douglas debates. Today, there are more than 3,600 historic buildings in the city's four National Historic Register Historic Districts. So, it's definitely worth visiting if you have an extra day or two after seeing Hannibal.

Hermann, MO

On a business trip to Missouri, I was told that, since I had a free day, Hermann would be a good place to fill the time, given my interest in history. The highway followed the Missouri River, with forested bluffs rising to my left, offering a delightfully scenic drive. A golden stag and a few antique houses marked the entrance to Hermann. Not a large city, with a population around 2,500, so it was easy to get around—but there is enough history here that it could easily have filled more than the one day I had. Named for a Germanic hero who successfully fought the Romans two millennia ago, Hermann was planned by the German Settlement Society of Philadelphia to be a German town. In 1836, land was bought and the town, which is sometimes called "Little Germany," was founded. The town developed an important wine and grape culture, and before Prohibition, it was home to one of the largest wineries in the U.S.

It was too early in May for the tourist-oriented activities, such as costumed interpreters at the Hermann Farm (which opens in late May), but my compensation was that all the flowering trees were in bloom. Plus, there was already too much to see in the time I had. I drove around for a while, as Hermann sprawls a bit, but I eventually just parked the car and walked up and down the streets, enjoying the very European feel of the place.

I started at the handsome Hermann Farm and from there walked up First Street, past the Hermannhof Winery and a large, retired mill (now repurposed as a beer hall and dining venue), into the historic heart of the town. Impressive red brick buildings lined the street for a couple of blocks, and then gave way to houses and gardens. Near the imposing Inn at Hermannhof, there was a park with information signs, and I stopped to read more about the town's history. Nearby, there was a train caboose, which has been converted into a museum of railroad history and how it affected westward expansion.

After a fair bit of exploration, I took another recommendation that had been made and stopped at the Wurst House, a store and restaurant where the owner is an award-winning sausage maker. At a mere 70 years old, this is far from as historic as the rest of the town, but a few German brats in natural casing (I enjoyed the one called "Best of Show"), with sauerkraut and red cabbage seemed too perfect for the setting to not include in the day's activities.

Continuing onward, I admired everything from the German Wine Hall to the old Concert Hall, stopping to read signs that offered more history. I then returned to my car and drove around a bit more of the charming, hilly town, turning eventually toward the Historic Hermann Museum. This museum is housed in a two-story red-brick building with a white clock tower. It was constructed in 1871 as a German School and was the town's elementary school until 1955. Today, it offers a collection that relates the story of the area, as well as of the individuals who immigrated here beginning in the 1830s.

Finally, I headed across town to the historic Stone Hill Winery. Established in 1847, this is among the oldest wineries in the country and is the oldest in Missouri. The winery sits atop North America's largest series of arched, underground cellars, which makes it noteworthy, but its wines get a lot of attention, too—and awards. Of particular interest is the Norton grape, a historic grape that, in the 1800s, produced internationally acclaimed red wines. The Norton, once feared to be extinct, is the state grape of Missouri— and the fact that a state has an official wine grape tells you something about their attitude toward wine. The small patch of Norton grapes discovered at Stone Hill was planted around the time of the Civil War. There are not enough Norton vines to make wine every year, I was told, but they had one available for sampling. So, happily, I got to taste this historic wine—and it was very good. Big red, incredibly smooth. And in case you think this sounds like a good story and should be in a book, it is: *The Wild Vine: A Forgotten Grape and the Untold Story of American Wine* by Todd Kliman (2011).

Ste. Genevieve, MO

For roughly a century before the United States won its independence, most of the region we now call the Midwest went by the name of New France. The "Bienvenue" sign at the entrance to Ste. Genevieve confirmed that French culture has not vanished from the region. A history lecture I'd attended a while back had alerted me to the fact that Ste. Genevieve in Missouri was home to the largest concentration of French Creole homes in the U.S., which got my attention. This town was, in fact, the first European settlement west of the Mississippi, established in the 1740s.

Simply driving around, admiring the architecture, was a delight. But then I parked the car and headed for the Welcome Center. There, in addition to offering me maps and brochures, the attendant urged me to head next for the Centre for French Colonial Life, both because it houses a history museum and because I'd be able to get tickets to tour some of the older houses. This was great advice.

The museum at the Centre offered a wealth of details about early settlement here. The hopes and ambitions of early settlers are reflected in the town's name: Ste. Genevieve is the patron saint of Paris. The ambition was not unfounded. Here, as elsewhere in New France, there was fur trapping, always lucrative, but there was a lot more. Lead mining became important, and the production of salt, maple sugar, and wheat led to the town being known as the "breadbasket" of New Orleans and other French possessions.

The Louis Bolduc House, built circa 1788 and 1792, is one of the remarkable vertical-log houses built by French settlers in Ste. Genevieve, the oldest permanent European settlement in Missouri. Today, the house is owned by French Colonial America. The photo by S. K. Hurt Photography is courtesy of the Centre for French Colonial Life.

Slavery arrived even before the town was established, with the first enslaved Africans arriving in 1719. By the mid-1700s, forty percent of the population was of African descent.

The town had to be moved to its present location in 1785, because the Mississippi River flooded the original location. So pretty much all the older buildings in town date to around this time.[1] The museum offered information on life, work, the French military, clothing, food, Native Americans, and so much more, but the thing that surprised me most was learning that many of the oldest houses were built with vertical logs. Apparently, this vertical-log construction exists in Quebec and New Orleans, as well, but most of the vertical-log buildings are here.

I signed up for a tour, and my guide shared even more about the vertical-log homes—including the fact that she was born in one of them. She said that the reason the homes in Ste. Genevieve survived the New Madrid Fault earthquakes in the early 1800s is because the vertical logs sway. She related that there are families in town who are descendants of families who settled here more than 200 years ago. I was guided past several styles of homes, all with handsome gardens. Then we headed to the Louis Bolduc House, one of the vertical-log houses. My guide related that the house, built in 1788, was patterned after a Medieval Norman farmhouse, with a Norman truss ceiling. It was actually a remarkably handsome and spacious house. In one spot, part of the plaster had been removed, to show clearly the vertical logs, supporting cross beams, and *bousillage*, a mixture of mud and straw packed between the logs.

After the tour and a bit more time back at the museum, I headed off on my own, both driving and walking. I stopped at the Green Tree Tavern, no longer in business, but a prodigiously large vertical-log building. I located the Bauvais-Amourex House and Bequette-Ribault House, and then I just wandered the streets, enjoying the general European air of the place. Finally, as evening fell, I made my way to the Old Brick House, the oldest brick building west of the Mississippi (1785) and now home to a restaurant. This was by no means the most highly rated restaurant in town. Several venues promised gourmet fare, but I couldn't resist that "oldest." The food was simple but quite tasty and the waitress was delightful. It was the perfect end to a day filled with history.

Nearby: Twelve miles from Ste. Genevieve, on the Illinois side of the Mississippi River, was Fort de Chartres, built to protect French interests in the area. Historian Lance Geiger, who first suggested the fort to me, shares his thoughts about this destination.

Located off Illinois route 155 in rural Randolph County, Fort de Chartres State Historic Site features a partial reconstruction of an impressive stone fortification built by the French in the mid-eighteenth century.

The first fortification near the site east of the Mississippi River was built in 1720 to protect mining interests in Illinois country and named after Luis, Duc de Chartres, the son of the regent of France. The initial fortification was a log palisade with wooden bastions at opposite corners, and served as a seat of government, a center of trade, and a military outpost to help control Native American tribes of the region.

Sitting in a floodplain, the location was subject to frequent flooding from the Mississippi River, and a new wooden fort further from the river was built in 1725. A third fort, this time built of native limestone with walls 15 feet high and three feet thick, was built between 1753 and 1754.

After the 1763 Treaty of Paris, the fort was occupied by the British until its eventual abandonment in 1772. The fort fell into ruin, and the location was acquired by the state of Illinois in 1913. The state restored the only remaining structure at the fort at the time—the powder magazine—thought to be the oldest existing building in the state of Illinois, in 1917. Reconstruction of several fort buildings occurred in the 1920s and '30s, and the fort's walls were partially reconstructed on their original foundations in 1989. The current partial reconstruction represents the more substantial third fort.

The fort and grounds include walking trails, a site museum, and a playground. Visitors can walk the walls and climb up into the gatehouse of a fortification that represented one of the first European attempts to establish authority in the Illinois country and served as a seat of French governance of the area for forty-five years. The site hosts an annual Rendezvous celebrating frontier French and Indian culture that is one of the largest and oldest in the nation.

Lance Geiger, better known as The History Guy, shares stories of forgotten history on his popular and worthwhile YouTube channel, "The History Guy: History Deserves to Be Remembered."

Windmill Island

Holland, MI

Dutch settlers arrived in North America in 1624, founding New Netherland (today's New York), but like almost everyone else (except the French), they didn't have access to the Midwest until later. The Dutch arrived in what would become Holland, Michigan, in 1847. Not too surprisingly, the town that grew up became famous for tulips (and there is an annual tulip festival), but this was not the only sign of Dutch culture. Though I enjoyed a tradi-

DeZwaan, a Dutch-built windmill on Windmill Island, is reached by crossing a traditional Dutch draw bridge. Photo by Cynthia Clampitt.

tional Dutch meal in a local restaurant (DeBoer's Bakkerij), my main reason for stopping in Holland was to visit Windmill Island.

Windmill Island is the location of DeZwaan, the oldest Dutch-built working windmill in the United States. DeZwaan (the Swan) is more than 250 years old. It was originally built in the Netherlands, where it operated for two centuries, milling grain, before being dismantled and brought to Holland, Michigan.[2]

The splendid windmill is the centerpiece of a 36-acre park that is planted extravagantly with flowers. It was spring, and daffodils, hyacinths, and tulips were in bloom. I wound my way through the gardens and headed for one of the classic Dutch drawbridges that gives access to the island and its windmill.

My more than casual interest in the mill and local food history led a costumed interpreter at the windmill to introduce me to Alisa Crawford, the miller at the windmill. Alisa has the remarkable distinction of being the only Dutch-certified miller in the United States, and the only woman in the Dutch millers' guild. Alisa is also the author of the authoritative book on this windmill, an impressive, heavily illustrated volume titled *DeZwaan*. We talked about local food history, the type of heirloom corn Alisa is growing now to grind at the mill, what it took to become a Dutch miller, and more about the mill's history. It made an already pleasant visit remarkably informative.

The other buildings here are not on the island. There are only a few, but all are constructed in Dutch style. One of the buildings features a re-creation in miniature of the Island of Marken in the Zuidersee. It was from this island that most Dutch emigrants departed from the Netherlands to sail to North America. Life as it was in the early 1800s has been re-created in loving detail. One surprising thing I learned was that Peter the Great lived in the Netherlands for a while, learning the ship-building trade to take back home to Russia. Other small buildings offered snacks, books, Delft china, and Dutch cookies for sale, as well as whole wheat flour and cornmeal ground at the mill. For children, there is a playground and hand-painted Dutch carousel, and for families, a lovely picnic area.

I ended my visit with a stop by the wonderful, old Amsterdam street organ. This once popular form of entertainment is something of a cross between a pipe organ and a player piano. A costumed interpreter related that the street organ was built in 1928, was long used on the streets of Amsterdam, and was given to Holland, Michigan, after World War II, as thanks for American help during the war. We listened to it play, and I was astonished by how loud it was. But as the guide noted, it had to be heard over the crowds on a bustling city street. Delightful way to end my visit.

Nearby: The Holland Museum, with a collection of more than 90,000 artifacts, tells the story of the Dutch in the U.S., particularly in Holland, Michigan. Just a few blocks from the museum, The Cappon House, a restored Victorian confection, and the Settlers House, a working-class cottage, tell different stories of the town's earliest settlers. Plus, downtown Holland is delightful, with many buildings dating back a century or more, but now home to shops and restaurants.

Traverse City, MI, and Vicinity

Traverse City is known as a destination for people who love food, and wine trails and chocolate trails certainly help reinforce that idea. It is also a place known for its physical beauty, with miles of glorious lake vistas, forests, sand dunes, hiking trails in the summer, and skiing trails in the winter. But there is also some interesting history here. Opportunities for all these things trail outward from the city up two peninsulas, Old Mission Peninsula and the Leelanau Peninsula.

Old Mission Village

On the Old Mission Peninsula, the Old Mission Village represents the oldest permanent settlement in the area, begun in 1839. The original church and general store are not only still standing but also still in use. The Old Mission General Store is great fun, packed with artifacts from across the area's history, but also stocking everything you need for preparing a meal or throwing a party. In addition to the pasties for which this area of Michigan is known, this store almost always has a block of astonishingly strong, aged cheddar cheese. That vintage cheddar makes this one place I consider a must-visit. In addition, there is a replica of the log schoolhouse built by Peter Dougherty, who established the mission that gave the peninsula its name. This offers a small but interesting museum that details the community's history.

Fishtown

As is true of many places on the Great Lakes, fishing was an early, important source of food. On the Leelanau Peninsula, a fishing village that came to be known as Fishtown developed in the late 1800s at the point where the Leland River connects with Lake Michigan. This wonderful collection of old fishing shanties is one of the last working fishing districts on the Great Lakes—but it's still here and still working. I really love the look of this place, with its wonderfully weathered wooden buildings hugging and even overhanging the water. Many of the old shanties that line the docks now house intriguing shops and galleries, but Carlson's Fishery keeps the old traditions alive. This fifth-generation operation, which has been located at Fishtown since 1904, is still processing fish, and it is a must-visit place for me for their smoked whitefish pâté, though I've heard that their whitefish sausage and fish jerky are also outstanding. But even if you don't like whitefish, stop to admire the charming village.

Two blocks from Fishtown is the **Leelanau Historical Society Museum**. From Native American crafts to the history of area lighthouses, shipwrecks to history of mapping the peninsula, though exhibits change, there is always something of interest here.

Within Traverse City, just a few blocks from downtown, is the **Grand Traverse Commons**, a great, sprawling, castle-like hospital built in 1884 that has been repurposed as a dining and shopping complex surrounded by hiking trails. You can visit for the myriad shops and restaurants or tour for the history.

This is just a few of the options offered by this delightful corner of Michigan. There are many more places I love here that aren't very historic, and many historic places that I haven't gotten to yet. But it's always good to have a reason to return.

Nearby: The Old Mission Peninsula also offers the Dougherty Mission House, also now a museum about the area and its history, and Old Mission Inn, constructed in 1869 and Michigan's oldest continually operational historic hotel. At the tip of the Old Mission Peninsula, you can find the Mission Point Lighthouse, which is discussed further in Chapter 5.

Amana Colonies

Iowa

The Amana Colonies are a destination you could get a feel for in half a day, but to really appreciate, you should probably allow yourself 1-1/2 days, and depending on your interest level, could take more. Because this isn't one museum or even one town—it's a cluster of seven colonies, where shared culture and history create a whole that is greater than the parts. That said, if time is short, just drive around the "loop" of U.S. 6/151 and 220 Trail, which takes you through all the colonies and some beautiful scenery, and then stop in Amana for a meal and perhaps to visit the Amana Heritage Society to

The charming, vintage buildings in downtown Amana invite exploring—and dining and drinking. Ronneburg Restaurant is on the left, but if you look at the front yard of the next building to the right, you can see a large wine barrel. There is a lot of good food in Amana, but there are also several wineries, offering more than sixty wines. Photo by Cynthia Clampitt.

see the excellent film about Amana history. Maybe you can also fit in a stop at Amana Meat and Smokehouse, but only if you've got a cooler in the trunk, because Amana prides itself in glorious meat products.

If you do decide to slow down and enjoy the *Gemütlichkeit* for a couple of days, there are a number of wonderfully historic hotels in the area. I chose Zuber's Homestead Hotel, built in 1862. (For more on Zuber's, see Ch. 6.) Homestead is the one colony that doesn't have Amana in its name. The others are West Amana, High Amana, Middle Amana, East Amana, South Amana, and Amana. Most of the colonies were established in 1855, when the Amanas moved to Iowa from New York, where they had outgrown the available land.

One thing you should know is that this is not an Amish community. (There are Amish in Iowa, and not very far away. But Amana isn't Amish.) The Amana started as a communal religious society, driven out of Europe by persecution. But they had the idea that you could embrace technology and still retain faithfulness, which led to the Amana name being associated with so many high-end electronic products, including everything from microwave ovens to washing machines.

If you can give this at least one day, I recommend taking a tour, simply because there are a lot of interesting details to Amana history and culture that you can't just pick up by looking around. The tour includes the previously mentioned movie at the Amana Heritage Society (though I recommend going back after the tour to see more of the museum). It then goes to the only remaining communal kitchen and dining area, where forty people were fed five times a day. (Five meals a day being common in farming communities everywhere before modern equipment made work less grueling.) At the kitchen, my guide pointed out the ice box (what people had before refrigerators, actually chilled with ice), and said that milk was stored in the basement, just under the ice box, because the cold water from the melting ice would flow down through a hole in the floor and keep the milk cool. Clever. Next stop is the High Amana General Store (note that the High Amana Store is historic while the Amana General Store is more oriented toward gifts and local delicacies). My guide told me High Amana was also the location of the Hahn Bakery, where an original stone oven still turns out great bread, but it was closed on the day I was there. Final stop on the tour is the old Homestead Church, where the beliefs of the Amana are explained.

The colonies are home to five wineries, all of them good, my guide assured me. You can also visit (and buy things at) a woolen mill, a broom maker, more than one furniture store (you can even pick out your wood and have something custom made), gift shops, and the impressive Amana Meat Shop and Smokehouse. I had a few meals in Amana, but my top restaurant recommendation is Ronneburg, named for the town and its castle in Hesse, where the Amana initially gathered for safety, before moving to the U.S. Definitely order the pickled ham appetizer—an Amana specialty that underscores a tradition of frugality (recipe follows). Most of the rest of the menu will look familiar to those who love German food, from *jagerschnitzel* to *rouladen*.

One additional thing worth noting is that the Germans in the Amana colonies came primarily from Hesse and Alsace (which was German at the time, though French now), so the Octoberfest they put on each year (massively successful as it is) is not really part of their culture, as lederhosen and dirndls are Bavarian, not Alsatian or Hessian.

Worth knowing if you do visit is that there is an Amana Colonies app that you can download. It offers maps, restaurant reviews, recommendations of things to see and do—and reaffirms that Amanas are still embracing technology.

Population of the colonies at their height in the 1890s was around 2,000. Today, the population is around 1,400, so the colonies are still small, warm communities. Because agriculture is so key to their success, farms cover a substantial part of the lovely valley in which the colonies are situated. This area is definitely worth visiting if for nothing other than the physical beauty of the old brick, wood, and sandstone homes and carefully tended farms nestled amid gardens and forests. But do try to enjoy a bit of the history and culture, as well.

Pickled Ham

I had heard about pickled ham before I saw it on a menu. It is an iconic Amana appetizer that offers a way to avoid waste while delighting the taste buds. In the Amana colonies, not only is it prepared at home, it also appears on restaurant menus and can be purchased in jars at the Amana Meat Shop. It is one of the most common appetizers in the colonies.

I first had pickled ham at the Ronneburg Restaurant in Amana. I had been told that pickled beets should also be ordered, so I got both. For those who might try both, I'd advise you to taste the pickled ham first, as the pickled beets are considerably stronger in flavor. But having had this now a couple of times, you can count me a fan of pickled ham.

Fortunately, the kind people at Ronneburg Restaurant gave me their recipe for pickled ham, along with permission to share it with you.

1 lb. precooked ham, trimmed of fat and cut into ½-inch cubes
1 small onion, sliced
1–1/2 cups water
1 cup white vinegar
1/8 tsp salt

Combine all ingredients and refrigerate at least 24 hours before serving. This will keep for several days in the fridge. Serves 4.

Monroe, WI

Green County, where Monroe is located, was settled primarily by Swiss immigrants. This is probably most evident in the delightful village of New Glarus, which has an abundance of Swiss architecture, celebrations, and even a Swiss Historical Village and Museum. But Monroe is the Swiss Cheese Capital of the USA and home to, among other things, the National Historic Cheesemaking Museum. So, for this food historian, that was a must-see.

National Historic Cheesemaking Museum

The museum is housed in a vintage train depot, which seemed fitting because, for many decades, trains were the primary way of moving cheese to market. My delightful guide, Donna, even exclaimed at one point, as we passed large carts and a scale, about the tons of cheese that were shipped from Monroe by train. In front of the museum, two large, copper cauldrons flank the museum's sign. These copper cheese kettles were used for cheesemaking up until the mid-1900s. (One kettle has a sign saying it was used until 1959.)

Inside, the museum offers a wonderful look at cheesemaking past and present. Donna pointed out an old phone booth and explained that this was once a direct line to the National Cheese Exchange, which used to be in Green Bay, Wisconsin. (It was moved to the Chicago Mercantile Exchange in 1997.) Calls would come in every week, setting the price of cheese, to help keep cheesemakers competitive.

The National Historic Cheesemaking Museum is easy to spot. The cow needs no explanation, though it's possible that some have not seen a full wheel of cheese or the old-fashioned milk can. Photo by Cynthia Clampitt.

A short video on cheesemaking, how it was done and how it has changed, gave context to much of the rest of the museum. In the 1900s, milk went straight from the cow to the cheesemaker, still warm when it arrived. Today, milk is cooled even as it is leaving the cow, which is safer, but it then needs to be warmed up before rennet is added. (Rennet is the substance that causes curds to form in the milk.) Fascinating to see all the steps that go into creating what seems like a fairly simple product.

As we continued through the museum, Donna pointed out and explained equipment old and new. It was interesting to compare what I knew from small-scale hobby cheesemaking with the larger scale traditions of the cheesemakers represented here. Life-size mannequins stand by a large copper kettle, ready to stir the warming milk. A pulley system lifts a loaded cheesecloth of what would be curds, if they were really making cheese, separating them from the whey. A cheese press nearby waits for the newly formed cheese, which must be weighted to get rid of extra moisture. A door opens to reveal a painting that appears to be a cellar with dozens of wheels of cheese on aging racks. There are photographs of notable cheesemakers from years past (including, of course, J. L. Kraft) and a display about master cheesemakers. Donna related that only Wisconsin has a Masters of Cheesemaking program. Cool. I appreciated the many kid-focused elements, too, such as a diorama of a farm. Donna said they get a lot of school groups through.

Leaving the main museum building, we walked next door to a century-old "factory," an old hut that was long used to produce cheese. All the equipment is traditional: huge kettle for heating the milk, brick oven for heating the kettle, rakes for breaking up forming curds, the cheese press. In fact, this place is so perfectly outfitted for cheesemaking that, once a year (usually the second Saturday in June), retired cheesemakers come here to make cheese the old-fashioned way.

Before I left, knowing I wanted to see the local Turner Hall as well, Donna contacted the Turner Hall historian, Sherry Anderegg, and Sherry offered to meet me at Turner Hall.

Turner Hall

Turner Halls (Turners being members of *Turnverein*, German gymnastic clubs) are not as common as they once were in the Midwest, but some still exist. Most were, in fact, German, but in Wisconsin, many of them were actually Swiss. Sherry said it is thought that Monroe's is the last Swiss Turner Hall in the United States. It is a beautiful Swiss-chalet style building, with white walls and dark-brown woodwork. The original building, constructed in 1868, burned, and this is a reconstruction, but it is a beautiful reflection of Swiss culture. I had just planned on stopping at the Ratskeller for dinner but having Sherry as a guide gave me the opportunity to see much more—because Turner Halls, even at their height, were never just for gymnastics. (As the sign out front states, it is a Swiss Heritage & Community Center.) There is still a gymnasium here, and Sherry told me one of the local women (Marie Blumer Hoesly) who trained here went to the Olympics in 1952. I was guided through the Grand Hall, where weddings and other important events are celebrated. I got to see the gorgeous old "smoking room," originally for men only, with its Alpine horn mounted on the wall. Sherry told me about the bowling alley, the celebration of Swiss Independence on August 1, the Christkindlmarkt in winter, and historic visitors, including Susan B. Anthony, Belle Boyd, Clara Barton, Jack Dempsey, and JFK. Sherry had brought an album of photos and showed some of the events (lots of Swiss entertainment, Swiss wrestling, and even a baking school), as well as some of the performers who have appeared here, from Lawrence Welk to the Mormon Tabernacle Choir. Quite a history. Sherry said, as she closed the album, "We love this place. This is the center of everything. We even vote here." Before parting company, Sherry recommended the Kalberwurst sandwich at the Ratskeller, a veal sausage covered with melted Swiss cheese and fried onions. I wanted to try the cheese pie, because this is the Swiss cheese capital, after all. The cheese pie was lovely (recipe follows), but I definitely look forward to returning and trying Sherry's recommendation sometime.

Nearby: The lovely town square in Monroe offers a few things worth seeing. At the center of the square is the Historic Green County Courthouse, an imposing, Romanesque-style building constructed in 1891. Self-guided tours are available and offer a chance to learn about the county and clock tower, and even to put on a judge's robe and sit at the bench. Facing the courthouse is Baumgartner's Cheese Store and Tavern. While not yet a century old (it opened in 1931), it is Wisconsin's oldest cheese store. There is lots of wood and a feel of the past—plus a lot of good Wisconsin cheese (I went for the smoked gouda). About seven miles north of Monroe is the Chalet Cheese Cooperative, founded in 1885 and the only place in the U.S. that still makes Limburger cheese. And, of course, there's New Glarus, which is about seventeen miles north of Monroe.

Turner Hall Käsekuchen/Käsechüechli

The reason I've given two names for this recipe is that there is a difference between German from Germany and German from Switzerland. *Käsekuchen* is German for "cheese pie" and *Käsechüechli* is Swiss German for "cheesecake." Käsekuchen was used on the recipe that was sent to me, but Käsechüechli is what you'll see on the menu at the Ratskeller.

This is very much like a quiche, but a bit creamier. It is surprisingly tasty for its simplicity, and, now that I've made it in my own kitchen, I'd say it's pretty close to foolproof. At the Ratskeller, they serve it with fresh fruit, but I've also served it with a nice salad. Also, because in Switzerland, there are a number of cheeses that qualify as being "Swiss cheese" (Emmentaler, Gruyère, Appenzeller, and more), recipes from Switzerland may use a blend of cheeses. However, of these, Emmentaler is the most like American Swiss cheese—and so Swiss cheese truly is a reflection of Swiss heritage here in Monroe. And Wisconsin makes such good Swiss cheese. Note: though I received this recipe from the Turner Hall historian, the executive director of the Cheesemaking Museum asked that I credit *Old World Swiss Family Recipes*, compiled by the Monroe Swiss Singers of Monroe, Wisconsin. So there's more history behind this than just the restaurant!

2 9-inch unbaked pie shells
3 cups grated Swiss cheese (not too sharp)
6 eggs
2 cups cream
1/4 cup grated onion
1 tsp. salt

Preheat the oven to 400 degrees. Beat eggs with cream, salt, and onion. Fold in the cheese and pour into the pie shells. Bake at 400 degrees for 10 minutes, then at 350 degrees for 35 minutes. Serve hot, garnished with fresh fruit.

Bayfield, WI, and Vicinity

Bayfield is a really splendid location. Surrounded by high, forested hills, the charming town perches on the shores of Lake Superior overlooking the Apostle Islands. It seems almost too perfect to be a place for serious history study, and yet the layers of history are remarkable. The Ojibwe were here when the first French explorers arrived. Then came French trappers and traders, next the British, and finally the Americans, initially for industry and then for fruit growing, fishing, and holidays.

There are a number of ways to explore the past, but the Bayfield Historical Society Museum and Bayfield Maritime Museum are good places to start, and they complement each other nicely.

At the **Maritime Museum**, I learned about the evolution of boat building, lighthouses, local shipwrecks, and fishing. Cartography in the area began with the French in 1670. British explorer Lt. Henry Wolsey Bayfield explored the area in 1823–25 (and yes, that's where the town got its name.) In the 1870s, Basswood Island was home to quarries for brownstone, a popular building material that was shipped to Milwaukee and Chicago. Another important commodity was ice. Ice harvesting was hugely important through the 1800s and even into the 1900s (when collecting ice in the winter and saving it for summer was the only form of refrigeration), but ice also gave mainlanders easier access to the islands during the winter. (Easier, but not always perfectly safe. If you visit, look for the image of the house falling through the ice.) The guide at the museum was a volunteer who grew up here but moved away—only to return for one week each summer to work in the museum. (The beauty of Bayfield makes it easy to appreciate why someone would do this.)

The **Historical Society Museum** is not large, but it offers interesting insights into life in the area. The various people who lived here over the centuries are recounted, along with an explanation of why this is a fruit "capital," especially for berries and apples. Most of the displays on the ground floor were contributed by people whose families settled here, including the contents of a few rooms and an entire barber shop. There are displays of maple-sugar making and diaries of people who lived on one of

The ferry to Madeline Island offers a wonderful view of beautiful, historic Bayfield, Wisconsin. Photo by Cynthia Clampitt.

the Apostle Islands. From more recent history, photos and stories from the devastating flood of 1942 are horrifying and moving.

In the basement—and worth seeing—is a large train set that offers a wonderful re-creation of Bayfield and the surrounding islands, reflecting the time when this was a more active commercial center, including brownstone quarries, lumber, fisheries, and more. The fisheries were a big draw for Norwegians who moved here looking for work. Given the nature of the Great Lakes, fishing was incredibly dangerous and took both skill and bravery. (And speaking of fisheries, while not historic, it's worth noting that there are a number of excellent fish restaurants in town.)

My second day in Bayfield, I was down at the ferry dock early for the 21-minute ferry ride across to Madeline Island. This is the only island here that is not part of the Apostle Islands National Lakeshore. One interesting aspect of the island is that it is the only off-reservation place in Wisconsin where the signs are bilingual, English and Ojibwe. Madeline Island is, I learned, the main Ojibwe "homeland." They dispersed outward from here.

While I enjoyed wandering around the town of La Pointe, where the ferry lands, my main objective was the **Madeline Island Museum**. The island is named for an Ojibwe princess, and the museum has a considerable amount of Native American history—though it covers the early history of European arrivals, as well. The museum is part new construction and part collection of wonderfully weathered old buildings.

Throughout the buildings, Native American and European history are interwoven. A short film offers an introduction to island history and observes that, though Chippewa and Ojibwe are the same people, the names are not interchangeable—some groups identify as Ojibwe and others as Chippewa. These groups are quite active in this region, and the docent told me there are powwows most weekends during the summer, because every Native American community has one.

The large room set aside for temporary exhibits did a lovely job of explaining the importance of birch bark to the Ojibwe, past and present. The French appear to have arrived in 1618 and built their first fort in 1693. Interestingly, rum and tobacco, while popular gifts, were never trade items. Trade items had to be practical—axes, knives, iron pots, glass, and so on. By 1816, John Jacob Aster's fur company was active up here.

Wonderful displays show how mobile Native American groups were early on. There is a dugout canoe, probably Huron, that predates the Ojibwe (who built birch bark canoes). There is pottery dug up here that was from Woodland and Mississippian people who greatly predated the Ojibwe. An Ojibwe guide in the museum explained to me that some pottery was Huron but made with Madeline Island blue clay.

A lot of the displays are inside the old buildings, which look as interesting inside as they did from the outside, and which further reflect what life was like in the past. Also reflecting that past are snowshoes and musical instruments, trade goods and a whiskey still—and so much more.

The French may have been the first Europeans, but they were followed by Russians, Danes, Scandinavians, and Brits. A Frenchman named Michel

Cadott married the daughter of a local chief—and it is for her that the island is named.

There is much more, inside and out, from early Native Americans up to the U. S. Coast Guard. There are some fun things for children, too, including touchable displays, Native American paper dolls, and other projects in the "kids' corner." Remarkable destination, with so much to learn.

I hiked around La Pointe, which has a few more interesting buildings, but which focuses mostly on tourists and artists (lots of galleries, restaurants that range from funky to posh, nice resorts, and a substantial marina). The real highlight for me was the museum, but it definitely looks like a nice place for a vacation. Then, after a delightful day, I caught the last ferry back to Bayfield.

Nearby: Apostle Islands National Lakeshore includes a section of shoreline in Bayfield but focuses more on the 21 rugged, water-carved islands scattered outward into the waters of Lake Superior. This is the northernmost point of Wisconsin. The historic elements include lighthouses and the Lucerne shipwreck, but the big draw tends to be natural beauty and abundant wildlife.

WisconsinShipwrecks.org

My fascination with the underwater world dates back to my youth. I loved Jacques Cousteau, but it was a book I got in high school about the sunken Swedish warship *Vasa* that triggered an interest in marine archaeology. From the *Mary Rose* in Portsmouth, England, to the Flagstaff Hill Museum on Australia's "Shipwreck Coast," I have always enjoyed discovering the history that often lies beneath the waves. And then I heard my first (of several) lectures by divers from Wisconsin Shipwrecks. I knew that the Great Lakes were dangerous and that thousands of ships had sunk over the years (conservative estimate is 6,000, but some say the number is much higher), but I hadn't realized that diving on those wrecks was an active pastime for many. I'm not a diver, but having seen so many photos and videos at these presentations over the years, I didn't feel I could leave out this important part of

Midwestern history. So I asked marine archaeologist Caitlin Zant to share some of her insights about exploring this alternative destination.

Before I turn it over to Caitlin, however, you should know that, if you wish to pursue this option, Wisconsin Shipwrecks is not a place; it's a website comanaged by the Wisconsin Historical Society and the University of Wisconsin Sea Grant Institute. Maritime museums across the state can help guide you to diving opportunities. But the Wisconsin Shipwrecks website offers information about all that you can find, both along the shore and under the waves.

The Great Lakes contain one of the most well-preserved collections of historic shipwrecks in the world. More than 750 historic shipwrecks lie in Wisconsin waters alone, representing a remarkable range of vessel types, genres, and histories. Centuries of exploration, commerce, and settlement have created a series of maritime cultural landscapes along shorelines and bottomlands.

Studying the shipwrecks of the Great Lakes allows for a better understanding of the development and growth of Wisconsin. It offers a new lens through which to understand the important role Wisconsin, and the Great Lakes region, played in the development of the country as a whole. Even Wisconsin's state seal, seen on the state flag, contains three references to the importance of maritime trade to the state: a sailor, an anchor, and a caulking mallet used in shipbuilding.

We certainly promote visiting these wrecks, but we have a strong educational message. Wisconsin's Maritime Trails Educational Initiative helps place these resources into the broader context of Wisconsin's rich maritime history. The "trail" this initiative forms links historic shipwrecks, lighthouses, historic waterfronts, historic vessels, museums, and shore-side historical markers and attractions. At the WisconsinShipwrecks.org website, as well as through public presentations, we encourage divers, snorkelers, boaters, and paddlers, to responsibly visit Wisconsin's maritime cultural resources.

160

Chapter 4

The Wisconsin Shipwrecks website makes underwater archaeological research available to the public and fosters the preservation of submerged archaeological sites. The heart of the site features detailed information on significant shipwrecks in the Wisconsin waters of Lakes Michigan and Superior. Each shipwreck profile includes information about the ship's archaeology, history, final voyage, sinking, and current condition. With several searchable databases, visitors are able to view shipwreck site plans, as well as historic and underwater photos.

But the website isn't all we do. To date, 43 shoreside historical markers have been produced featuring shipwrecks and other important remnants of Wisconsin's maritime past. These shoreside markers are colorful signs that inform visitors about historic waterfronts, allow non-divers to "visit" shipwreck sites, and interpret historic vessels. The markers contain historic information, historic and underwater images, archaeological site plans, and information about the Maritime Trails program.

Additionally, five interactive kiosks promoting shipwreck preservation are located at the following maritime museums: the Wisconsin Maritime Museum, Manitowoc; the Wisconsin Historical Museum, Madison; the Wisconsin Historical Society's Madeline Island Museum in LaPointe; and both branches of the Door County Maritime Museum, at Sturgeon Bay and Gills Rock.

We strive to spark interest in maritime history by bringing glimpses of these unique resources to the public's attention. Our underwater archaeological investigations and historic research, coupled with underwater images and video, help attract those interested in history, whether they dive or not. In fact, many things are located near shore and in shallow water, allowing paddlers and boaters to see resources in their natural setting.

Probably not too surprisingly, state and federal law specifically prohibits the removal of artifacts. Because title to Wisconsin's historic shipwrecks is held in public trust by the State of Wisconsin for the benefit of all citizens, the Society's Maritime Preservation and Archaeology Program's public outreach initiative is a statewide endeavor. Educating visitors, whether divers or paddlers, about the historic and archaeological value of these shipwrecks remains the key to reducing negative impacts and fostering long-term preservation. As we like to say, "Take only pictures, leave only bubbles."

Caitlin Zant is a Maritime Archaeologist at the State Historic Preservation Office at the Wisconsin Historical Society.

Historic Fort Snelling

St. Paul, MN

Though it is only minutes from the heart of the Twin Cities, Fort Snelling almost seems to still be in the wilderness. It sits on a bluff overlooking the junction of the Mississippi and Minnesota Rivers, surrounded by forests. The parking lot is far enough from the fort to maintain that sense of isolation—and it suits the place.

This is a destination that deserves time, not just because there are several buildings to explore, but also because of both the history and people associated with the place. Half a century before Minnesota would become a state, explorer Lieutenant Zebulon Pike was ordered to find a place along the Mississippi River to build a fort. In 1805, Pike chose this site and negotiated with the local Dakota for the land needed for the fort and a trading post. In 1820, an Indian Agency was established near the site, with instructions to manage the fur trade and build positive relations with the Native Americans. When it was built, St. Louis, MO, was the nearest city—so it really was remote. The fort was an active military base for roughly 120 years, from the 1820s until 1946, but with a short blip of inactivity between Minnesota gaining statehood (1858) and the beginning of the Civil War.

Work on the stone fort began in 1820, under the command of Lieutenant Colonel Henry Leavenworth (for whom Fort Leavenworth in Kansas would

Surrounded by forests and bordered by two rivers, Historic Fort Snelling looks almost as remote as it did when it was built 200 years ago. The Round Tower in the forefront of the image is the oldest building in Minnesota. Photo courtesy of Minnesota Historical Society.

later be named). The Round Tower, which is the first thing one sees on approaching the fort, is where they started, and it is the oldest building in Minnesota. The fort's first commander, Colonel Joseph Snelling, arrived in 1820, and four years later, General Winfield Scott, after touring the fort, recommended it be named for Snelling. Future U.S. President Zachary Taylor commanded the fort for a short time. On the grimmer side of history, the time Dred Scott spent here eventually became a major element of his claim that he should be free. As is true of most history, this story is much more complicated than what we learned in school. Scott arrived here in 1836 (and met and married his wife here), but the tragic decision about his fate that was handed down by the Supreme Court wouldn't occur until 1857.

And those are just the best-known names associated with the fort. There are layers and layers of history here. Perhaps not surprisingly, there were lots of "first in Minnesota" elements (first library, first hospital), and the commandant's house is the oldest residence in the state. Every building is packed with artifacts and information about what happened at the fort and how it connected with what happened beyond the fort. The hospital displays medical equipment and details of the worst health problems: scurvy, malaria, dysentery, cholera, and tuberculosis. When smallpox threatened the local Native American population in 1832, Dakota chiefs, Indian Agent Lawrence Taliaferro, and surgeon Robert Wood acted quickly, vaccinating 333 Dakota, and thus preventing a major epidemic. I found it interesting that surgeons were also expected to record weather conditions and report the information quarterly. This was part of an effort to determine how much climate affected disease. At Fort Snelling, it appeared that the coldest weather, while brutal, reduced the amount of illness.

Whatever happened at the fort, there is a building or room to highlight it, from the operating room in the hospital to the bakeshop, storage rooms to the blacksmith, single men's quarters to the carpentry shop. The commandant's house was remarkably lovely. Everywhere, there are displays of archaeological finds, from buttons to pottery to animal bones.

The fort offers both self-guided tours and docent-led tours (general or specific theme). Information signs are excellent, but for younger visitors, there are also activity stations and demonstrations.

Nobles County Pioneer Village

Worthington, MN

In more densely populated areas, a county museum might take up a building. In areas that have a little more space, they can spread out a bit. Nobles County is among those that have taken advantage of the extra room to preserve local buildings that they've salvaged, and it has done an excellent job of creating a fairly extensive village with those buildings. It also has the advantage of being so close to the Interstate that you don't have to search for it.

This is a remarkably handsome restored village. I was greeted in the welcome center by Diane Murray, from the Nobles County Historical Society, who was enthusiastic about all that the village had to offer, and who offered some interesting details about the place. For example, the preservation of the 1870s parsonage was funded by the Nystrom family, as it was at one time the home of earlier Nystroms and was moved to the village from the Nystrom farm. (I would learn as I moved through the village that there were many stories like this.) Diane also mentioned that the large barn can be rented for parties and other events, and people still get married in the churches here (there are two).

I spent close to three hours exploring the nearly 50 buildings and objects (merry-go-round, windmill, train cars) here. Every building has wonderful displays that reflect their purpose (land office, barbershop, library, general store, hospital, blacksmith, school, firehouse, and more) or the lives of those who lived there (including a tiny prairie house, once home to a family of five, a handsome farmhouse, and even a sod house). Signs throughout relate dates, the names of owners, and the lives of residents. One thing I'd never seen before was a sand tower. Sand was stored in the tower and then loaded onto a train engine, to be released as needed through tubes in front of the drive wheels, to create traction when the train wheels slipped. I was also interested to see a series of panels offering details about the different ethnic groups that settled the region, along with contributions they made.

This was not the "big" history of wars and discoveries, but rather the more intimate history of lives lived near the edge of the frontier as the state began to develop. It is a history beautifully and lovingly restored because it is still connected to the present. While the village is open Memorial Day to Labor Day, one can gain entrance other times if one has a group of five or more.

Homestead National Monument

Beatrice, NE

Abraham Lincoln was not the first to dream of a nation of small farmers. Thomas Jefferson had envisioned that, as well—and set the stage by establishing the ideal small farm as being 160 acres. But it was Lincoln who signed into law the act that would cause that dream to explode.

The Homestead Act, signed into law in 1863, offered free land—that 160 acres—to anyone who would settle, build a home, and farm. All you had to be was 21 and the head of a household—and that applied equally to women

The Heritage Center at the Homestead National Monument is, appropriately, set amid the sweeping grasses and flowers of the Great Plains. Photo by Cynthia Clampitt.

and African Americans—an unparalleled opportunity for many. The idea was that this would reduce poverty by drawing excess workers away from overcrowded cities—but so much of the world was poor that people began flooding in from overseas, as well.

Philosophers of the day were calling the Midwest a new Eden and talking as if it were paradise. Scientists promoted the idea of "rain follows the plow"—that is, farming would, by adding moisture to the soil, make it rain even in very dry areas. The fact that this was not true would not be the only issue faced by people out west. It didn't help that the Civil War was raging at the same time as this act was signed—but, again, it was only one issue among many. Droughts and plagues of locusts destroyed farms, record snow and cold killed settlers and livestock, and many who came simply had no experience farming. However, hope drove them on. It has been said that individualism was born on the plains, through hardship and tenacity. Only about 37 percent of those who attempted homesteading actually succeeded, but those who did succeed had a huge impact. Today, roughly 93 million people worldwide are descended from those homesteaders.

The Homestead National Monument, operated by the National Park Service, is a splendid place to learn about homesteading, from its beginning through to the last homesteader (a Vietnam vet in 1974—and then the act was repealed). The monument actually has a few parts—but if you can only see one, make it the Heritage Center. Here, a 23-minute movie introduces the issues faced by Native Americans and homesteaders and explains the long-term impact. The center does not focus solely on the Midwest, because homesteading occurred just about everywhere, from Florida to Alaska, but the largest influx was here.

The Heritage Center combines great artifacts with effective presentation to demonstrate life at the time—including striking images of earliest houses (made from logs, tar paper, even sod) and the few implements available for farming. There are clever displays geared for younger visitors that compare life in the 1800s to life today for diet, play, and schooling. Overall, the impression one has is that it was a stunning amount of work, all too often heartbreaking, but a real start on a new life for those who could stick it out.

Out the back door, a short distance away, the tiny Palmer-Ephard cabin demonstrates just how basic living conditions could be—but the walk also rewards visitors with views across an unbroken stretch of prairie.

About a mile away from the Heritage Center is the Education Center. Here, in addition to changing art exhibits, there is a long room that houses a collection of implements that would have been common on the prairie, along with information signs and videos that explain and show how they were used. Here, I learned that 10 percent of the total area of the U.S. was transferred to private ownership by the Homestead Act. Remarkable. I also saw how sod was cut for building sod houses. Clever device. I then followed the hiking path across a small suspension bridge to a glorious native plants prairie. The goal here is to re-create what the first settlers would have seen when they arrived. There are detailed signs identifying the many plants and relating their importance.

Last stop for the Homestead Monument was just another quarter mile down the road—the Freeman one-room schoolhouse—because many did succeed, and their children needed to go to school.

Nearby: Also in Beatrice (pronounced BeATrice), near the railway tracks, is the **Gage County Historical Society and Museum,** inside the old Burlington Passenger Terminal. This is a thoughtfully laid-out museum that covers the history of the county in detail (including the genesis of what would become Beatrice Foods, when it moved to Chicago). There is a considerable amount of information on the county's most famous resident, actor Robert Taylor, as well as some about silent film great Harold Lloyd, also from Gage County. However, the collection, while wonderfully detailed, is in many ways similar to other county museums (local businesses, medical equipment, war heroes)—perfect if you live in the area and want to learn more and also perfect if you've never visited a county-level museum, because it reminds us that interesting things happened everywhere. For example, the stories of two people stood out for me: Nan Aspinwall, aka "two-gun Nan," was a sharp shooter who could also do trick roping and bronco busting and became a star in Buffalo Bill's Wild West show; and Elizabeth Wiebe, who was the first anesthesiologist at Beatrice's Mennonite Hospital.

Pioneer Village

Minden, NE

In south-central Nebraska, amid miles of handsome farmland, there is a remarkable collection that represents the vision and life work of Harold Warp. A sign at Pioneer Village states that this is the nation's largest private collection of Americana, and what I saw made that claim easy to believe. The complex, which includes both a sprawling museum and charming "village," is home to more than 50,000 artifacts that cover the full spectrum of the region's settlement and development, all carefully grouped by function and era. The entire venue is well sign-posted, so it is easy to learn about everything displayed—and there was a lot to learn.

Starting in the museum, I explored a century of technology from fields as disparate as art, transportation, farming, and food preparation. I wound among wagons and coaches, many of the more than 350 antique cars, more than a dozen airplanes, and a hundred antique tractors, plus toys, sculpture, and machines for every possible task. Among the many fascinating things I learned was the extent of operations for moving freight. Before Henry and

Clem Studebaker made cars, they made huge Freight Wagons, and these wagons moved a tremendous amount of goods (from trade goods to private households) along the Oregon Trail. The operation of one freight company alone—Bussell, Major, and Waddell—required 6,000 wagons and 75,000 oxen to move freight over the trail. I thought that was pretty stunning.

Leaving the indoor museum, I strolled into the "village" itself—twelve historic buildings around a broad, tree-shaded lawn. Each building—barns, houses, church, store, schoolhouse, Pony Express station, print shop, doctor's office—is home to its own collection. The toy store is filled with antique toys. The barns are crammed with tools and inventions that were once vital on farms. The shelves and counters of the general store are crowded with once exciting goods. The schoolhouse has all its original furnishings. The collections are fascinating, but the buildings themselves are wonderful, as well. They are all original buildings that have been rescued, moved here, and restored.

One surprise was the "soddie"—a house built of what came to be known as Nebraska marble, the local sod. If you have seen only nice, soft, grassy sod being unrolled onto lawns, it may be hard to imagine what sod was like on the Great Plains when the first settlers began trying to farm the region. Sod here was almost a solid mass of tough roots and rhizomes extending four or more inches into the earth.[3] The plants growing on the prairie were ideally suited to an environment where flood and drought alternated and brush fires were common. Deep, strong roots meant survival. Sod was so tough that the earliest settlers to attempt farming here often resorted to using axes to chop through it, to get to dirt where they could plant seeds. That is why farmers in the region became known as "sodbusters."

However, sod was useful. It was thick and heavy and nearly indestructible. In a region literally defined by a lack of trees, this rough, thick, woody mat provided the only readily available building material. Houses built of sod became a common sight on the early prairie. It took eleven acres of prairie sod to make up the three-foot-thick walls of this soddie. Walls inside and out were "plastered" with clay, to keep dirt from crumbling into the house and to protect the exterior from the weather. I thought that, for all its roughness, the soddie was surprisingly handsome. Definitely "prairie style." And I was surprised by how much cooler it was inside the soddie than it was outside. A sod house, with its thick, insulating walls, would have been ideal in this region of temperature extremes.

There is vastly more to see than I can describe here. I haven't even mentioned the splendid art gallery with literally thousands of items to examine. If you're driving across Nebraska, or if you have a keen interest in Americana, this is definitely a place you'll want to visit. Open year round.

Frontier Village

Jamestown, ND

For fans of Western novels, Jamestown is best known as the birthplace of Louis L'Amour. That said, it's also pretty well known for buffalo (or American bison, if you want to be precise). If you head for Frontier Village, you get both the writer and the buffalo, plus a hefty dose of local history and culture.

Located half way between Bismarck and Fargo, Frontier Village is a celebration of North Dakota's frontier past. All of the roughly 20 stores, offices, and cabins are original buildings that have been moved to this site from frontier villages around the state. Each building invites exploration. (Though for those traveling with children, you may be more interested in the pony rides or the stagecoach ride, both offered at the end of the street.)

My visit to Jamestown's Frontier Village was on a Tuesday, so it was pretty quiet, as is often the case on weekdays. But that meant no rushing, uninterrupted photos, and the chance to talk to locals. The buildings are set up on either side of the road, so it has the feel of being an actual town, and buildings were selected to represent the variety typical of a town, with a blacksmith, trading post, dentist, barber shop, fire department, print shop, sheriff's office, train station, bar, and so on. Most of the buildings are filled with appropriate antiques and artifacts.

The Northern Pacific Railroad Depot here was the first railway depot in Jamestown, arriving in 1880 and still in use until 1965, when it was moved to Frontier Village. The Writer's Shack is a memorial to Louis L'Amour. It offered a good bit of the writer's history, plus a display of all of his books (an impressive collection at more than a hundred titles). I loved a L'Amour

Among the buildings on Frontier Village's main street is the white cabin that was Louis L'Amour's writer's shack. Photo by Cynthia Clampitt.

quote that was posted: "I am a product of libraries." I think most writers are. The jail cell in the sheriff's office was interesting: essentially, a large cage. A wonderful early cabin is furnished with a great eye for detail, including a pump out front, clothes on the line in back, and a table set for dinner inside. In other buildings, everything from blacksmithing tools to early telephone switchboards to surveyor's chains offered insights into early history.

A few buildings, rather than focusing on history, offer local specialties, as well as artwork and crafts produced in the area. I learned at the Dakota Store that they grow a lot of horseradish in the area. I was also informed that chokecherry is very popular here, which seemed proven by the range of products. I sampled a bit of chokecherry candy—and later looked it up to find out that it is a species of bird cherry that is native to North Dakota. So, a fun bit of food history.

Looming at the end of the street is the massive form of what is said to be (and I have no reason to doubt this) the World's Largest Buffalo—a huge monument to the animals once so key to the culture and economy of both Native Americans and early settlers.

Nearby: At the bottom of the hill on which Frontier Village perches is the National Buffalo Museum. Next to that is a field where a small herd of bison graze during the summer.

Fort Abraham Lincoln State Park
Mandan, ND

This state park offers two destinations historically separated by roughly a century: the fort that was General Custer's last home before he headed in 1876 for Montana's Little Bighorn and, prior to that, a Mandan Indian village.

Sprawling Fort Abraham Lincoln was one of the largest forts on the Northern Plains, with a total of 650 men, both infantry and cavalry, stationed there. Built on a high bluff overlooking the Missouri River, it was created in 1872 to offer protection to surveyors and workers who were laying tracks for the Northern Pacific Railroad. By 1873, it was home to George Armstrong Custer, a Lieutenant Colonel at the time and the fort's first commander. Decommissioned in 1891, when the railroad was done, the fort lost its original buildings to arriving settlers faced with the reality that the treeless plains did not naturally supply much in the way of building materials. Fortunately, in the 1930s, the Civilian Conservation Corps (CCC) took on the project of reconstructing a number of the original buildings.

First stop was the visitor center to sign up for a guided tour. The guide, dressed as a soldier from the 1870s, led us out along the wooden sidewalk in the direction of Custer's house. A sign welcomed us to the year 1875. Along the path, markers showed where other buildings once stood.

The house to which Custer brought his wife, Elizabeth (Libbie), was surprisingly large and handsome. I counted five brick chimneys as I approached the Victorian-style white frame house, which was reconstructed in 1989. The elegant interior, with its tall windows, great fireplaces, and Oriental rugs, hardly seemed to be a place on the edge of the frontier. I imagine Mrs.

Custer (a successful author and speaker from a wealthy family) would have been very comfortable here. One of the interesting tidbits the guide shared was that Custer was fond of taxidermy, and there were samples of his work in several rooms. His wife, on the other hand, fancied sewing, making most of her own clothes on the still relatively new invention, the sewing machine. While exploring the spacious, modern-for-the-time kitchen, we were told that Custer's favorite food was onions. He would even eat them raw. The guide explained that some items were reproductions, but the camp desk in Custer's office is an original. There were so many personal touches (don't miss the his-and-her buffalo coats in the trunk room). Photographs of Custer with the lovely, young Libbie were a good reminder that historic characters were real people.

Next, we hiked toward the barracks. These were among the buildings rebuilt by the CCC. The two things that struck me as we walked across the parade ground were the great view of the Missouri River and the wonderful fragrance of the prairie grass. In the barracks, the guide pointed out details of everyday life, from sleeping quarters to storage to dining areas. Because it was a reconstruction (though nearly a century old at this point), it looked as new as it probably did when soldiers first arrived in 1872.

Our next destination was the museum for the nearby Mandan village. Situated on a sloping plain, the village was named On-a-Slant (Miti O-pa-e-resh). On-a-Slant village was deserted a century before the fort came into existence. In fact, when Lewis and Clark passed through in 1804, they noted the spot as "ruined village." Fortunately, while the original earth lodges were gone, six of them, including the Council Lodge, were reconstructed by the CCC.

Between the guide and the great signage, I garnered a great deal of fascinating information. The Mandan were unusual among Native Americans in building permanent homes. They were skilled farmers who grew more than they needed in order to have plenty to trade with the nomadic tribes that passed through. Interestingly, though they didn't see their first European until 1738, they had European goods thanks to extensive trade networks.

Photos, foods, tools, and other artifacts in the museum helped create a sense of Mandan society. I was of course interested to learn that they grew thirteen different varieties of maize, many of which were on display.

Then we headed out to the earth lodges. These are wonderful. An astonishing amount of work went into the wood frames and roofs, but the thick, earth-covered walls would certainly have provided good insulation. Lodges are filled with items that would have been common when the Mandan lived here, including trade goods, rough beds, baskets, snowshoes, animal pelts, hatchets, and a large wooden mortar and pestle for grinding corn. I loved the backrests that had been devised for elders. Very practical.

At one time, there were at least 86 of the earth lodges and a population of about 1,500. Women outnumbered men, because hunting was dangerous. As a result, men often had more than one wife, but they would marry sisters, so they only had one mother-in-law. Women built the earth lodges and did the farming, while men did the hunting and fishing.

This thriving community remained here for about two centuries (1575–1781), but the Mandan burned their village and moved away when the Sioux became powerful and threatened to take over the area.

A drive around the perimeter road offered further delights. The views out over the river and surrounding countryside were wonderfully open and evocative, and I took a fair number of photos. This also gave me the opportunity to see the other buildings the CCC had reconstructed.

Lewis and Clark Interpretive Center/Fort Mandan

Washburn, ND

The handsome, twelve-foot-tall steel statue of three figures—Meriwether Lewis, William Clark, and Mandan Chief Sheheke—let me know I'd found the Lewis and Clark Interpretive Center. I would return shortly, but my initial reason for stopping there was to get a ticket that would give me access to both the center and nearby (just over two miles) Fort Mandan.

Nestled amid trees not far from the banks of the Missouri River, this fort is a full-size reconstruction of the fort the Corps of Discovery constructed near this spot in 1804 to help them survive the winter. The original Fort Mandan was built in six weeks in subzero weather.[4] Daunting task. Constructed entirely of tree trunks, the fort is handsomely geometric. Upon entering, I was greeted by a buckskin-clad explorer/tour guide, who

Meriwether Lewis's desk at the reconstructed Fort Mandan shows his serious interest in nature and Native American culture. Photo by Cynthia Clampitt, used with permission of North Dakota Parks & Recreation.

explained all that we were seeing and detailed life at the fort. There were numerous interesting, revealing items in every room. Shaving gear, candles, and toothbrushes spoke of life's minutia, while fire-starting kits, powder horns, and metal-working equipment spoke of the practicalities of survival. Beds, desks, shelves, and chairs were, like the fort, made of rough wood. All the food in the kitchen and storage area reflected the customs of the Mandan people for whom Lewis and Clark had named the fort: corn, squash, beans, and sunflower heads. There was also evidence (maps, notebooks, plant cuttings) of research already done and planning for what was ahead, once spring returned.

One of my favorite details that the guide pointed out was that, while most of the living quarters were filled with bunk-beds, in the room shared by Lewis and Clark, there were two separate beds. This was intended to communicate to all that the two men were coleaders, and one was not above the other.

Many notes and photos later, I turned back toward the Interpretive Center. I've been a fan of the Corps of Discovery since grade school, so I was in heaven. When you visit, be prepared to look everywhere, as the center has used every possible inch of space to relate the history of this area. There are hundreds of artifacts, both Native American and European (and, in the case of the wooden canoe on display, European imitating Native American). Permanent exhibits besides those on Lewis and Clark include ones on the Mandan and Hidatsa nations, foods from this region, and others who came in the 1800s to learn and record what they saw. There is also additional information on Knife River and Fort Clark, which I visited previously (see Chapter 3).

I learned that Sacagawea was actually one of Toussaint Charbonneau's two wives, though the only one to go on the expedition. There are several reasons why there are numerous spellings for Sacagawea's name: different tribes had different ways of pronouncing her name (she was a Shoshone living among the Hidatsa), plus Native American languages were not written, so all spellings were phonetic. Lewis and Clark, in their journals, spelled her name a dozen different ways. The Hidatsa of this region prefer "Sacagawea," which is what I saw at the center, though "Sakakawea" is also frequently seen in North Dakota.

I had learned at Fort Clark that Prince Maximilian of Weid and Karl Bodmer had been in the area. Here I learned that the prince was a naturalist who traveled for a year with Lewis and Clark and later (1833–1834) documented Indian culture. As for the Swiss artist, Bodmer, this center is one of only four galleries in the world to have a complete collection of his prints. Maximilian's writing and Bodmer's art are among the most important records extant of Native American cultures in the upper Midwest.

Food exhibits offered more than just a repetition of women doing the farming. Mandan squash is drought resistant. Sunflower seeds provide three times the protein and eleven times the fat of corn. Shield beans were the forerunner of the Great Northern bean. And the Arikara yellow bean (a popular heirloom variety today) was developed locally.

I have quite a few books on this area and era (including George Catlin's work, if you want a recommendation), but in the gift shop, I did succumb to the temptation of buying *The Essential Lewis and Clark*, which is an abridged version of the journals kept during exploration. All too soon, it was closing time, and I had to leave.

Mitchell, SD

While the Corn Palace is what draws most people (including me) to Mitchell, I soon learned that the Prehistoric Indian Village and the excellent Dakota Discovery Museum are also definitely worth visiting.

Prehistoric Indian Village

First stop at this site is the Prehistoric Indian Village Museum, where you are introduced to the culture of the people who inhabited this point of land around A.D. 900–1000. A short, excellent movie is followed by a docent-led tour, and then you can explore on your own. It is not a large museum, but the exhibits are rich with artifacts and information. A full-size reconstructed lodge with wood-pole roof offers insight into both living conditions and one reason the people here moved away: there is very little wood on the Great Plains, so after about 100 years, the people migrated northward. It is thought that they were the ancestors of the Mandan, people who hosted Lewis and Clark when they arrived eight hundred years later.

Abundant maps and signs relate where people settled and how they moved around, where languages originated, and what trade goods passed through. Native Americans had vast trading networks, and examples of trade goods here include pottery that can be traced to Cahokia in Illinois. The primary trade good produced here appears to have been pemmican, a handy "energy bar" made of dried meat (generally bison), dried berries, and fat.

From the museum, I headed across the broad, green lawn that borders Mitchell Lake toward the Archeodome, a building created to both protect and exhibit the ongoing archaeological exploration of the prehistoric village site. More than 1.5 million artifacts have been found here already. A broad ramp winds around the dig site, leading up from the ground floor to a second floor filled with displays, artifacts, and more information about what has been discovered here and how it fits into what we know about North America a thousand years ago.

Dakota Discovery Museum

On the attractive, tree-shaded campus of Dakota Wesleyan University, I located my next destination: the Dakota Discovery Museum. The museum starts with Native Americans and then progresses through different layers of history as one continues around the first floor. Just inside the entrance was an impressive Native American pictograph, painted on buffalo hide, of a battle between Sioux and Crow, painted by the Lakota at Pine Ridge in 1891. One exhibit showed how Native American quillwork morphed in time into beadwork, as glass beads became available with the introduction of the fur trade. The displays evolved from Native American to fur trade, pioneer to farmer, growing towns, and into the 20th century. There were a few large objects, such as a threshing machine and an old sheep wagon fitted out as a horse-drawn mobile home. However, most exhibits focused on the intimate details of daily life.

One particularly interesting thing I learned was about geographic versus political borders. The Missouri River, which cuts the state roughly in half, constitutes South Dakota's "middle border." People to the east of the river moved here from the East, and those west of the river moved from the West. The two regions are identified by locals as East River and West River. West River tends to be more Wild West. That's where you have Deadwood, the Badlands, and the Black Hills. There is more tribal influence in West River and more ranching. East River is more farming, and the landscape is flatter. Mitchell is solidly in Middle Border Country.

The second floor of the museum is an art gallery. One section is dedicated to Sioux artist Oscar Howe. Other displays include bronzes by Remington and Russell, plaster casts of Gutzon Borglum's miniatures of the faces destined for Mt. Rushmore, work by Western painters Harvey Dunn and Charles Hargens, and the model created by sculptor James Earle Fraser of his most widely circulated work—the buffalo that graced the buffalo nickel.

Outside, I joined a tour of the four historic buildings that have been moved here: a 125-year-old Methodist Church, a prairie schoolhouse (the one-room variety), a train depot, and Beckwith House. The Beckwith House is a handsome, Victorian confection built for Louis Beckwith, the booster who got Mitchell to build the original Corn Palace in 1892.

Corn Palace

Displays celebrating the agricultural abundance of the Midwest became popular in the late 1800s, with the first Corn Palace being built in Sioux City, IA, in 1887. But it is the Corn Palace in Mitchell that survived. Inside and out, grand murals made entirely of corn display whatever aspect of South Dakota life or history is chosen as the year's theme. In the lobby, the walls are covered with historic photos and timelines of Corn Palace history, along with photos of the mural themes through the years. The support columns are shaped and tiled to look like giant ears of corn. It is wonderfully over the top. Videos relate the state's history and detail other sights to see in South Dakota. Around the periphery of the main arena (because the Corn Palace is a sports and event venue), there are great exhibits on corn through the centuries, including background on harvesting, whiskey-making, and processing—plus an opportunity to test out Native American tools for grinding corn.

Carnegie Library

While not a major draw, if you are in Mitchell, you might want to drop into the local Carnegie Library. Built in 1903, the library is now owned by the Mitchell Area Historical Society and offers displays of Mitchell history and

Corn Palace memorabilia, as well as records tracing the history and genealogy of people in the Mitchell area. The building is also notable for being one of only three surviving buildings in Mitchell built of local red quartzite.

Sioux Falls, SD

Looking for history doesn't often involve premium ice cream or the sound of rushing water, but it does in Sioux Falls. (Though there are plenty of more usual sources of historic information.) My first day in Sioux Falls, I sought out the **Falls Overlook Café**, because it is inside a building that was once a hydroelectric plant. The building is perched on the edge of the Big Sioux River, just past the beautiful waterfalls for which the town is named. The rushing water, which plunges along amid a chaos of pink quartzite boulders, was the source of power for the plant, as well as for a few other water-powered businesses (including the Queen Bee Mill, the ruins of which are near the café). Inside the café, aside from the impressive architecture, with its soaring ceiling and tall windows, there are numerous photos that recount the planning and history of the hydroelectric plant, which opened in 1908. From blueprints to construction (all done by hand) to rows of turbines once it was operational, the photos show how it happened, and nearby signs offer details of the importance of supplying electricity to the rapidly growing town. And then there is the ice cream, though they also offer lunch, snacks, and beverages. But outstanding ice cream combined with the view of the nearby waterfall makes this a fairly remarkable bit of historical exploration.

But it is just the beginning of places to learn about history—the city's, the state's, and the territory's (before statehood). The pink quartzite so evident at the falls is also the building material used for many of the city's historic buildings, including the **Old Courthouse Museum**. Built in 1890, this impressive edifice, with its tall clock tower, is one of two Siouxland Heritage Museums. The interior is as imposing as might be expected of a county courthouse—high ceilings, abundant wood paneling, and a massive iron stairway. On the ground floor, there are three permanent exhibits: a bison (with descriptions of how Native Americans used such parts as the bladder and stomach), the 1908 Fawick Flyer (a car that would go 60 mph at a time when the limit was 7 mph), and the "tornado tree"—a tree that was pierced

I'm betting there are not a lot of cities with parks like this downtown. These falls on the Big Sioux River give Sioux Falls its name. The ruins of the Queen Bee Mill can be seen in the background. Just out of sight to my left is the Falls Overlook Café. Photo by Cynthia Clampitt.

by a steel girder from a bridge that was lifted off the river and torn apart by a tornado. The other exhibits are generally changed about every two years, I was told. When I was there, the exhibits included a photographic history of the city; a large Norwegian rug loom, which both reminds visitors of the large Norwegian presence in SD (approximately 14 percent of the population) and is used to make rugs one can buy in the gift shop; and, on the second floor, exhibits on the suffrage movement and the evolution of medicine (with a kid-friendly activity that compares treatment in 1900 with what we do today). A photo of an attractive young man bore the legend, "Constant Toohey was the first person in Sioux Falls to die of Spanish flu in 1918"—so a good reminder that pandemics are not new. There were also biographies of many of the early doctors in Sioux Falls, including the first doctor, George A.

Pettigrew, who began his practice in 1883. He was a cousin of South Dakota Senator Richard Franklin Pettigrew—which made a nice segue to my next destination, the **Pettigrew Home and Museum**.

Richard Franklin Pettigrew, I soon learned, was quite a character. More commonly known as Frank, he was, in essence, the primary force behind the creation of Sioux Falls. He was a surveyor who had studied law, an adventurer who traveled the world, and an investor who knew Calamity Jane and went on buffalo hunts with local Native Americans. After seeing the falls on the Big Sioux River, he decided this was the perfect place for a city, so, with the help of his brother and a partner, he brought in five railroads, a woolen mill, a flour mill, a school for the deaf, a post office, stockyards, a meat-packing plant, a soap factory, a horse-drawn trolley system, and more. He invited his friend Andrew Carnegie to build a Carnegie Library here, and he donated his own land and money to help build Augustana University. He was also an amateur archaeologist, and the house contains some of the ancient tools and other artifacts that he dug up. As a perfect Victorian in an age defined by collecting, he gathered souvenirs from his travels and rocks from all over the territory (including a lot of petrified wood, which is built into the exterior wall on one side of the house). Throw in all the glorious furnishings of that time period, and there is a lot to see. The museum section also related that by 1904, thanks to the railroads and Pettigrew's aggressive PR campaign, there were 10 hotels with roughly a thousand rooms, because there were so many visitors (the falls were a big draw). Pettigrew willed his home, library, and museum to the city of Sioux Falls, with the hope that it would help future generations learn about the past.

As wonderful as the Pettigrew Home and Museum are, from the outside, it is just one among many splendid Victorian mansions on Duluth Avenue. Each home has a sign in front relating the year it was built and who built it. A lot of the city's first families lived in this area. A nice bonus, if you're interested, is that the impressive home right next to the Pettigrew Home is now a hotel: the **Historic Victorian Inn**. Built in 1888, this grand Victorian confection has eight rooms, four with private baths, an elegant, wraparound veranda, and a play area well enough equipped to keep children busy for hours. The location is a bonus.

A few minutes away is Augustana University, where the **Heritage Park** is home to a small cluster of historic Great Plains buildings, including two related to novelist Ole Rölvaag, author of the classic novel *Giants in the Earth*, which relates the hardships faced by Norwegian pioneers when this area was first being opened up. (Great book. I recommend it highly.) The Berdahl-Rölvaag House, built in 1883, is where Rölvaag heard the family stories that inspired him to write his pioneer tales. It's also where he met his wife. Nearby is the Rölvaag Writing Cabin, where he worked. The other buildings are the 1892 Beaver Creek Lutheran Church and the one-roomed Eggers School House, both victims of declining rural population.

Last stop for me was the **Stockyards Ag Experience**, a museum that reflects the history of farming and food processing in Sioux Falls. This is a largely agricultural area, so this represents a major part of the city's history. The previously mentioned Mr. Pettigrew had a hand in much of this, from building a flour mill to beginning plans in 1889 for a stockyard. Meatpacking began in the 1890s. In 1909, meatpacker John Morrell and Company (now Smithfield) opened and was for a long time the largest employer in Sioux Falls. Then construction of Pettigrew's Sioux Fall Stock Yards began in 1915, opening in 1917 and operating until 2009. This and other information about the history of agriculture is on the top floor of the museum, related through videos, touch screens, and signs, mixed in with some hands-on elements. The lower level, "Farm to Table," is more geared for younger visitors and explores current food production, from field to kitchen.

Finally, I headed back to the falls, to sit and watch the tumultuous water and the fish trying to swim upstream. There is definitely no shortage of history in Sioux Falls. However, I almost think the waterfall that inspired that history is enough reason to visit.

Eating History: Chislic

If you are traveling in South Dakota, especially the southeast of the state, you may encounter a local specialty called *chislic*. And if you don't encounter it, you may want to look for it. It is iconic here. In fact, there is an annual chislic festival in Freeman, SD, considered the heart of chislic country.

Chislic is simply small, deep-fried cubes of meat. Traditionally, the meat would be mutton or lamb, threaded on a skewer, and served with garlic salt and saltine crackers. This traditional form is still widely available, and delicious, but the history of food is rife with altered traditions, and that is true of chislic. Beef is now a common substitute for mutton and lamb, but I've also seen menus offering pork, chicken, and even fish (though the fish is breaded before frying). Some even skip the step of threading the cubes on skewers, simply tossing the cubes in the fryer (which is just as tasty).

There is some debate as to the origin of both the food item and the word, but it is often pointed out that *chislic* is similar to the Russian word *shashlik*, which is cubes of meat on skewers, though grilled rather than fried. Russians and Russian Germans were coming into South Dakota in the 1870s, when this dish first appeared, so it seems like a reasonable argument.

CHAPTER 5

Experiencing History

There are numerous ways to connect with history on a more active level. Attending a reenactment or a rendezvous is a great way to engage with past events. You can just be a spectator, but these often offer opportunities to participate in a variety of activities or at the very least try food from the period being re-created. But perhaps you'd like something where you can participate more fully.

Most of the places in this book actually represent opportunities to get involved, because museums and living-history venues rely heavily on volunteers, from extra costumed interpreters to people doing research or working behind the scenes. So, if there is a place that "does history" near where you live, ask about available opportunities. You may be surprised at how many options are open to you—and how happy they will be that you asked. (This is why many venues have a lot more interpreters on weekends; that's when people with jobs can volunteer.)

As you think about getting involved, one major consideration is level of commitment. Some opportunities are for a few hours, such as taking a class, while an event might take a whole day or even a weekend. Involvement may be no more than listening to a reenactor talk about medical care in the late 1700s, but it could be joining in a folk dance or trying your hand at making candles. Historic vacations can take more time, whether a luxury bus tour that follows Louis and Clark's route or the re-creation of one of the famous trail rides, with horses and/or covered wagons, where you might be gone for a week or more. An hour or a week, these are still one-time events. Volunteering is generally a bit more long-term, perhaps all summer or every weekend. Reenactors often pursue "the hobby," as they call it, for years, with most of each summer's plans built around the dozens of places in the Midwest that reenactments are held.

The following is just a sampling of options, both short- and long-term, to help you start thinking about this. Then I'll discuss reenacting, which can be a weekend away or an entire lifestyle. However, more can be found as you visit historic sites and explore the past.

Garfield Farm Museum

Campton Hills, IL

I first visited Garfield Farm to attend a class. I then had the pleasure of doing the full tour, which offered some fascinating facts, such as there being about 14,000 related Garfields in the country. The Garfields who owned this farm were third cousins of President Garfield (and 3rd cousins of Aaron Burr, as well). So, the family, as well as the farm, are anchored in history.

Timothy Garfield bought the 366-acre farm in 1841. In addition to farming, he built a log inn and then, in 1846, upgraded to brick—and the brick inn is still here. After 136 years, the final Garfield to own the property, Elva Ruth, decided the entire place should be preserved as a museum, so that future generations could see what inns and prairie farming in the 1800s were like—and also see what the natural environment was like, as several areas were never plowed. So vintage buildings abound: houses, barns, sheds, and the inn, but also wetlands and prairie. In keeping with the thought of revealing what things were like, the crops planted and animals raised are all heirloom varieties.

During the tour, we visited many of the buildings, and all were remarkably well preserved. The inn, however, offered the most novelty for me. In the 1800s, you didn't rent a room at an inn or tavern, just an area of floor in one large room, along with everyone else staying at the inn. But having everyone in one room was actually the standard at the time. Or, rather, all the men in one room; this was a teamster inn, and pretty much only men were driving teams of horses and oxen. However, there was a ladies' parlor for when women did travel that road. There were 41 inns on the St. Charles-to-Chicago road, approximately one every mile, which suggests the impressive level of traffic. The kitchen, which was well equipped (loved the wood-burning stove), was in a different wing than the tavern. For 37 cents, you got dinner, breakfast, and that space upstairs to sleep. The inn usually hosted about 15,000 customers per year. Our guide attributed this in part to the farm, as that made it possible to serve something other than the salt pork and beans common elsewhere.

There is so much more to learn here, even if all you do is take the 90-minute tour. But Garfield Farm really takes seriously the idea of educating people. They offer classes and seminars on such topics as fruit tree grafting, blacksmithing, and wetlands management, as well as special events that focus on heirloom seeds, antique farm tools, and rare livestock breeds. Taking it a step further than just offering classes, Garfield Farm Museum also offers internships in museum management and natural areas management. In addition, reaffirming the earlier comment about volunteers, this museum relies on roughly 300 volunteers during the year, with a wide range of options. Just as there is history all around, there are also opportunities to connect with it.

Sycamore Steam Show & Threshing Bee

Sycamore, IL

For one weekend each summer, the Taylor Marshall Farm roars into noisy, smoky life as the location of the annual Sycamore Steam Show & Threshing Bee. Hundreds of collectors bring their restored steam traction machines— the predecessors of tractors—to the show. Your first impression of these astonishing machines may be that this is a steampunk fantasy, but these machines are all real, and they were vital to farm work in their day. They didn't just pull plows; they supplied power wherever it was needed. At the show, you can see them run threshing machines (fascinating machines in their own right), as competitors race to load the most grain. You can also watch a steam traction engine run a sawmill that cuts logs into planks throughout the day. And, of course, you can see them pull a plow. You can watch engineers shoveling coal into the engines, to keep them running, or watch the demonstration of an early steam shovel (invented in 1839). Early afternoon, there is a narrated parade that shows oldest to newest, so you can watch the machines evolve before your eyes.

There are a lot of activities—flea market, farmers market, activities for children, food, music, and more—but the big draw is the machines. And when you arrive, no matter how far away you park, you'll be okay, because mule-drawn wagons circulate through the lots and give rides to the entrance.

The people who own these machines generally love talking about them, and they are usually intimate with every detail of a machine's operation, as well as the applications to which the machine can be put. So, while there are some signs around offering background (especially in the buildings on site, where there are exhibits of stationary machines), the greatest source of information is likely to be the exhibitors.

Because there are a lot of folks across the country who have refurbished these astonishing machines, this is not the only show that features them. If you don't live near Sycamore, check for listings (Steam Show, Power Show, Threshers Reunion, or similar) that might be scheduled near you or near somewhere you want to visit.

Michigan Maritime Museum

South Haven, MI

The exhibits in this lovely little museum focus primarily on 20th-century events. However, the fleet is more historically oriented. The *Friends Good Will* is a faithful replica of a sailing ship built in Michigan in 1810. It's a graceful vessel, and you are welcome aboard. Simply exploring the ship is an option, without leaving the dock, asking questions of the docent and crew, who are always at work on the ship, keeping it bright, clean, and, as they say, shipshape. However, during the summer, the ship sails daily, if you want to try that out. The crew, dressed in clothes appropriate for an early 1800s

During the summer, visitors can sail in, and even help operate, the lovely sailing ship *Friends Good Will*, shown here leaving port. Photo courtesy of the Michigan Maritime Museum.

sailor, will show you what life was like on a merchant ship on the Great Lakes. Participation by guests in raising and lowering sails is encouraged, so you can get a real feel for the work on a ship of this type.

The *Lindy Lou* is a smaller boat. This vessel is electric powered, rather than wind driven. It is a replica of an 1890s Truscott river launch. Rather than re-creating a sailing adventure, this boat recaptures the charm of excursions upriver that were popular during the late 1800s and early 1900s.

In addition to these vessels that reflect travel in the 1800s, the museum has a 1921 racing yacht, a 1929 luxury Chris Craft Cadet, and a 1941 U.S. Coast Guard Motor Lifeboat. This means you can view, or even cruise in, nearly 150 years of maritime history.

Lighthouses are vital on the Great Lakes. This one at Mission Point offers a "keeper program" for those who might want to spend a week in this lovely location. Photo courtesy of Ginger Schultz, Mission Point Lighthouse Manager.

Mission Point Lighthouse

Traverse City, MI

The Old Mission Peninsula offers abundant history—and there is more about the area under Traverse City in Chapter 4, as there is much to explore. The lighthouse, which is both a State and National Historic Site, is lovely, and the surrounding area offers delightful options for hiking and enjoying nature. I was interested to learn that the lighthouse is near the 45th Parallel, so roughly halfway between the Equator and the North Pole. However, it was the remarkable beauty of the location, perched between forest and lakeshore, along with the wonderful appearance of the pristinely white lighthouse, completed in 1870 (construction having been delayed by the Civil War), that really delighted me.

Aside from being a remarkably lovely destination, the Mission Point Lighthouse is one of only a handful of Michigan lighthouses that has a "keeper program." This is a program that offers people (energetic and 18 or older) a chance to spend a week as lighthouse keepers. Don't worry—no lives depend on your keeping the light burning. That is now automated and offshore. But you would be expected to climb the lighthouse (37 steps) to clean the windows, help in the gift shop, chat with visitors, and possibly do a few other tasks. The objective is both for the temporary keepers to appreciate the life of a lighthouse keeper and to keep the lighthouse "alive" for other visitors. And when you're not working, there are those forest trails and lovely beaches to explore. Check out the Mission Point Lighthouse website if you want more details.

State Fairs

Throughout Region

While the Midwest is far from merely agricultural, there is no doubt that farming is a big part of what the region does. A nation of farmers was, in fact, the vision Thomas Jefferson had when he considered the stunning amount of land available once he concluded the Louisiana Purchase. After Jefferson, the president most associated with promoting Midwestern agriculture was Abraham Lincoln, even as he handled the Civil War. The

Morrill Land Grant Act of 1862 gave states the means of creating agricultural colleges. The Homestead Act of 1862 offered any adult head of household 160 acres of land, as long as the they occupied and improved (that is, farmed) the land. Also in 1862, Lincoln signed legislation establishing the U.S. Department of Agriculture.

There were, however, few aspects of agriculture Lincoln valued more than the state fair. He didn't create state fairs, but he appeared at them—and praised them. Lincoln, along with many others, realized that communication was a key to success. In a speech at the Wisconsin State Fair in September 1859, Lincoln shared his vision of the prime virtue of these gatherings. "But the chief use of agricultural fairs is to aid in improving the great calling of *agriculture*, in all its departments, and minute divisions—to make mutual exchange of agricultural discovery, information, and knowledge; so that, at the end, *all* may know everything, which may have been known to but *one*, or to but a *few*, at the beginning—to bring together especially all which is supposed to not be generally known, because of recent discovery, or invention."

Lincoln also understood the value of a little competition, noting that it could, "by exciting emulation, for premiums, and for the pride and honor of success—of triumph, in some sort" motivate even more discoveries and improvements.

Today, the communication aspect of state fairs is less important, as there are so many alternatives for disseminating discoveries and updates. However, the competition aspect is still important, whether it's for a prize hog or blue-ribbon preserves.

There is still so much of history at the state fairs that I think everyone should visit at least one. It is a good way to sample the iconic foods of a place, such as the cream puffs that showcase dairy at Wisconsin's fair or the iconic pork chops at Iowa's fair. You can attend some of the competitions. (If you can, see a horse-pulling competition, where well-trained teams of draft horses will astonish you with the power of pulling together.) Visit the animal barns to see which sheep, goats, cattle, hogs, rabbits, chickens, turkeys, or geese might have won ribbons. Check out what youngsters have done for their 4H and FFA projects. It is truly a place where the past and present are one.

A great illustration of the interconnectedness of history, family, food, and state fairs, is the Family Heirloom Recipe Contest created by Catherine Lambrecht, founder of the Greater Midwest Foodways Alliance (GMFA). So I asked Catherine to share with us a little about this remarkable project. Perhaps this will inspire you to think about your own family history.

Since 2009, Greater Midwest Foodways Alliance has sponsored a family heirloom recipe contest at Midwestern state fairs. Contestants enter their best scratch family heirloom recipe suitable for a family or community dinner. The recipe should originate 50 years ago or earlier. Contestants bring a prepared dish along with a history of who passed the recipe down to them; ethnicity, if relevant; number of years the recipe has been in their family; and any interesting information about their recipe. The all-important history of the recipe would account for fully half the score, with execution and taste (40 percent) and display and appearance (10 percent) accounting for the other half.

The foods are sometimes submitted simply in their transport container, or more elaborately on the family's china with relevant props of family pictures, kitchen paraphernalia, and their loved one's handwritten recipe.

Some of these recipes originated when oven temperatures were difficult to regulate, or temperature was taken literally by hand: stick your hand in the oven chamber and count the seconds before your hand cannot tolerate it.

Unlike many sponsored contests which rely on state fair–appointed judges, we send our members to judge the Family Heirloom Contest. This contest is unique because the final decision is not solely dependent on the recipe's execution. We weight the history at 50 percent to emphasize it is a major consideration. Consequently, an excellent history can trump a recipe's execution, but an excellent dish with no history will never go far. We recognize that participation would be greater if we dropped the requirement of a history, though the lower numbers are a cost we can live with to achieve our goal of breathing new life into old recipes.

At the end of the state fair season, these recipes, histories, and images are loaded to our website: www.GreaterMidwestFoodways.com.

For the long haul, the original histories and recipes will be archived at the University of Michigan Library Special Collections Research Center at the Janice Bluestein Longone Culinary Archives in Ann Arbor. This culinary archive is a mecca for researchers. We want to encourage the continued use and study of these Family Heirloom Recipes, because these recipes and their histories will live on as long as they are not forgotten.

If nothing else, we hope this contest inspires a family to document their favorite recipe to be shared with loved ones. Then we have accomplished our mission.

After our judging duties are over, we review the domestic arts (cakes, candy, cookies, and preserved foods) and agricultural contests (flowers, herbs, fruits, and vegetables: from green beans to giant pumpkins). We visit the dairy barn for a glass of milk, ice cream made with Guernsey cream and admire the butter cow. At least once, we enjoyed seeing a life-sized chocolate moose[1] at the Iowa State Fair.

When it is time to eat, we go to food stands sponsored and manned by farmers who raise beef, lamb, pork, and poultry. Often, we are sitting among farm families and their ambitious children who participate in Future Farmers of America. The net income from these food stands go to agricultural education.

We leave the fair by walking through the barns housing 4-H and adult-contestant's animal husbandry projects. We try to keep our visit agricultural centric in keeping with the state fairs' original premise since 1841.

Catherine Lambrecht is a founder of the Greater Midwest Foodways Alliance, LTHforum.com, a Chicago Food Chat site, and the Chicago Foodways Roundtable section of Culinary Historians of Chicago.

Reenacting

A gathering of reenactors may be called an encampment, a rendezvous, a reenactment, or some combination of these terms. Almost every reenactment or rendezvous also includes an encampment, whether it appears in the name or not. An encampment refers to the setting up of and moving into a camp-site, with simple tents for soldiers, more elaborate tents for officers, and tents that can be opened for trade for the merchants or entertainers at the event. If something is simply called a reenactment, you can probably expect an imitation of combat at some point, but there will likely also be an encampment, as all the reenactors need someplace to stay for the weekend. A rendezvous is generally the reenactment of a gathering of trappers, traders, voyageurs, and others, and often includes Native Americans. There are several rendezvous in the Midwest, with variations based on the history of the location. The Spirit of Vincennes Rendezvous is a reenactment of the Battle of Vincennes (one of the few Rev War battles actually fought, and won, in the Midwest), and appears in some listings as Rendezvous & Encampment. Just know that these terms, in whatever combination, will at least offer people in costume reliving a period of history, most likely from the 1700s through the 1800s.

The Feast of the Hunter's Moon

I've been to a fair number of reenactments and encampments, but my favorite event so far is The Feast of the Hunter's Moon, the re-creation of a 1770s trading post held each fall in West Lafayette, Indiana. I first went with friends about twenty-five years ago, and we returned for the next three years. Then I became a Revolutionary War reenactor and went two years in that capacity—actually sleeping in a tent at the Feast. Then life got busy, and reenacting got dropped and a weekend at the Feast became an every-few-years outing. But I'm still going. It's a great event. It has changed a bit over time, as things must. It now caters a bit more to people who aren't hardcore history enthusiasts, offering more food and beverage options, but it's still remarkable.

The Feast is held at Fort Ouiatenon (in the 1700s, one of New France's earliest military bases) on the shores of the Wabash River. While the event is not quite as big as when I first went, it still involves more than 3,000 costumed volunteers. Dozens of sutlers (the people who sell the goods needed by, originally, soldiers, but now, those who portray them) set up tents where they can offer reenactors and visitors alike all the trappings of the time period: clothing, canteens, cooking gear, and vastly more. Native Americans encamp and offer presentations on dance (which visitors are invited to learn) and crafts, as well as information on the groups that lived (and may still live) in the area.

Almost half of the sprawling property where the event takes place is covered with the tents of the military reenactors. They are organized by era or focus: French Marines, Voyageurs, French and Indian War, American Revolution (Colonial and British), War of 1812. Reenactors not only dress authentically, they also camp, cook, and eat authentically. Over two days, reenactors demonstrate everything from flint-lock rifles to French colonial dancing. While many events occur simultaneously, there are a couple of "big" things that tend to draw most visitors together. In the morning, there is a flag-raising ceremony, where all the flags that have flown over the fort are raised: French, Spanish, English, American. For this, all military units and all bands assemble. Then, down by the river, everyone gathers to welcome the arrival of the Voyageurs, who steer their big canoes to shore welcomed by cheers. While there is music almost everywhere throughout the day, I particularly love the massed bands near the end of the day. Really rousing.

One can simply wander and enjoy. The sutlers hope you'll shop. But there are lots of things to do, including working with a blacksmith, using a two-person saw to saw logs, learning how to throw a tomahawk. For those with children, there are numerous kid-friendly options, as well. This event is also where I met the members of Hamilton's Artillery, the unit I joined when I did my stint as a reenactor.

Northwest Territory Alliance

Hamilton's Artillery is one of the many units that are part of the Northwest Territory Alliance (NWTA). The NWTA is a reenactment group that focuses on the American Revolution. The organization's more than five hundred members are spread across the original Northwest Territory (Ohio, west-

Members of NWTA portray a wide range of military units from the American Revolution. In this photo, taken at an event in Vincennes, Indiana, the four soldiers in helmets are 1st regiment of Light Dragoons, and the other three soldiers are members of Hamilton's Artillery. Vincennes was the site of one of the few Revolutionary War battles in the Midwest. Photo courtesy of Cindy Jackson.

ward), though with some members in bordering states. But they come together for the many events during the year (hence the need for encampments). This organization is wonderfully supportive and even offers opportunities to try out "the hobby" without commitment. You can borrow a costume and venture out to a couple of events before deciding whether you want to invest in the outfits and paraphernalia. The NWTA has just about all the groups who fought in the Rev War, including Hessians, Brits, Scottish Highlanders, and colonists ranging from Hamilton's Artillery to ragtag militia. The people involved are fun and interesting and love history—and usually know it well. Check out their website to learn more, to find out what events might be near you, or even to ask for an opportunity to sample what it's like: https://www.nwta.com/.

Some of the ladies of the NWTA enjoy the Ladies Tea at an event held at Dollinger Family Farm in Channahon, Illinois. Note the one very young reenactor on the right. At these events, there are children of all ages in costume, not just adults. Also note that there are Red Coats in the background, as both sides of the Revolution are portrayed. Photo courtesy of Cindy Jackson.

As a reenactor, I was involved in events across Illinois, Wisconsin, and Indiana. Women had a lot of tasks around camp (as did everyone), but they actually got to see "combat." Most commonly, they took water to the wounded in the field. (On hot summer days, carrying water to those in the field is, even now, often still really important.) Because women during the Revolutionary War occasionally stepped in and helped when men were killed, they trained me for the cannon crew, which I loved. My favorite job was vent tender, but I learned all four positions for the cannon. You definitely want to be wearing ear plugs, however.

As noted earlier, there are also groups that do the War of 1812, the French and Indian War, and more. But another popular war to reenact is the American Civil War.

Civil War Encampments or Reenactments

There are Civil War Encampments or Reenactments all over the country, and I've been to several, but the two largest Civil War events I've visited are both in Lake County in Northern Illinois. These are impressively grand, sprawling events. As with many reenactments, there is a lot more than just combat on display. At these events, while visiting the reenactors, I've talked to an undertaker about embalming techniques; a doctor about medicine in the field; a cook about the different types of camp ovens available, including a wonderful, light tin oven; a couple of men from a Zouave regiment about their unusual uniforms; and so much more. The impetus for my first visit to the larger of the two Lake County events was an invitation to be a judge of an interesting competition: which unit was not only preparing authentic food but also had created the best story to explain how they got the food. Actually, because the Union had a lot more food during the war, their stories were a little less compelling than those of the Confederates, who had to dig through burning rubble or catch a rabbit to come up with a meal. But it was also a good reminder that, whatever your interests are, there is a good possibility that you can find something at a reenactment that will connect with one or more of those interests.

While the internet offers many options for connecting with reenactors, the best way to connect with a group, should you wish to investigate reenacting, is to go to reenactments. Talk to people. See who has a story that resonates for you—or uniforms you want to wear. Know that there are a lot more options than just the American Revolution and the Civil War. I've met groups that do the French and Indian War and the War of 1812, as well as groups that represent other aspects of early history, from backwoodsmen to voyageurs, early pioneers to French Marines, and just about any other character to be found on the prairie in the 1800s. Sutlers can help outfit you, but they too are reenactors. An online search will turn up a surprisingly large number of outfitters, but you may find that any group you want to join will have recommendations.

Even if you never become a reenactor, attending the events is both great fun and a great way to connect with the past. And remember, most reenactors love talking about the time periods they represent, so feel free to ask questions.

If you are interested in what eating authentically is like for a reenactor, though you can learn a lot about food watching and talking to reenactors encamped at an event, YouTube is probably a more readily available source for historic culinary inspiration. One of the most popular channels for cooking from the 1700s is Townsends, which may surprise you with some of the dishes available during that period (even fried onion rings). This channel focuses on foods that can be prepared with period equipment, all of which they offer for sale. However, a search on YouTube for food of any era (such as the Civil War) or "historic cooking" in general will turn up instructional videos that can show you not only what was eaten but how you can prepare it. It is worth noting that canning was invented in the early 1800s to feed Napoleon's fighting forces in the field, and this new technology moved swiftly to Britain and then North America, evolving from glass jars to tin cans. As a result, canned foods were available in the U.S. shortly before the Civil War and were happily adopted by the military. This means you may have more options available than you'd expect, if this is your chosen time period. Of course, the menu will vary depending on the time period you're re-creating.

CHAPTER 6

Eating and Sleeping History

Attending the reenactments and opportunities mentioned in Chapter 5 will no doubt introduce you to some historic foods. The groups that put on these events are generally very careful about authenticity, from costumes to cuisine. However, there is much more to consider when talking about food rooted in history, including foods indigenous to the region, foods introduced by settlers from many lands, and foods that evolved here. A few of these are introduced elsewhere in the book. But in this chapter, the focus is on restaurants and taverns that long ago popped up along trails and in early towns—and that are still in business. Not too surprisingly, given the slow speed of travel at the time, hotels and inns also popped up. Many of the historic hotels and inns that remain in business also have historic dining facilities. In these cases, there is just one listing for the combination.

Here, we'll look at some of the oldest places still in operation where you can dine or sleep. Of course, "oldest" often comes with other modifiers—oldest continuously operational, oldest family owned, oldest between Detroit and Chicago, oldest west of the Mississippi, oldest in the state, and even vintage buildings that were not originally restaurants. To narrow this a bit further, this chapter's restaurants and accommodations are not located in towns covered in Chapter 4, so you will find additional options if you visit those destinations. (For example, the oldest restaurants in Missouri are in Arrow Rock and Ste. Genevieve and are covered in those entries.)

In some of the old restaurants, the food is historic, or at least classic Midwest, which frequently means steak, unless you're near the Great Lakes, in which case it is just as often fish. In many of these spots, farm-to-table never went out of style. A few offer local specialties or reflect the culture of the people who settled an area. Some capture the "tone" of the restaurant, rather than an original menu: burgers in a stagecoach stop, cutting-edge cuisine in a more upscale place. The food ranges from outstanding to, at the very least, tasty and wholesome.

The region's settlers were and are astonishingly diverse, a reality that has only become greater over time. Those who came brought traditions from their homelands but also adopted foods indigenous to the Americas. Because of this, there is a degree to which anything you might eat in the Midwest is, in fact, Midwestern and, to an even greater degree, reflective of our history. So even though the items at the listed restaurants might be more varied than when they opened in the 1800s, know that, at some level, if you are eating well, that reflects Midwestern history.

Like the restaurants, there is a range of options with accommodation, though I'm happy to say there are a lot of splendid and even occasionally award-winning places to stay. You can spend the night in accommodations that have hosted presidents and literary giants or that simply have interesting histories, from being private homes to serving as hospitals. The variety is wonderful. Note that the hotels included here are not located in larger cities. Major urban settings generally offer multiple historic options. For example, Chicago has the splendid Palmer House, rebuilt in 1875, following the Great Chicago Fire; the Staypineapple, a National Historic Landmark built in 1895; or The Blackstone, opened in 1910 and favored by Presidents, to name a few. Cities offer many opportunities that are more easily located by being more numerous. However, many of the oldest places are outside the large cities, built in vintage towns, along rivers, or on once-well-traveled trails.

There are vastly more options than are listed here. This is just a sampling, to give you some ideas and to encourage exploration. Almost every old town has at least one vintage bed and breakfast, and many have refurbished hotels from the 1800s. In addition, some places offer rustic but new accommodations where you can overnight amid historic surroundings (some of the more remote state and national parks do this). However, the places included in this chapter are noteworthy. I have eaten in all the restaurants, and I'll mention the food (though please do not consider these restaurant reviews—a good review takes multiple visits). As for the hotels, I have stayed in some and toured others. But I believe the surroundings, along with the histories, make these accommodations worth considering, even if just to visit them for their historic value.

The Golden Lamb

Lebanon, OH

About forty-five minutes out of Cincinnati, I drove into the town of Lebanon, which was officially founded in 1802, one year before Ohio became a state. The abundance of beautifully preserved architecture from this era suggested to me that this would be a good place to explore, but I was here for the Golden Lamb, an inn and restaurant that is the oldest continuously operating business in Ohio.

In 1803, Jonas Seaman was licensed to open a "a house of Public Entertainment." Seaman's wife, Martha, was a good cook, and the Golden Lamb became hugely popular. Then, in 1815, Seaman sold the property to Ichabod Corwin. Corwin, the town's first settler, had arrived with his family in the area that would become Lebanon in 1796 and was actually the original owner of the property occupied by the Golden Lamb. Corwin replaced Seaman's original two-story log cabin with the handsome, white-trimmed, red-brick building that I now approached, but he kept the name—and the tradition of good food and hospitality.

The inn's antiquity is what attracted me, but it was the inn's elegance that drew the likes of Charles Dickens, John Quincy Adams, Ulysses S. Grant, and most of the key figures of the history of opening up Ohio and the rest of the Northwest Territory. Located on the road that connected Cincinnati with the National Road, the Golden Lamb continued to grow in popularity as traffic increased. The operation changed hands a few times in the ensuing centuries, and it was even temporarily renamed, but it never stopped being important.

The hotel rooms at the Golden Lamb are decorated to honor the illustrious people who have stayed here during the more than 200 years the hotel has been in business. This room is the Charles Dickens Room. Photo courtesy of the Golden Lamb.

Today, just as it did in the 1800s, the Golden Lamb offers elegant surroundings and splendid food. As delighted as I was with the handsome décor, I was really taken with the menu, which managed to be both historic and contemporary. One section of the menu was, in fact, labeled "Historic Fare" and included lamb shanks, roasted turkey, and prime rib. A few items caught my eye because I'd encountered them while researching my book on pigs and pork. One was a Tri-State Ham Tasting, which featured a sampling of ham from the top purveyors in Kentucky, Tennessee, and Ohio. I opted for the Sauerkraut Balls, since I knew they were an Ohio specialty. They were outstanding. They consist of beef, pork, and sauerkraut, rolled into one-inch balls, breaded, fried, and served with mustard sauce and cocktail sauce, both excellent. A dish that involved smoked chicken, andouille sausage, and ale cheese was tempting, but I decided I should go with something that was potentially portable, since I still had two and a half hours of driving ahead of me, and I didn't want to eat to sleepiness. The Tavern Cheeseburger seemed a good option, and the excellent beef served with Tillamook cheddar and garlic aioli could not have been better. I got it with a side salad, and the creamy balsamic house dressing was another delight.

The nice thing about dining at four in the afternoon is that one can wander a bit more without annoying other diners, so I explored the varied dining rooms. A sign near the stairway to the upper floors listed all the luminaries who have stayed here, and I stopped to read it. I then headed upstairs to explore the hotel part of the Golden Lamb. The rooms have been decorated to reflect the time periods of the famous guests who have stayed at the hotel. Though these rooms can be booked, when they are not, they are left open, with a chain to remind visitors to not enter, but without obstructing the view. I think the Charles Dickens Room and Ulysses S. Grant Room were my favorites, but all were impressive. Then it was time to get back on the road.

Rathskeller

Indianapolis, IN

While the name clearly reflects the German influence that created this venue, the thing that tickles me most is the fact that Kurt Vonnegut's grandfather was a partner in the firm (Vonnegut & Bohn) that designed the impressive building that houses the Rathskeller. It's a good reminder that even famous people often have deep roots in this region.

Opened in 1894, the Rathskeller is actually part of a larger complex known originally as *Das Deutsche Haus*. However, in February 1918, with Americans fighting Germany in World War I, the name was changed to Athenaeum, to reassure everyone that the Germans in Indiana were dedicated Americans. The massive red-brick edifice, which is almost a block long, once housed a *Turnverein*, or gymnastics club, always the center of German community in the 1800s. The multi-use venue houses a number of facilities, including a theater. That theater, still in use, is the city's oldest. And the Rathskeller restaurant, which is in the basement (*keller* means "cellar"), is the oldest continually operating restaurant in Indianapolis.

After stopping to read the historic markers outside the entrance, I headed downstairs to the restaurant. I was seated near a huge fireplace in the main dining room, which was busy enough that I was glad I'd made a reservation. The general ambiance of the building is solidly Old World, with wood beams and wood paneling, but much of the décor and the displays of beer steins in the restaurant made the German heritage clear. The lengthy, diverse menu offered a fair number of non-German items, but I was there for the classics—of which there were many. The oxtail soup (*ochsenschwanz suppe*) was delicious. The bread service included, in addition to good rolls, a huge pretzel served with mustard mixed with horseradish. Really wonderful. The *jägerschnitzel*—a veal schnitzel buried under wild mushrooms and shallots—was splendid. Of the included sides, the creamed spinach was the standout.

After dinner, I strolled down the hall to see the Kellerbar, a stunning room with a ceiling that rises up two stories. Here, stone and wood and mounted deer and moose trophies on the walls evoke a hunting-lodge feeling, while flags overhead make it clear it is a German hunting lodge. I then strolled through one of the empty banqueting halls (not in use on a Tuesday night) on my way back to the handsome wooden staircase, and up to street level again.

DeSoto House Hotel

Galena, IL

Galena is an almost perfectly preserved town from the 1800s, and there is a tremendous amount to see. However, while I don't feel I've spent enough time there to really do the town justice, I do feel that my stay at the delightful DeSoto House Hotel is worthy of a report on its own. Opened in 1855, the imposing, red-brick DeSoto House is the oldest continuously operated hotel in Illinois.

Hotel management has an interesting way of sharing the building's history, as well as the history of Galena. They have created documentaries that you can watch at the hotel or buy and take home. I chose to watch there, and I learned a lot. The hotel was named for the Spanish conquistador and explorer Hernando DeSoto, who, in 1541, became the first European to see

The DeSoto House Hotel, the oldest hotel in Illinois, is in the heart of historic Galena. Photo by Cynthia Clampitt.

the Mississippi River—the river on which booming mining town Galena depended for its success. When it opened, the DeSoto House was the largest hotel in the West (because in 1855, everything from Ohio onward was "the West"). It became the center of Galena's life. Abraham Lincoln spoke here multiple times, and Ulysses S. Grant made the hotel his campaign headquarters when he ran for the presidency.

But not everything was easy. Both the hotel and the town were devastated by floods (levees now keep the Galena River from overflowing). At various times, the hotel experienced a fire and an explosion. And when in 1880 it was determined that the five-story hotel was too heavy for the terrain, the top two stories had to be removed, a remarkable feat. More recently, much of the interior had to be rebuilt, to bring the accommodations up to modern standards, but the entryway, with its huge, wooden reception desk and sweeping stairway, is still what you would have seen a hundred years ago.

Like many hotels of its age, there are stores across the front of the building. The open courtyard, once necessary to let light into center-facing rooms, has a skylight now but still creates a bright, airy space that makes the hotel feel very open and welcoming. The word "gracious" comes to mind.

Galena is justly proud of the nine Union generals the town contributed to the Civil War, most notably General Grant, and this is reflected in the name of the upscale restaurant on site, The Generals, as well as my room, the Ulysses S. Grant room (right next to the Abraham Lincoln room). The rooms have high ceilings and tall windows, and a décor that might best be described as understated late-nineteenth-century elegance. Delightful and comfortable. And I loved the view of Galena's Main St. that I had from my window.

For dining, in addition to The Generals, there are two other venues: the Courtyard and the Green Street Tavern. While everything at each venue was fresh and tasty, and I enjoyed each of my meals, for me, the most memorable item on any of the menus was the house specialty: blue cheese soup.

While I was there for the antiquity, I would go back for the beauty, comfort, and excellent service . . . or perhaps for one of their special events.

Nearby: The setting for the hotel, the town of Galena, could keep you busy for days. Just about every travel magazine in the last twenty years has written about Galena, so information is abundant and readily available. Also, if you're interested in a scenic drive, one of the roads leading out of Galena is the Stagecoach Trail, part of a route established in the mid-1830s for stagecoaches traveling between Galena and Chicago. The road curves through green hills, passing historic towns and beautiful farms. I drove a bit more than half of the trail's 37 miles, as I needed to head north, but the section I drove was wonderfully worthwhile. Living history indeed.

The Village Tavern

Long Grove, IL

The Village of Long Grove was settled in the 1840s. Because I grew up only about 20 miles away, Long Grove was a destination long before my interest in its history had developed. Back then, in the historic downtown of this largely German rural settlement, every store sold antiques, which was what drew my mom there. But it was the determination of residents to preserve both the old buildings and the feel of the town—no neon, lots of trees, gardens and open spaces, one-lane road, original covered bridge—that earned it the designation of first historic district in Illinois. It was the town's charm, and reliably good food in several venues, that kept me coming back over the years. The things being sold in the stores have changed, though they remain interesting and unusual. The old cider press is gone. But the old buildings still stand. And the Village Tavern is still in business. Opened in 1847, it is the oldest restaurant in Illinois.

The food is the kind of classic, fresh, made-from-scratch cuisine one would expect from a small-town restaurant, though with a lot more options than would have been available when the restaurant first opened. Mary Ann Ullrich, who, with her husband, has been the owner since 1962, says the fried fish is hand-breaded using a recipe that was given to them by the previous owner. The restaurant is known for hand-cut steaks and hefty burgers, but they have added gluten-free, vegetarian, and vegan options. Guacamole, buffalo wings, and a tasty Tavern House Cheese are among the offered appetizers. Ullrich noted that they work to keep the feeling old-fashioned and historic, but they also know that customers want variety and quality. She also related that when repairs and an expansion were needed, they used wood from old barns that had been torn down, which enables them to keep the antique look throughout the restaurant. (I actually think it's nicer now than when I first went, so many years ago.) Photos of Long Grove's earliest days decorate the walls, and it is fun to note what has not changed.

If you plan to visit, be aware that Long Grove is famous for its festivals and concerts, so check before going if you're looking for a quiet day in the country. Crowds can be surprisingly large on special weekends. But whenever you go, do give yourself some time to wander around town and enjoy the ambience, the shops, and the antiquity, as well as the food. The visitor center offers a nice map for walking tours and can share more of the town's history.

Eating History: Shrimp de Jonghe

Sometimes foods live on long after the restaurants where they originated have vanished. This is the case of Chicago's De Jonghe's Hotel and the hotel's restaurant, which was fabulously popular from the 1890s to the 1920s, enchanting diners with its gourmet fare. The De Jonghe family had emigrated from Belgium in 1891, and it was Henri de Jonghe who was credited with the shrimp dish that continues to appear on menus all across, and far beyond, Chicago. However, in all fairness, it is likely that the hotel's chef, Emile Zehr, had a hand in developing the dish. Regardless, shrimp De Jonghe is still popular, and few think of it as being a dish that arose in the Heartland. So next time you order this rich, garlicky shrimp dish, know that this is Midwestern cooking.

The Whitney

Detroit, MI

If you need to impress someone, this is a good choice. The Whitney Restaurant is inside the stunning, almost overwhelming mansion of timber baron David Whitney, whose company was, in the mid-1800s, the largest lumber dealer in the United States—though that was only one of Whitney's sources of income. Begun in 1890 and built of rose-colored South Dakota jasper, the mansion has 52 rooms, 20 fireplaces, and 218 windows, many of them designed by Tiffany. The gardens are glorious. Entering the grand hall, one is immediately surrounded by gorgeous architectural elements and artwork. For those who want to see more than the splendid rooms set aside for dining, they actually offer tours. Oh—and they have good food, too. I took my mom for her birthday, and we had the house specialty of beef Wellington. Yum. But if all they had was potato chips, it would almost be worth it just for the opportunity to see the opulence of this stunning home. Definitely recommended if you want to see what wealth in the "Gilded Age" looked like. But it's a good choice for dining, as well.

Stagecoach Inn

Marshall, MI

The first time I turned off the highway and headed for Marshall, Michigan, I was looking for lunch, rather than history. I knew about Schuler's Restaurant primarily because even in Chicago stores carry their cheese spread, or "Bar-Scheeze" as they call it, and I also had a recent recommendation from a friend. The restaurant dates to 1909 and has always been in the Schuler family, so it is clearly well established. However, it is wildly popular, and I had several hours of driving ahead, so I accepted a small table in a corner of the bar rather than waiting 45 minutes for a table in the dining room. Then, after a pleasant lunch, I went for a bit of a walk, and that's when I began to discover Marshall.

Signs along the main street (Michigan Avenue), a map of historic locations, and a few informational posters let me know that this was one of those delightful towns with lots of history. In fact, Marshall, founded in 1830, was originally considered as Michigan's state capital. Streets are lined with vintage buildings.

Half a block from Schuler's, at the corner of Eagle Street and Michigan Avenue, the Stagecoach Inn caught my eye. The pillars across the Greek Revival façade made it look like a government building, and the signage, gas lamps, and impressive double front door definitely made it look 19th century. But it was the sign on the side of the building that let me know I needed to stop here on my next trip across Michigan. "Built in 1838, it stands directly on the famous Territorial Road, following Indian trails from Detroit to Chicago. . . . Today, this is the oldest continuously operated inn between Detroit and Chicago." It is still a hotel, as well as a dining establishment. And now it was on my "must visit" list.

On my next trip, while I spent a bit more time admiring the charm of Marshall, photographing old buildings and historic markers, I was really there for the Stagecoach Inn. The menu offered a long list of sandwiches, burgers, fries, and other essential bar food—which seemed appropriate, as the vintage wood-beamed dining room was definitely dominated by its bar. And I'd say the menu was appropriate for a place that still refreshes weary travelers keeping to a schedule. Online reviews said the burgers were outstanding, so I ordered the Swiss-and-mushroom burger with sweet-potato fries. I heard them drop the fries in the fryer, so definitely fresh. The burger looked hand-formed and had a generous amount of mushrooms, and the bun appeared to be freshly baked. So they aren't just relying on the historic surroundings to make customers happy—which probably explains the steady stream of diners.

Breitbach's Country Dining

Balltown, IA

Jacob Breitbach bought this restaurant, which was ten years old at the time, in 1862. Today, six generations later, it is still in the Breitbach family. It is the oldest restaurant and bar in Iowa. However, though the Breitbachs have served food continuously since Jacob's day, the comfortably handsome white building I pulled up to is not the original building. In 2007, a gas explosion destroyed the original restaurant, and less than a year after Breitbach's reopened, there was another fire. However, the restaurant never stopped serving food, using a smaller building across the parking lot to keep the tradition, and business, alive. The restaurant is so much a part of the local community that Balltown residents supported rebuilding, and the current restaurant, built on the original foundation, reopened in August of 2009.

So, in reality, it is the building's foundation, the concept, the recipes, and the family that have been around, rather than the roof and walls. I was stopping here because I wanted to sample the cuisine and service that have kept this place in business since 1862.

The word *country* in the restaurant's name is a good indication of both the décor and the cuisine. It is attractively rural, with pots of flowers on the veranda adding color to the exterior and, inside, wood beams supporting the ceiling, large fireplaces, and interesting antiques placed strategically. Breitbach's is famous for its all-you-can-eat buffet, but it was 3:45 when I arrived, so the dinner buffet was not ready. However, I was happy with the menu, which offered locally sourced Black Angus beef. My steak was excellent: good meat perfectly cooked. This came with chunky potato soup, tender-crisp vegetables, and a salad bar that was simple, but fresh and thoughtful. Service was warm and enthusiastic. Easy to see why Breitbach's would be around for close to 170 years.

A short walk from the restaurant, a couple of overlooks offered splendid views of verdant farmland, the Mississippi River, and Wisconsin in the background. But I had a speaking engagement the next day and another hundred miles on the road before bedtime, so I had to keep moving. As I continued on, I smiled at the stories the town names told me about the area's settlers: Guttenberg, New Vienna, Manchester, Waterloo. History everywhere.

Nearby: The Black Horse Inn is just down the road from Breitbach's, in Sherrill. Built in 1856, it is one of the few pre–Civil War hotels in Iowa still in business. I passed it on my way to the restaurant, as I wound through the green countryside bordering the Mississippi River. The inn sits at the point where Sherrill Road joins Balltown Road. The commanding, hillside location of the sturdy three-story brick building clearly shows that this was once the focus of the town.

Zuber's Homestead Hotel

Homestead, IA

Turning onto a narrow road, I soon crossed railroad tracks, and almost immediately afterward, I saw a charming red brick building enveloped in greenery and flowers. It is, in fact, because of the train tracks that this building is located where it is. The community of Homestead was started in 1842, but in 1861, the nearby Amana Colonies purchased this land from the railroad, to give the Amanas access to the train. (The other Amana colonies are discussed in Chapter 4.) In 1861, if you had a train station, you probably needed a hotel—and one was built here in 1862. Originally, there were 15 rooms and one bathroom, but that has changed. Brian James, who, along with wife Bonnie, owns the hotel, related that not only do all rooms now have attached baths, they are also all up to code when it comes to safety features. So old doesn't mean decrepit. In fact, the hotel is delightful. The section of the building that houses accommodations was built of bricks created right here in Homestead. (Brian pointed out a wolf's pawprint in one brick, where a wolf ran across the bricks before they dried.)

Zuber's Homestead Hotel, built in 1862, is charming and perfectly located for visiting the Amana Colonies. Photo by Cynthia Clampitt.

The bricks were also in evidence on one wall of my room. A high, wooden headboard on the bed added a touch of elegance, while the wine-colored walls reflected the theme of this room. (Each room has an Iowa-related theme, and I was in the Vintner, reflecting the extensive wine making by German settlers here.) There is much to love in this hotel, but one of my favorite items was the door mechanism in my bedroom, an iron contraption that seemed almost Medieval.

The breakfast room, which is primarily wood, used to be the woodshed. Today, a large window on one side of this room looks out over a green field dotted with trees. "That area used to be home to chicken coops and kitchen gardens, to feed guests," Brian explains. He also points out an unusual sculpture. "A tree died, and we brought in one of those chainsaw artists, and he turned it into a baseball bat and ball, in honor of Bill Zuber." Zuber was a major league baseball player and Amana resident who owned the place for a while, turning it into a restaurant bearing his name. The building was turned back into a hotel in 2007, but it retained Zuber's well-known name. Brian relates that, in its heyday, when trains were the primary mode of transportation, celebrities and luminaries often stopped here to eat. "Bob Hope ate here," Brian notes happily. Brian then (with my encouragement) launched into a history of the Amana colonies, from "The Great Change," when they gave up communal living, to the reasons people had for some of the things I would see elsewhere in the colonies. "People often grew grapevines on the outside walls. It kept a building cooler in summer, but also provided grapes for making wine."

The hotel is quiet and homey, filled with antiques and character. Photos and documents in the lobby offer insights into the history of the area—and, I imagine, reflect Bonnie James's years as a school teacher. (She's even the author of a children's book about the colonies). Breakfast (included in the room rate) was fresh, hearty, and delicious. And the hotel is a short, easy drive from Amana, so it's an ideal location for exploring the other colonies. Of course, for me, having a resident source of local history and advice made it especially delightful.

Union Hotel

De Pere, WI

Driving from adjacent Green Bay into De Pere, down tree-shaded Riverside and onto Broadway, my route was lined with impressive old homes on the side of the street that backs onto the Fox River. Then the trees parted, and within a block, the pale brick, three-story Union Hotel appeared. Opened in 1883, the hotel and fine-dining establishment has been owned and operated by the Boyd family since 1918.

Outside the hotel, among gas lamps and large flowerpots, I stopped to read the information signs. The first was a Packers Heritage Trail sign that relates the long association between the hotel and the football team. The hotel opened the year before the Green Bay Packers came into existence, and from the start, people associated with the team lived or dined here. The second sign was about Wisconsin's history from the standpoint of the nearby (across the street) Fox River, from the French Voyageurs arriving in the 1600s up through the growing city's reliance on water power.

When time for my reservation approached, I stepped inside and understood immediately why the place remains popular. I was led through

The Union Hotel, in addition to being a venerable accommodation, is also a popular dining destination and historic hangout for people associated with the Green Bay Packers. Photo by Cynthia Clampitt.

the handsome, wood-heavy bar area into a cozy dining area of dark wood booths. In the best tradition of Wisconsin supper clubs, a plate of crudités immediately appeared, accompanied by ham salad, cheddar cheese spread, and chicken liver pâté. The dinner menu leans heavily toward steaks, though with chicken, lamb chops, pasta, and fish available. I overheard one waitress praising the lobster ravioli special, which sounded appealing—and it proved to be very nice. Good bread service. Cranberry vinaigrette was a good choice for the salad. Very nice meal overall—though watching plates go by, the steaks were impressive.

Because I was busy taking notes, my waitress, Heidi, mentioned that, if I was interested in the place, the owner was nearby and would probably like to talk to me. Of course, I said "yes," and soon, McKim Boyd had joined me. McKim is the fourth-generation owner and manager. Seeing that I had enjoyed the bread service, he related that the garlic rolls (which were very good) were his grandmother's recipe.

McKim related that, in 1883, when it opened, this hotel primarily served two groups of clients. Travelers in that day (normally arriving by coach or on horseback) could rely on finding a nice hotel every 15–18 miles, but it was also a boarding hotel for rural high-school students who lived too far from school to commute daily. The school was one block from the hotel. Rates were $1 a night for travelers and $4–5 per week for students (meals included).

McKim, who is clearly delighted with the hotel's history, then offered to take me on a tour. I discovered that the cozy dining room I'd eaten in was just for slow nights. There was a much larger, more elegant dining room nearby. Then we went upstairs to see the rooms. McKim explained that initially all rooms were small and shared bathing facilities. But now, some rooms have been combined to make them larger—and McKim and his family lived here for a while. Today, of the twenty rooms, four have attached baths and sixteen share facilities. The rooms I saw, both large and small, were attractive and looked comfortable. Then we went back down to the lobby. Even here, the past is retained. Keys are in wooden cubby holes behind a polished wooden desk. The phone on the desk is a heavy, black antique that still works—as does the old public phone in a booth across the room. (McKim explained that the phone company charges extra for supporting these older phones, but he thinks it's worth it.)

While this is a historic site that draws a fair number of travelers, it is also clearly a local favorite. Everywhere we went in the hotel, people called out to McKim, and he knew everyone's name. I love the idea that the history of hospitality is preserved, as well as the history of the objects in the building. I can't imagine being near Green Bay and not dropping in.

Wilmot Stage Stop

Wilmot, WI

A quiet road leading through a rural area is not that uncommon in Wisconsin. But this road was leading me to a once-busy intersection where, long ago, the handsome white clapboard buildings welcomed the Kenosha-to-Galena stagecoach, rather than cars. One of those buildings, the Wilmot

The Wilmot Stage Stop stands on what was once a busy stagecoach route. Today, it is a popular spot for great steaks and potatoes with a lot of butter. A museum upstairs reveals details from when this was also a dance hall and hotel. Photo courtesy of Wilmot Stage Stop.

Stage Stop, built in 1848 (the year Wisconsin became a state), lays claim to being "Wisconsin's Oldest Tap and Dining Room." (Perhaps the distinction lies in the definition of restaurant, as there is another 1848 establishment that is identified as the oldest restaurant, while the Wilmot Stage Stop was once considerably more, as I would learn after dinner.)

A broad, white-pillared veranda stretches the full width of the three-story building. Inside, the combination of a little rustic and a little polished makes it comfortable while still delightfully historic. Steaks and chops flow in a steady stream from the kitchen to the grill master, who stands by the impressive fireplace, tending the meat (and often lobster, which can be added to any entrée). Chicken breast is also available, but it is clear that that is not why people are here.

The abundance of steaks may represent a Midwestern standard, but the abundant dairy products and brandy-based drinks are pure Wisconsin. Dairy takes the form of "heaps of butter," as the menu states (roughly a quarter pound on each large baked potato), though sour cream is also served. As for brandy, that is as much a part of Wisconsin history as the restaurant. It is said that Wisconsinites discovered their passion for brandy at the 1893 World's Fair. Today, Wisconsin is the top consumer of brandy in the country, with a Brandy Old Fashioned being the state's top cocktail and Brandy Ice or Brandy Alexander being almost requisite desserts.

Every meal starts with warm rolls (with, of course, butter) and a small, fresh salad with three house-made dressings (Roquefort, French, and Thousand Island). A children's menu and à la carte options are also available.

Dinner finished, I headed up the steep stairs to the second floor, where the space that was once a dance hall now houses a museum that displays not only this recreational past but also other aspects of the building's history. For one thing, back when travel was slow and towns were farther apart, the Stage Stop was also the post office, and the cubbyholes needed for sorting mail stood in one corner. The enthusiastic young woman in charge of the museum pointed out the ivory balls used for playing pool, related that the handsome Brunswick pool tables were purchased in 1880, and noted that the piano that would have provided music for dances came from Boston. After pointing out several other items of interest, the docent related that the third floor is where overnight guests would once have stayed. Like the second floor, the rooms on the third floor are now solely for display, decorated with the modest furnishing of earlier years along with evocative collections of things travelers might have carried with them. Worth the climb.

The Old Mill

Austin, MN

This is a case where the building is older than the restaurant. As its name suggests, this place was originally a flour mill, built in 1872 by British brothers just back from fighting in the Civil War. As is true of most mills of this vintage, it sits at the edge of a river. Before entering, I walked around the building for a better view of Red Cedar River, as well as the short, exuberant waterfall created by the original owners to power the milling operation.

However, the big mills in Minneapolis made it hard for a small mill to survive, so this operation shut down after the turn of the next century. Then, about seventy years ago, new owners envisioned the shuttered mill as a restaurant. Wooden beams and hand-hewn post were preserved, with photos of the original operation hanging on the walls as reminders of the building's history. The interior is really handsome, with wood used extensively. The menu is both impressive and fun. Because Austin is home to Hormel Foods, there are a couple of bar-food items that involve SPAM®. But the offerings are varied and interesting and make it easy to see why a reservation is advisable. I didn't order an appetizer, though Thai peanut flatbread, stuffed Medjool dates, and Brussels-sprouts chips were all tempting. Fish, steaks, salads, and burgers were on offer, but I opted for one of the "House Favorites," garlicky chicken and sautéed shrimp served with mushrooms and wild rice. I enjoyed the dinner, but the historic surroundings and the view out over the river were easily as good as the food.

Nearby: The mansion of George Hormel, the first man to can a ham and creator of the company that bears his name, is worth visiting. I enjoyed touring the handsome, 1871 home and appreciated the insights about the man and his dedication to the food business. In addition, while not dating to the 1800s, there is a SPAM® museum in Austin. (For more on Hormel and SPAM, see my book *Pigs, Pork, and Heartland Hogs*.)

Hays House Restaurant

Council Grove, KS

Leaving Wichita, I chose a circuitous route through the undulating and handsomely carved Flint Hills region, which on the day I was driving was so green, all I could think was that this must have been the inspiration for the Emerald City in Dorothy's Oz. (A friend would later tell me that the Flint Hills are not always as astonishingly verdant as I was seeing them, but what I witnessed was glorious. However, the Flint Hills are home to the world's largest continuous tallgrass prairie, so even if not always so green, I imagine they will always be remarkable.)

My destination was the Hays House Restaurant in Council Grove, a small (population roughly 2,000) town in the midst of the Flint Hills.

Hays House is plugged into history on many levels. It is the oldest, continuously operational restaurant west of the Mississippi. Seth Hays, who built the restaurant, was the great grandson of Daniel Boone, and also

Hays House, built by Daniel Boone's great grandson, is the oldest continuously operational restaurant west of the Mississippi River. It is, however, far from being the only vintage building in the history-heavy town of Council Grove. Photo by Cynthia Clampitt.

Kit Carson's cousin. When Hays arrived here in 1847, he was the first white settler of Council Grove. He had been sent to trade with the Kansa Indians (also known as the Kaw—the people for whom Kansas was named). He soon found himself also handling steadily increasing traffic along the Santa Fe Trail, on which Council Grove sits.

Hays initially built a log cabin and trading post, but by 1856, he needed to expand, as the number of people traveling on the Santa Fe Trail had grown. So, in 1857 he opened the restaurant that still bears his name. In addition to the restaurant, Hays also started a newspaper for the town and opened the first bank.

Council Grove is as charming as one might hope. I drove through, admiring the layers of history evident in the tidy little town. I parked near Hays House and walked around for a while, discovering a few other places to add to my "next time" list, and then headed for the restaurant. While it was clearly kept in good repair, it was also evident that the building was old, with heavily weathered wood still visible. It was too early for lunch and too late for breakfast, but there were still a few small clusters of people enjoying the quiet and their coffee.

I asked the waitress what the fastest thing was I could order—because, sad to say, I was on a tight schedule. She suggested biscuits and gravy. I said yes, plus coffee. I still had a long drive ahead. I enjoyed my late breakfast and was delighted when the waitress offered me a large, lidded cup of iced water for the hours ahead on the road. So thoughtful. Then I had to leave.

Definitely need to get back here sometime, to explore further.

Nearby: Kaw Mission State Historic Site displays items that reflect both the lives of early settlers and those of the indigenous Kaw people. The Post Office Oak is a tree that, from 1828 to 1847, was the place where travelers on the Santa Fe Trail left messages about trail conditions ahead. The museum of the Morris County Historical Society occupies a brick house built by Seth Hays in 1867, after 20 years in his original log cabin. The Cottage House was also built in 1867, as a cottage and blacksmith shop. Today, this handsomely restored historic building is a well-rated hotel/motel.

Glur's Tavern

Columbus, NE

In 1856, a group of adventurous souls from Columbus, Ohio, decided that they wanted to build a town farther west, near a soon-to-be-created railroad line. They moved to a valley in Nebraska that seemed a likely train route and began to build, calling the new town "Columbus." The Union Pacific Railroad soon came across the valley, and the town grew quickly. In 1876, two immigrant brothers from Switzerland, Joseph and William Bucher, decided the town needed a saloon. That saloon is still in business and still near the tracks that run through Columbus. Originally called Bucher's, the saloon changed names when the Buchers sold it to Louis Glur, who was originally hired by William as a bartender. The bar is recognized as the oldest continuously operated saloon west of the Mississippi, with a listing on the National Register of Historic Places. Other than antiquity, Glur's Tavern is also famous for being a place Buffalo Bill Cody liked to stop for a drink in the 1880s through to the early 1900s.

The exterior looks vintage—white clapboard with a wraparound veranda—except for the signs blazoning the location's antiquity. The interior is somewhat changed from the days when Cody visited (they now have TVs and a few sports posters, because staying in business involves keeping your regulars coming back). However, there are elements that clearly reflect an earlier time, including wood paneling, a mounted deer head, and a few taxidermic game birds, plus the old wooden bar.

That bar was lined with locals when I entered, each clearly acquainted with everyone else. The cheerful gentleman behind the bar who greeted me turned out to be current owner Todd Trofholz. It speaks well of a place that a new face is so readily identifiable. Todd offered me a menu, a little apologetically since it wasn't historic. However, while I doubt that Buffalo Bill ever had access to jalapeño poppers, the food is classic bar fare, and so is in keeping with the tavern's original objective. Most tables are set up for families or groups, so it's still a community gathering place. The menu states that their burgers are famous, so I went for the 5-ounce cheeseburger. I also had the excellent onion rings. Not a meal to write home about, but solid and tasty. Combined with the history and the friendliness, I was glad I'd come. Besides, how often do you get to walk into a place that Buffalo Bill used to frequent?

CHAPTER 7

Locating More History

As noted in the introduction, no single volume could include all the delightful places one can learn more about Midwestern history. I have highlighted many of the larger or more notable venues, as well as some smaller but still interesting sites—but there is more. In fact, there are thousands of places, large and small, all across the region, where you can learn about the people and events that helped create the world of today. In this chapter, we look at some of the ways you can locate other places of interest. In addition to tips, I'll mention a few destinations that I found by using these techniques.

Worth noting is that a lot of these search options will help you find numerous other things to enjoy, because the Midwest offers many delights: rock formations, forests, sand dunes, wildlife, zoos, state and national parks, art galleries, and lots of museums for things other than history, as well as for periods of history not covered by this book. So, there's no need to limit yourself. Our history is remarkable and worth knowing, but so is everything else. This book is simply designed to get you started. (That said, the places in this book could certainly keep you busy for a while.)

History of Historians

Perhaps it's because things were moving so fast that people didn't want to lose track of what was happening. More likely, it was that people realized the significance of the events whirling around them in the 1800s. Most of the Founding Fathers were still alive as the Northwest Territory opened, and many who headed west had served during, or at least been affected by, the American Revolution. The Louisiana Purchase took place because Napoleon Bonaparte needed money to continue fighting the British. Philosophers whose ideas affect us today (Emerson, Mills, Thoreau, Kant) and writers we still read (Dickens, Whitman, Twain, de Tocqueville) were working and enthusiastically read. The Civil War touched almost everyone. So, people knew that things were changing and that they were part of it. Plus, we were no longer British colonies and now had our own evolving history to record. As a result, the Midwest developed historical societies and gave rise to respected historians very early in the region's history. (In fact, Indiana's Historical Society is one of the oldest in the United States, having been founded in 1830.) Happily, many people continue to pursue that preservation of the past. Their efforts led to the publication of some wonderful books about the history of the Midwest but also gave us a remarkable number of delightful collections, events, and venues pretty much everywhere one travels.

All these options offer a way to better know a region, state, county, or village. Some are epic and give detailed insights. Many offer pieces of a bigger picture, because some events (wars in particular) draw everyone in, even from very remote areas. For example, it was in a one-room historical society in a rural part of Illinois (Putnam County) that I first saw trench art, artwork created during World War I by soldiers hunkered down in trenches, hammering beautiful objects out of the brass from empty artillery shells.

In addition, while local societies are likely to offer one destination, a search for some state historical societies may turn up much more. For example, the website for the Minnesota Historical Society lists 26 historic locations all across the state, and also identifies everything from events to research libraries. These lists do not include everything in a state, just the places with which the historical society is involved. But historical societies alone could keep you busy for a long time.

With that in mind, my first tip for finding places to learn is an internet search for historical societies. Using your favorite search engine, type in the name of a town, suburb, city, county, or state, plus the words "historical society" or "historical museum." Alternatively, you can simply type "historical society near me." Be aware that, while built-up areas may have a society in every town or suburb, in more rural areas, there may just be a county society. In some cases, the buildings that house the societies are historic themselves—from log cabins to Victorian mansions, and more. But all of them will offer a look at the past.

Allies in Your Search

Fortunately for us, these places want to be found, so there are plenty of resources, both online and off.

To start with, the majority of old places, including most of the places in this book, are on the National Register of Historic Places. Of course, every year, a few more places qualify, so the number keeps growing—but at present, there are more than 85,000 listings for the entire country. Granted, some of these places are not specifically educational. There are food purveyors, office buildings, historic districts, and more—but all must be nominated and proven to have historical significance, so it's not just random old stuff, either. You can search by state or county at https://nationalregister ofhistoricplaces.com/.

The National Trust for Historic Preservation does not simply register old places, it works to save them. They understand how important the past is for facing the future. And they, too, have an excellent database of worthwhile historic destinations. Just click on "Exploring Places" on their website: https://savingplaces.org/.

It won't come as a surprise to anyone that the Smithsonian is interested in history, but some may not know that the country is dotted with places that are Smithsonian Affiliates. For example, Conner Prairie, described in Chapter 2, is a Smithsonian Affiliate. Affiliates are museums, living-history venues, or cultural organizations that partner with the Smithsonian to share resources. These are carefully vetted alliances, so Smithsonian Affiliates are

excellent destinations in the pursuit of knowledge: https://affiliations
.si.edu/about-us/affiliate-directory/.

Numerous National Historic Sites, Historic Trails, Monuments, and
Heritage areas are under the oversight of the National Park Service. In
addition to offering information about potential destinations, the National
Park Service website includes historical information about sites, as well as
practical information, such as fees, accommodations, hours, and special
events. It also has a section offering Trip Ideas. Select a state and discover
what is available: https://www.nps.gov/index.htm.

Once you reach one destination, there will probably be information
about other destinations nearby, or other places associated with the park
district or whatever other organization is involved in operating the venue
(especially if the National Park Service is involved—they have great maps
and brochures).

States themselves are excellent allies when planning travel. You can just
type in the state name, or if you have seen an ad, use the marketing tag:
Pure Michigan, Enjoy Illinois, Travel Wisconsin, or Visit Wichita, for example. Otherwise, just put in the state name and "tourism."

In addition, almost every rest area or oasis along the major interstate
highways offers maps at the very least and often have a wide range of
brochures of the state or surrounding area. Generally, the first rest area as
you enter a state will have the most information, but there is almost always
something. Keep your eyes open for "bonuses" at some rest stops. Many
have memorials, historic markers, or information signs about people who
lived or events that occurred nearby.

If you find yourself in an unfamiliar town, know that hotels and motels almost always have a tremendous amount of information available. At the lower
price end, this usually consists of a rack of flyers and maps somewhere in the
lobby. At the higher end, it may take the form of a concierge service, ready
to help you find anything of interest nearby. Sometimes there are things
you wouldn't even have known to search for until you saw the brochure. In
addition, many hotels place magazines about the town or area in their rooms.

Often, areas or organizations work together to help you find other
locations. Some create "passports," to actively encourage exploration. For

A rest area off I-90 in southern Minnesota, near Adrian, has both a historical marker and this wonderful information panel, which offers a description of the surrounding prairie ecosystem, details about nearby places of interest, and a map suggesting a short driving trip that would take in the Pipestone National Monument, Laura Ingalls Wilder Museum, and Blue Mounds State Park, among other delights. Photo by Cynthia Clampitt.

example, when I visited the Kansas African American Museum in Wichita, I received a "passport" for The Kansas African American History Trail, which listed seven other places in Kansas to visit, as well as offering a website (TKAAHistoryTrail.org) where I could learn more about African American history. At the Naper Settlement in Illinois, my "passport to adventure" was a joint effort of the Kane and DuPage Counties and offered 90 pages of local museums, historic sites, and nature centers. So be on the lookout.

If you're a member of AAA, you have access to a range of trip aids. They offer books by state or region that identify places to see, as well as places to stay. If you're planning a trip, you can order maps. Plus, AAA has an online program that will not only outline your drive but also tag some places of interest along your route.

Numerous other options appear and disappear online, so it is likely that, once you start searching, you'll find other resources.

Other Internet Options

There are three additional ways I have benefited from the internet: accessing lists created specifically to guide visitors to places, looking up places along a planned route or at a required destination, and posting on social media that I'd be traveling.

Everyone seems to love lists. People have created a wide range of lists that can lead you to the oldest, largest, or most interesting aspects of towns, states, and regions. (Though remember that, while oldest and largest are verifiable, "most interesting" or "best" are opinions—so double check recommendations.) Your search terms can be general, such as "things to see in North Dakota." You may also be more specific, such as "oldest restaurants in Wisconsin." Sometimes, you can find lists related to a particular historic interest, such as "windmills in Illinois." This search actually turns up an entire website dedicated to this topic—http:/www.illinoiswindmills.org— which lists not only surviving Illinois windmills but also Illinois windmills that have been destroyed and all surviving windmills in the U.S. (This search item is not as random as it may seem. In a region defined by grain and bread, the existence of mills is inevitable.)

If business is taking you to another town, or if a road trip will be taking you through unfamiliar territory, look up specific spots along your route or near your destination, to see what is available. It's almost difficult to find a town in the MW that doesn't have a historic district or old mansion or some other bit of history. Search for history in the town—but know that other things may show up, as well. A speaking engagement in Keokuk, IA, gained me the fact that this is the geode capital of the world, while a gig in Burlington, IA, turned up Snake Alley, built in 1894 and said to be the crookedest street in the country. There is always something.

And, of course, there is social media. I have found that posting something on an online profile or on one of my blogs often gets surprising responses. Suddenly, everyone you know will have a relative in a state you'll be visiting or will have just visited and can make suggestions.

Carnegie Libraries

Writing a biography of Andrew Carnegie, back when I still worked almost entirely for textbook publishers, I was impressed with how his impoverished youth influenced the way he later spent the fortune he earned. Carnegie started working at age 12, shortly after his family arrived in the United States in 1848. He was a "bobbin boy" in a weaving factory. He worked hard, but he understood that the most important thing for getting ahead was education. He read constantly and went to night school. The efforts paid off, and he found himself with increasingly important jobs. By his mid-20s, Carnegie was superintendent of railways in Pittsburgh. He used his income to invest in new technologies and inventions, including sleeping cars for trains and steel mills. He recognized the potential of steel and bet everything on the belief that steel would become vital in the U.S.—which it did. The Carnegie Steel Company built the country and enriched Carnegie.

The rags-to-riches story was delightful, but Carnegie's belief that "A man who dies rich dies disgraced" was what drove him later in life. He set up charitable agencies, museums, and child-welfare centers, both in the U.S. and the British Isles. He never forgot the impact of books and learning, so much of his fortune went to aiding colleges, funding scientific research, creating museums, and building libraries across the United States, Canada,

Europe, Africa, and beyond—2,509 libraries. (In the book *Up from Slavery*, Booker T. Washington related that it was Carnegie who contributed the library at Tuskegee Institute.)

Today, Carnegie Libraries and Carnegie Museums make up the single largest group of related historic buildings in the country. Of the 1,795 libraries Carnegie built in the U.S., roughly 800 are still libraries, while another 350 have been "repurposed" (like the one mentioned in the exploration of Mitchell, SD, where the Carnegie Library is now a museum). Because these libraries were built more than 100 years ago, they are inevitably located in older towns and generally in the oldest part of each town. Doing a search for Carnegie Libraries in a state or region gives you an easy way to locate places with a past.

It's a Sign

Highways throughout the Midwest are lined with signs intended to alert you that you are passing along a historic corridor or through a notable region, or that someone hopes will attract you to a nearby ethnic museum, historic site, or birthplace of someone famous. Keep an eye out for signs, as you never know what you might see (the house portrayed in Grant Wood's *American Gothic*, for example).

Some signs will suggest future options for research. Driving across Iowa, I saw signs in several places for Silos & Smokestacks National Heritage Area. When I got home, I looked that up and discovered that National Heritage Area was a designation bestowed by the National Park Service on areas rich with history. The Silos & Smokestacks website listed a treasure trove of historic sites, scenic routes, museums, events, nature centers, and vintage B&Bs across Iowa. It was another reminder that, no matter how much you see, there will still be more to discover.

A few signs, even on smaller roads, will offer information about events that happened near where the sign is planted. Often, names you know well will pop up in places you don't expect them—such as the sign I encountered on a winding road on the Illinois side of the Mississippi River not far from the bridge that would take me over to Keokuk, Iowa. The sign, titled "Thy Wondrous Story, Illinois," offered a surprising number of names and events associated with this area, including French explorers Louis Jolliet and Jacques Marquette, Revolutionary War hero George Rogers Clark, and a young Lieutenant Robert E. Lee (who had been sent to supervise attempts to make the river more navigable).

While driving through Ohio, visiting places I knew I wanted to include in this book, I saw a sign near my hotel that read, "Welcome Center and Fulton County Museum, 1 Mile." This museum, or even the town of Wauseon, where it is located, wasn't on my radar at all, but I thought I'd give it a try. What a surprise. This was not a huge museum, but it more than made up in splendid detail, insightful presentation, and brilliant planning what it lacked in size. I had no idea so much interesting stuff happened in Fulton County, Ohio.

The museum starts in the area's prehistory and moves up through the centuries—Native Americans, early European settlers, Civil War, and well into the 20th century (including Wauseon native Barney Oldfield, pioneering auto racer). When artifacts are particularly abundant, drawers beneath primary displays hold the carefully labeled overflow. While all the exhibits were interesting, the one I found most surprising was about local showman, Woodson T. Campbell, a performer and entrepreneur who worked with Buffalo Bill and P. T. Barnum and was friends with fellow Ohioan Annie Oakley. For a while, in addition to performing, he had his own museum. His success was enough to allow him to have several homes, including one in Florida. Quite a character.

The museum took me only about 2 hours to view—so this isn't a place you'd likely plan a vacation around. However, if you happen to find yourself on the Ohio Turnpike near Hwy 108 (which you likely will if you visit Sauder Village), you might consider stopping. This place is a good reminder of the fact that big things can happen anywhere. Of course, the real lesson is, when you see a sign telling you there is something of interest a mile ahead, if you have a little time to spare, you might want to check it out. It may not always be this good, but it will probably offer something of interest.

Read Maps

Often, place names will suggest possibilities. For example, Norway, IL; Holland, MI; or Lindsborg, KS. Such places generally have long histories and may offer museums or ethnic/heritage festivals. Do check, once you identify a potential target, because some places offer more than others. But names often offer clues as to where history can be found.

Scan along waterways. Rivers and lakes were the super highways for centuries, and the oldest settlements were almost inevitably close to water. Often, these are towns that once were prosperous but have declined, so a waterfront destination may not always be large. But it will almost always be historic.

Consider famous trails. The Oregon Trail started in Missouri, as did the Santa Fe Trail. Lewis and Clark crossed most of the Midwest, and their memorial trail follows their route, including Ohio, Illinois, Indiana, Missouri, Iowa, Kansas, Nebraska, South Dakota, and North Dakota. Even if you don't want to follow the entire trail, the places along these trails will usually offer some interesting history.

Listen

Among the places I've visited over the years, a few are ones I simply heard about from someone. Sometimes, it was a recommendation and sometimes simply an overheard conversation. But if I had free time, I often followed up.

For example, I was speaking at a conference at John A. Logan College in Carterville in southern Illinois. During a break, I heard someone mention that there were several historic buildings on campus. I asked around and learned there were tours twice a day. So, at 1:00 p.m., I was ready to tour the Harrison-Bruce Historical Village.

This was not a big village—just four buildings, two of them replicas—but there were still things to learn. The one-room Purdy School, which dates to 1860, is one of the real antiques. The original, two-story Harrison House was built in 1868 out of bricks made on the site with clay dug up while creating the basement. The house in the "village" is actually a replica con-structed by descendants of the original owners (who still own the original) and is decorated with antiques from the original Harrison House.

The Harrison Storefront re-creates the cabin the Harrison family lived in while Harrison House was being built. I found this building interesting because I'd never heard of a double dog trot cabin. This is a cabin divided into two large rooms with a space (the dog trot) between. This design was created to separate the kitchen from the living quarters, in a time when cooking fires in wood buildings posed a considerable risk. However, here, it separated home from business, because the second room was both a general store and the post office. The building was created entirely without nails. The guide also noted that, while the doors now open out, as required by state regulation (safety reasons), the original doors would have opened in—easier to defend/barricade if the family was attacked.

The Hunter Cabin reminded me that some of the Midwest was settled by people who were given land in lieu of payment for military service. Knowing this happened is one thing, but seeing a place that was actually an award seemed more meaningful. Here, the soldier in question, Emmanuel Hunter, served during the War of 1812, and in 1818, when Illinois became a state, it offered land to veterans of that war.

That's just a small part of what I learned at this location. The point is that there are opportunities everywhere. So, keep your ears and eyes open. It might lead to some special little discovery that will brighten a business trip or add to a vacation.

And sometimes the recommendation isn't a place, but rather a resource. For example, when I was planning a trip to Kansas, a friend urged me to get *The Kansas Guidebook*. It turned out to be an amazing resource—information about everything in the entire state that you might ever want to see. It will make you want to stay for weeks. (If you're intrigued, it's by Marci Penner and WenDee Rowe and is published by the Kansas Sampler Foundation: https://kansassampler.org).

A Few Odds and Ends

The more you search, the more resources you will find for searching. You might want to create your own list of sites that will help guide you to possible destinations—or perhaps inspire you to put together your own tour.

For fans of Lewis and Clark, here is the site for their National Historic Trail, which includes events, accommodations, and everything you need to know to pursue the exploits of the remarkable Corps of Discovery: https://www.traveliowa.com/trails/lewis-and-clark-national-historic-trail/13/.

For fans of Laura Ingalls Wilder, one can plan a trip around places she lived or museums that celebrate her books. Here is one site that offers suggestions for a road trip: https://www.mprnews.org/story/2015/01/12/books-wilder-attractions.

The Underground Railroad offers an inspiring look at a hard time. There are many state-specific sites, such as this one from the Indiana Department of Natural Resources, which offers a list of Underground Railroad sites: https://www.in.gov/dnr/historic/4120.htm. While state-specific sites offer more detail and more locations within the state, there is also a list on the National Park Service website: https://www.nps.gov/nr/travel/underground/states.htm.

A bit quirkier is the Historical Markers Database: https://www.hmdb.org/. You can search this site by topic (forts, Lincoln, folklore, canals) or location. Entries include links to photos and offer information about the marker, and also include connections to maps, showing locations of and routes to the markers.

Finally, you can look at tour companies that cover the Midwest. For example, there are a number of elegant steamboats that offer tours up and down the Mississippi and Ohio Rivers. While tours offer advantages, such as lectures and guides, simply looking at itineraries can suggest places worth visiting as you plan your own adventure.

These are just a few of the possible topics to pursue across the Midwest. If you look, you will find more.

APPENDIX A

Destinations by State

ILLINOIS

INDIANA

IOWA

KANSAS

MICHIGAN

MINNESOTA

MISSOURI

NEBRASKA

NORTH DAKOTA

OHIO

APPENDIX B

Order of Statehood

Areas and venues within the region have multiple layers of history, and destinations often reflect history that predates statehood, American independence, and even the arrival of Europeans in North America. However, to simplify organization, within each chapter, destinations are listed in the order in which their states obtained statehood. Then, within a state listing, destinations are in alphabetical order by town. Hence, for example, Sauder Village in Archbold, OH, comes before Historic Roscoe Village in Coshocton, OH.

State	Date of Statehood
Ohio	March 1, 1803
Indiana	December 11, 1816
Illinois	December 3, 1818
Missouri	August 10, 1821
Michigan	January 26, 1837
Iowa	December 28, 1846
Wisconsin	May 29, 1848
Minnesota	May 11, 1858
Kansas	January 29, 1861
Nebraska	March 1, 1867
North Dakota	November 2, 1889
South Dakota	November 2, 1889

Notes

INTRODUCTION

1. Literary critic Norman Foerster's relating of the Emerson quote, along with comments about the many others who shared the opinion, appeared in the essay "Emerson and America's Future," by Robert C. Pollock, in *Doctrine and Experience: Essays in American Philosophy*, edited by Vincent G. Potter, Fordham University Press, New York, 1988. The Lincoln comment is from Lincoln's 1862 State of the Union address. The insights from Turner come from Turner's *The Frontier in American History*, especially the chapter "The Middle West."

2. "Great Facts About the Five Great Lakes," *Live Science*, Kim Ann Zimmermann, June 30, 2017. "Major Landforms of the Midwestern Region," *Sciencing*, Diana K. Williams, April 25, 2018. "River Facts," National Park Service.

3. John Steinbeck, *Travels with Charley: In Search of America*. New York: Penguin Books, 1962, p. 106.

CHAPTER 1. CREATING AND DEFINING THE MIDWEST

1. Hudson, *Making the Corn Belt*, p. 16.

2. Ibid., pp. 17–18.

3. "The New Madrid Seismic Zone," U.S. Geological Survey, https://www.usgs.gov/natural-hazards/earthquake-hazards/science/new-madrid-seismic-zone.

4. Hudson, p. 15. "Adena Culture" and "Hopewell Culture," *Ohio History Connection*, http://ohiohistorycentral.org/w/Adena_Culture and https://ohiohistorycentral.org/w/Hopewell_Culture. Mann, 1491, pp. 280–318.

5. Biles, *Illinois: A History of the Land and Its People*, p. 21. Nicholas P. Hardeman, *Shucks, Shocks, and Hominy Blocks*, p. 21. Shortridge, *The Middle West*, p. 14.

6. Walter T. Durham, "Southwest Territory," *Tennessee Encyclopedia*, https://tennessee encyclopedia.net/entries/southwest-territory/.

7. John Opie, "Family Farm," *Encyclopedia of the Great Plains*. "Land Ordinance of 1785," *Ohio History Central*, https://ohiohistorycentral.org.

8. Northwest Ordinance (1787), https://www.ourdocuments.gov/.

9. Donald J. Berg, "Railroads, United States," *Encyclopedia of the Great Plains*.

10. Christian Wolmar, *The Great Railroad Revolution: The History of Trains in America*, pp. 172, 178–179.

11. Brian W. Beltman, "Ethnicity," *The Greenwood Encyclopedia of American Regional Cultures: The Midwest*, pp. 125–145.

12. Encyclopedia of the Great Plains, "All-Black Towns."

13. Shortridge, *The Middle West*, pp.16, 20–21, 25.

14. *Encyclopedia Britannica*, "Corn Belt."

15. Shortridge, *The Middle West*, pp. 19–20.

16. Pryor, "The Invention of the Plow," *Comparative Studies in Society and History*, p. 727.

17. Turner, *The Frontier in American History*, p. 10.

18. Different people date the closing of the frontier differently, largely because the term *frontier* had been redefined in the United States. The original and still primary meaning is the border between two countries. There is a frontier between France and Spain. In North America, the term came to refer to the region that, to a certain extent, formed the boundary between the known and the unknown, the unsettled beyond the settled. Some consider the completion of the Transcontinental Railroad in 1869 to have marked the end of the frontier, as the two halves of the continent had been connected. However, what might be called the "official" end was announced in a bulletin issued by the Superintendent of the Census for 1890, who noted that "Up to and including 1880 the country had a frontier of settlement," but that the frontier line had been so broken up that it no longer belonged in the census reports. For more on what constituted the frontier, its impact, and how it ended, check out Turner's influential essay, "The Significance of the Frontier in American History."

CHAPTER 2. WITNESSING HISTORY

1. Kim Krieger, "Erie Sauder's Sauder Village," *Midwest Open Air Museums Magazine*, Fall 2017, p. 10.

2. Ronald V. Morris, *History and Imagination: Reenactments for Elementary Social Studies*, Chapter 8, "Extracurricular Social Studies at the Conner Prairie Interpretive Park." Roman and Littlefield Publishers, Maryland, 2012.

3. Cynthia Clampitt, *Midwest Maize: How Corn Shaped the U.S. Heartland*, p. 111.

4. ALHFAM stands for Association for Living History, Farm and Agricultural

Museums. It is an organization that shares resources and information, offers classes, arranges hands-on experience (such as working with farm animals), and has conferences to ensure accuracy throughout these venues.

CHAPTER 3. PERUSING HISTORY

1. Clarence D. Long, "Wages by Occupation and Individual," *Wages and Earnings in the United States, 1860–1890*, p. 94, Princeton, NJ: Princeton University Press, 1960.

2. City of Dubuque, https://www.cityofdubuque.org/712/Shot-Tower.

3. I checked the story when I returned home, and indeed, millions of koalas were killed, and Hoover did stop the importing when he became U.S. Secretary for Commerce in 1927. Among the numerous sources that confirm this is the website of the Australian Koala Foundation.

CHAPTER 4. EXPLORING HISTORY

1. Finding conflicting dates for some of the buildings led me to contact the Centre for French Colonial Life, and Director of Museum Operations, Robbie Pratte, explained that dating the buildings presents some interesting difficulties. Tests can be done on wood to determine age (dendrochronology), but some homes were dismantled and moved from the older location. Other places, such as the Bolduc House, were built and then expanded, which Pratte thinks explains why different dates appear in some sources (most commonly, 1788 vs. 1792). Pratte says the 1792 date is unlikely for initial construction, however, because a 1791 census indicates that Louis Bolduc was already living in the house then. In addition, tests done on some of the wood support the 1788 date, but the building was expanded in 1792–1793, which is why some wood tests later. This is why one often encounters different dates.

2. This is not the only Dutch-style windmill in the Midwest, nor is it the only windmill in the U.S. to have been designed and even built in the Netherlands. However, because DeZwaan was not created for export and in fact had a long history actually working in the Netherlands, it is often billed as the only authentic or most authentic windmill in the U.S.

3. Illustrations generally show roots extending far deeper into the soil—ten feet or more. Roots this long do exist, but this does not represent the depth of the dense mat of grass roots that formed the heavy sod the settlers were "busting." There were/ are hundreds of different plants growing on the prairies, all with different root depths. It's actually a remarkably complex ecosystem that still keeps scientists busy. However, grasses dominate, and research has shown that the roots of those grasses get their water

and nutrients from a relatively shallow layer of soil—maybe as much as six to ten inches, but not ten feet. Of course, the longer roots would have contributed to the toughness of the sod, but the density of roots thins quickly below the top layer of grass roots. This is good, because if there had been a dense, impenetrable mat ten or more feet deep, the land would have been useless for agriculture.

4. Cold enough to be noteworthy. On December 8, 1804. Clark wrote, "The thermometer stood at 12 degrees below 0, which is 42° below freezing. . . . Several men returned a little frost bit." Landon Y. Jones, editor, *The Essential Lewis and Clark*, p. 28, New York, NY, Ecco, an imprint of HarperCollins, 2000.

CHAPTER 5. EXPERIENCING HISTORY

1. This is not a typo. It's not a mousse. It's a massive bull moose—10 feet, 6 inches from hooves to antlers—created out of chocolate at the Iowa State Fair in 2012. As for the butter cow, that is a life-size cow sculpted out of butter. The butter cow is an annual tradition. This is not unique to Iowa, however, as I've seen butter cows at the Illinois State Fair and read that Ohio's State Fair has a butter cow. There may be others.

Sources

Listed here are sources from which substantial information or insight was gained. Books and other resources that supplied only a single fact, idea, or statistic will be referenced only in endnotes.

BIBLIOGRAPHY

Biles, Roger. *Illinois: A History of the Land and Its People*. DeKalb: Northern Illinois University Press, 2005.

Bogue, Allan G. *From Prairie to Corn Belt: Farming on the Illinois and Iowa Prairies in the Nineteenth Century*. 2nd ed. Lanham, MD: Ivan R. Dee, 2011.

Cronon, William. *Nature's Metropolis: Chicago and the Great West*. New York: Norton, 1991.

Danbom, David B. *Born in the Country: A History of Rural America*. 2nd ed. Baltimore, MD: Johns Hopkins University Press, 2006.

Hudson, John C. *Making the Corn Belt: A Geographical History of Middle Western Agriculture*. Bloomington: Indiana University Press, 1994.

Hurt, R. Douglas. *American Agriculture: A Brief History* (rev. ed.). West Lafayette, IN: Purdue University Press, 2002.

Kopp, Elizabeth Z. *The Life of Dr. John Albert Kennicott: A Visionary Horticulturalist*. Glenview, IL: The Grove National Historic Landmark, 2014.

Lauck, Jon K. *The Lost Region: Toward a Revival of Midwestern History*. Iowa City: University of Iowa Press, 2013.

Mann, Charles C. *1491: New Revelations of the Americas Before Columbus*. 2nd ed. New York: Vintage Books, 2011.

Pryor, Frederic L. "The Invention of the Plow." *Comparative Studies in Society and History* 27, no. 4 (October 1985).

Quaife, Milo Milton. *Chicago and the Old Northwest, 1673–1835: A Study of the Evolution of the Northwestern Frontier, Together with a History of Fort Dearborn*. Chicago: University of Chicago Press, 1913.

Shortridge, James R. *The Middle West: Its Meaning in American Culture*. Lawrence: University Press of Kansas, 1989.

Slade, Joseph W., and Judith Yaross Lee, eds. *The Greenwood Encyclopedia of American Regional Cultures: The Midwest*. Westport, CT: Greenwood Press, 2004.

Turner, Frederick Jackson. *The Frontier in American History*. Mineola, NY: Dover Publications, Inc., 2010.

Wolmar, Christian. *The Great Railroad Revolution: The History of Trains in America*. New York: Public Affairs, 2012.

Sources

ONLINE RESOURCES

Encyclopedia of the Great Plains, http://plainshumanities.unl.edu/encyclopedia/.

National Park Service, http://nps.gov.

Encyclopedia of Chicago History, http://www.encyclopedia.chicagohistory.org.

ON LOCATION

The locations mentioned in the book were all rich sources of information about the history they preserve, re-create, or display.

Index

Cynthia Clampitt is a food historian and travel writer. She is the author of *Midwest Maize: How Corn Shaped the U.S. Heartland* and *Waltzing Australia*.

The University of Illinois Press
is a founding member of the
Association of University Presses.

Composed in 10.5/15.5 Lora
by Jim Proefrock
at the University of Illinois Press
Manufactured by Sheridan Books, Inc.

University of Illinois Press
1325 South Oak Street
Champaign, IL 61820–6903
www.press.uillinois.edu